INFORMATION TECHNOLOGY

INFORMATION TECHNOLOGY:
The Human Use of Computers

Harry Katzan, Jr.

ASSOCIATE PROFESSOR OF COMPUTER SCIENCE
PRATT INSTITUTE

FIRST EDITION
1974

petrocelli
books, NEW YORK

Copyright © Mason & Lipscomb Publishers, Inc. 1974

Published simultaneously in the United Kingdom by Mason & Lipscomb
Publishers, Inc., London, England.

First Printing

Printed in the United States of America

Library of Congress Cataloging in Publication Data

Katzan, Harry.
   Information technology.

   Bibliography: p.
   1. Electronic digital computers. 2. Programming
languages (Electronic computers) 3. Computers and
civilization. I. Title.
QA76.6.K36   001.6'4   74-1453
ISBN 0-88405-059-9

Contents

Preface

Although the computer is idolized by some and hated by others, the attitudes of most people fall somewhere in between. One marvels at the manner in which the computer is employed in space research and is totally frustrated when the billing procedures of a particular concern somehow become confused. Generally speaking, most people desire to know more about the computer and how it is used to serve the needs of the individual and of society. The objective of this book is to serve these needs.

Our interest is primarily personal. Even though we are members of organizations that use computers, we are keenly interested in automation, privacy, artificial intelligence, libraries, computer networks, and what all of this means to us. The book is designed to aid the reader in understanding the impact of computers on people. However, the approach taken here is that the reader must participate, to some degree, in the process of computing to comprehend the significance of the basic concepts fully. As a result, the book covers basic computing concepts, programming languages, topics in "computers and society," and some philosophical issues in the computer field.

The subject matter contained in this book has been class tested and has therefore evolved to some degree. Side issues that are interesting but not necessarily germane to the basic objective of the book have been omitted. The treatment of programming languages has been "beefed up," because once students see the computer and realize what it can do, they want to use it themselves.

The book is intended to be used as a text for one of the following general types of courses:

xi

Introduction to computers
Computer appreciation
Introduction to computers and programming
 for liberal arts students
Computers and society

Some comments on the use of the book are necessary. Ordinarily, all topics presented in this book would not be used in a given course. For example, the book includes a parallel treatment of BASIC and FORTRAN. If programming languages are covered, then the instructor would probably make a choice between the two. Similarly, the individual instructor may choose to omit many of the details associated with any given topic. However, most topics are covered completely to provide as much educational flexibility as possible. The book does not require the use of a computer even though there is much to be gained by giving the students a short programming problem to be run on the computer. However, the material is presented so that the student can obtain a general familiarity with the art of programming without actually using a computer.

The subject matter is designed for a one-semester or one-quarter course for nonmajors. No prerequisites are required and no special background is needed for full comprehension.

It's a pleasure to acknowledge the helpful comments and suggestions of Mr. Morton B. Lurie, who reviewed the complete manuscript, and the contribution of my wife Margaret, who provided valuable assistance throughout the project.

PART I

COMPUTER CONCEPTS

CHAPTER 1

Computers and People

TOWARD A POINT OF VIEW

The computer is an advanced technological innovation and, as such, is the product of our modern society. Yet, even though the computer is "our child," many people approach the subject with apprehension and, in some cases, actual fear. The reasons are almost obvious. The computer came upon the scene quickly and it affects our everyday lives in many ways. These facts coupled with a general lack of knowledge of computer technology have given rise to a wave of anticomputer feelings. Most technological innovations are received in pretty much the same way. The automobile is a case in point. Today, most of us have a good idea of what the automobile *can* do, without necessarily being automobile experts. Two of the objectives of this book are to introduce what the computer can do and how it affects people.

The computer industry is new and, in spite of its age, has acquired a controversial reputation. The industry is controversial because there are both advantages and disadvantages of computer utilization and because the computer directly or indirectly affects our daily lives. Many business ventures in the computer field have been failures, and many organizations have had disastrous results from attempting to use the computer. People have been inconvenienced and frustrated with computerized billing. Even computer education has had its ups and downs. The problem is not the computer but people with their normal shortcomings. However, one has reason to be optimistic. Because the computer industry *is* relatively new, it will probably evolve to some degree before things actually settle down.

The people employed in the computer field—as designers, builders, technicians, and users—are both benefactors and victims of their own creations. These people are admired by society, and at times, are classed as outcasts. But as in any new industry, the reputation of a whole class of people should not reflect the actions of a few. We have all heard of bearded programmers with Mickey Mouse T-shirts, salesmen who "promise you everything," and fly-by-night companies that cash in on the ignorance of unsuspecting customers. The intention here is not to condone or defend anyone or any group of people, but to approach the subject maturely and systematically. In this case, knowledge is the best medicine.

The advantages of using the computer to serve the needs of society are available only at a price: the price being the cost of goods and services, of increased control and responsibility on the part of vendors and users, and the reorganization of certain aspects of our lives to utilize the new technology. The investment by governments, business concerns, and other organizations, including individuals, in computer technology has been truly phenomenal. Overall, the use of computers has been tested and has proved successful. Computers are here to stay and it is the responsibility of an informed society to best utilize this vast resource.

INFORMATION AND POWER

Computers have an enormous capacity for storing information and for making that information available at a moment's notice. This is construed by some people to mean that the computer is a tremendous source of power. And indeed it can be. Knowledge about a person, a group, the future products of a business, and so on, can be used as a control mechanism. However, knowledge of this sort has always been useful to a few. The key point, of course, is that the computer merely extends the capability for using knowledge as a source of power or control. The situation is like a two-sided coin, and knowledge can be used to people's advantage as well as to their disadvantage.

To say that the computer is "good" or "evil" is like saying a writer's typewriter is "good" or "evil." There are, however, bona fide issues over which we can be concerned: automation, reliability, and privacy and security—to name only a few. Perhaps we can only understand the problems. Issues of morality are left to the philosophers and social scientists.

The issue of computers is somewhat analogous to that of atomic energy several years ago. There was a time when the subject of unleashing the energy of the atom was surrounded with suspicion and guilt and engineers and scientists involved therein were regarded, by some, as serving immoral purposes. The use of atomic energy has been controlled and has also been made to serve a variety of societal needs, from medicine to electric power.

It is felt by some that the impact of computers on mankind can be as great as that of atomic energy.

AUTOMATION AND RELIABILITY

It has been said that the horse was replaced by the motor vehicle not because the motor vehicle is that much more convenient, but because the horse had become inefficient from an economic point of view. Next, consider the manual operations necessary to compute the payroll for 30,000 employees or handle the billing for a major utility. The costs are numerous: personnel costs, turnover costs, training costs, benefits, absenteeism, retirement, management and overhead, scheduling costs, and so on. Enter the computer. For big jobs, there are big computers; for small jobs, there are small computers. The simple fact is that some jobs are done more accurately and more reliably by machine and at a lower cost than by human employees. So, what else is new? The computer is nothing more than an electronic machine.

What happens to jobs that are replaced by the computer? Some people say that they are gone forever. Others say that the computer industry has created more jobs than it has eliminated. One thing is certain. Prospective employees entering the job marketplace can no longer stop at the clerical level but must proceed to become accountants, business analysts, organizational specialists, and the like. It is true that some people are unemployable and must be retrained. It is also true that some people are not retrainable. But this has been a problem of society from the medieval sword maker, to the recent blacksmith, to modern times.

Modern electronic computers operate very quickly and can also perform new tasks that were previously left undone because of the time factor. In business, reports can be generated in time for the decision-making process. In science and engineering, calculations can be performed that would take more than a lifetime to perform by hand. In government, complex processes can be simulated and future events can be predicted. In education, computers are used to give the students new insights into the subject matter and additional capability for data analysis and research.

Computers are also used to improve the efficiency and reliability of mechanical components—both in their manufacture and in their substitution. Computer control of chemical processes, message switching, and computerized telephone systems is already as common as the ballpoint pen.

As society relies more on the capability of computers, the need for a level of systems reliability, previously unknown except in the military electronics field, has become necessary. Hardware reliability lies in the domain of the computer and component manufacturers. There is, however, an important need for software* reliability in the sense that a computer program should be validated to insure correctness and to guarantee an effective systems design, that is, the manner in which a computer system interfaces with its environment, that truly reflects the informational needs of an organization.

In short, the use of computers gives rise to a myriad of operational problems that cannot be solved overnight. As part of a dynamically changing society, it is our responsibility at least to understand the problem areas so as to be able to assess their impact on our lives and on the organizations of which we are members.

SCOPE OF THE BOOK

The book is designed to aid the reader in understanding the impact of computers on people. The approach taken is to have the reader participate in the process of computing so as to comprehend the significance of many of the problems mentioned above. To achieve this goal, the reader is first presented with the "Fundamental Concepts" of computing so that he can appreciate the mechanism being dealt with and the manner in which it is used. Next, the reader is given an introduction to computer programming using the BASIC language or the FORTRAN language as a learning vehicle. Both languages are presented in the second part of the book. The treatment is arranged so that the reader can learn to write programs of his own. The third part of the book provides a look into "Computers and Society," as related to computer applications, organizations, and the individual. The last part of the book, entitled "On the Philosophy of Computers and Information Systems," is designed to encourage the reader to think about conceptual and philosophical topics associated with modern computer technology.

QUESTION SET

1. List as many computer applications as you can that were not mentioned or implied in the chapter.
2. Ask several people with different occupations and with different backgrounds the question "What is a computer?" Answer the question yourself. Try to categorize the answers and relate them to the attributes of the respondents.
3. Some people feel dehumanized when they are identified by "account num-

---

*Generally speaking, software is classed as the programs used to control the operation of a computer. This is discussed later.

ber" or "student number." Why do you think this is so? Do they have a good point? How can this be avoided?

4. Try to make a list of applications for which the computer is used and for which you feel manual procedures would be more appropriate. An example is computerized dating (or mating)—or is it?

5. Give reasons why the federal government is the largest single user of computers.

6. Computer systems are used to hold information about people. Typical uses are in legal, criminal, credit, and educational fields. How does this relate to the assertion that "Everyone deserves the right to start over again"?

7. Poetry and abstract art are frequently used to convey an emotional experience or an imprecise "feeling" for which ordinary language is often inadequate. Write a short poem or draw a simple sketch that reflects your feelings about the computer.

8. Computers have been the object of many cartoons and jokes. Why do you think this is so? How do people develop cartoons and jokes of this type?

9. Describe how you "think" one of the following would operate:

   a. Computerized library
   b. Checkless society
   c. Society with no books, newspapers, reports, or periodicals in which the computer and appropriate consoles were used as a communications medium
   d. Computerized school with no teachers—that is, those that do teaching
   e. Household robots and/or computers

(Can you add any items to the list?)

10. Is it possible that computers could control the world? Could there be a "computer's lib" analogous to the popular "women's lib"? Do you believe in the concept of a self-producing automaton?

CHAPTER 2

Introduction to Computers

KEY TO UNDERSTANDING COMPUTERS

Understanding computers is like understanding many aspects of the physical universe. On the surface, an event or a physical entity may appear to be too complex to describe or understand. Once the event or entity is broken down into its component parts and basic laws or principles are applied, the complete system becomes understandable and is frequently manageable, as well. The same kind of thinking applies to computers and to computer applications. Some typically complex computer applications are:

1. An on-line information retrieval system. The user has a remote terminal that is connected to the computer via telecommunications facilities. The user is allowed to query the system to satisfy his informational needs and is normally provided with the requested information within seconds.
2. A computer is used to guide an airborne missile. The precise location of the missile and the target is obtained from radar units, electronically, and converted to computer numbers. A precise direction for the missile is computed and that control information is sent to the missile via radio devices. There is no human intervention in the process.
3. The motion of physical particles is simulated using a high-speed computer. The trajectory of each particle is traced as it collides with other particles and the boundaries of the container. Results are summarized automatically.

Obviously, these applications are complicated—even for the most experienced computer professionals. Yet each application can be analyzed in terms of its component parts and easily understood. The same concept applies to the computer. The precise operations that the computer performs and the manner in which they are performed can be analyzed individually. Each operation executed by the computer is implemented through electronic circuitry; and each operation is well defined and is easily understood by the designers and builders of the computer. In fact, any reader of this chapter could understand the electrical properties of the computer—if he were interested and wanted to go through the trouble of learning them.

The following key point must be emphasized: *As in the case of the automobile and the airplane, a person need not be capable of designing and building a computer in order to realize and use its capabilities.* A working knowledge of the functional components of a computer is all that is needed to integrate one effectively as a component in an overall business or scientific data system or utilize one in academic or research activity.

A SENSE OF THE BEGINNING

The processing of information is present in almost every activity of our lives and takes place whenever two or more persons or pieces of equipment interact. Throughout history, many devices have been developed to aid in this information (or data) processing. One of the first aids was the *notched stick* that served as an aid to counting and remembering. The first machine, per se, was the *abacus* developed by the Romans in ancient times. A more popular version, the *Chinese abacus,* was developed in the twelfth century and is still used in China today.

The next major advance in computing machines was the *slide rule,* invented in 1621 by William Oughtred, an Englishman. Since that date, many improvements have been made to the slide rule for both general- and special-purpose applications. The first adding machine is credited to Pascal, the famous French mathematician, in 1642. This gear-toothed machine was followed in 1673 by a machine that performed multiplication by repeated additions; it was developed by the mathematician Leibnitz. The machines of Pascal and Leibnitz are the forerunners of modern desk calculators.

The modern era in computing began in 1804 when Joseph Marie Jacquard invented a loom in which the weaving operations were controlled by punched cards. The first automatic computer was designed by Charles Babbage in 1822; it could perform numerical calculations. The machine, called the *automatic difference engine* was originally proposed by J. H. Mueller in 1786 and finally built in Sweden by George Scheutz in 1853. Another of Babbage's machines, the *analytical engine* was designed in 1833 but was never built. It is the forerunner of today's stored program computers.

The punched card and related processing equipment were developed in the 1880s for use in the U.S. census. As it turned out, the development of the punched card became one of the most significant events in the widespread acceptance and use of data processing equipment.

The first automatic computer was completed by Harvard College and IBM in 1944. This machine, called the Mark I, was constructed from mechanical components and handled 23 decimal digit words. The inherent slowness of the Mark I resulted in the design and development of the first electronic computer, the ENIAC, at the Moore School of Engineering at the University of Pennsylvania in 1946. Modern computers are an outgrowth of this pioneering research of the middle 1940s.

Every advance in computing machines was associated with an actual need. For example, ancient cavemen and shepherds needed the notched stick to count their flocks. Similarly, the adding machine resulted from tax computations in France; Babbage's computers resulted from a need for difference tables; and the Mark I and ENIAC efforts were largely influenced by World War II.

The computer explosion, which we are now witnessing, is not simply the result of a new invention or a new technique—although a multiplicity of technological innovations have been made in the last 25 years in the computer field. Other factors have contributed to this widespread growth.

In the area of scientific computation, computers have played a major role in many significant advances, and as a result of these advances, computer use has snowballed. Concrete examples in this area are missile guidance, simulation studies, and computer control systems—in addition to the traditional scientific problem solving. In general, scientific computing has received its fair share of publicity.

Computers play an equally important role in business and government, although the glamour seems to be lacking for various reasons. The volume of business and governmental data processing has grown enormously along with the growth in size of businesses and the expanding scope of government. The use of computers for diverse operations, such as check processing, has given rise to a variety of advanced input, output, and mass-storage devices. Many management problems created by geographical locations and distances are presently relieved through the use of telecommunications facilities that permit information to be transmitted between remote locations at electronic speeds. Here again, reasonable success in using the computer to reduce the volume of clerical operations has caused the use of computers to snowball. Another important factor in the growth of computer utilization is that we are now more adept at identifying computer applications and at applying the computer to those applications.

In computers, it seems as though success breeds success. To summarize, the computer era is the result of three major advances:

1. The development of the punched card and card processing equipment.
2. The development of the automatic electronic digital computer.
3. The development of telecommunications facilities for transmitting computer data between remote locations.

Each of these major advances utilizes its own technology and has contributed in its own way to the vigorous growth, at home, and abroad, in the use of computer technology.

FUNDAMENTALS

A computer can be viewed as a "numerical transformation machine," as depicted in Figure 2.1. The process of computing involves three "basic" steps:

1. *Input,* whereby data on which the computer is to operate are entered into the machine.
2. *Computing,* whereby the data are transformed to meet the needs of a given application.
3. *Output,* whereby the results are made available for subsequent use.

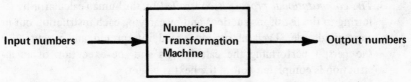

Figure 2.1 The computer can be viewed as a numerical transformation machine.

The notion of computing in this sense is certainly not new. For example, an ordinary mathematical operation, such as addition, uses a similar concept, shown as follows:

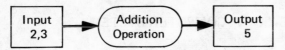

In general, the computer can be viewed as a device that performs a "well-defined" operation on the input data and that produces appropriate output data. As we shall see later, however, all input and output data are not numerical and may be descriptive in nature.

If the computer is to be viewed as a "black box," then it must be capable of operating automatically without human intervention—at least between elementary operations such as addition or division. This is, in fact, the precise manner in which it does operate.

As a means of introducing the concept, it is useful to outline the steps a person follows when solving a computational problem with the aid of a pencil and paper, and a desk calculator, slide rule, or ordinary adding machine. The human calculator usually has a list of instructions he is to follow and a set of input data. The process by which the calculations are performed is summarized as follows:

1. *Information is stored* by writing the list of instructions, as well as input data, on the piece of paper. During the course of performing the calculations, intermediate calculations are also written on the paper; however, the person frequently keeps some information in his brain while using charts and tables, and other information is held temporarily in the calculating device.

2. *Information is processed* by utilizing the computing device—that is, the slide rule, desk calculator, or adding machine—to perform the elementary calculations required by the computational process. Each operation is performed by taking data values from one place on the paper, performing the specified operation, and by recording the result in a definite place, elsewhere on the paper.

3. *The computational process is controlled* by the human calculator by referring to the list of instructions and by carrying each instruction out in a specified order. Each instruction is read, interpreted, and executed by the person performing the calculations and the execution of an instruction is completed before the next is begun.

Although this is an oversimplified analogy to the functional structure of a computer, hardware components that correspond to the piece of paper and the human calculator and his computing device actually exist; they are covered in the next section together with representative input and output devices.

OVERVIEW OF A COMPUTER SYSTEM

The major hardware units in a computer system (see Figure 2.2) are main storage, the processing unit, and intput/output devices. *Main storage* is analogous to the "piece of paper," mentioned in the previous section, and is used to hold computer instructions and data. The *processing unit* is analogous to the human calculator and his computing device and consists of a control unit

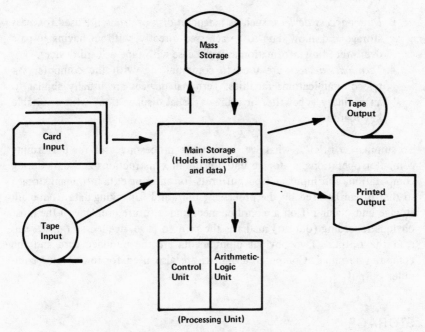

Figure 2.2 Functional structure of a computer system (simplified).

and an arithmetic/logic unit. The *control unit* is the means by which the computer can operate automatically. The control unit reads an instruction from main storage, decodes it, and sets up the circuitry necessary to have the instruction executed. When the execution of an instruction is completed, the control unit reads the next instruction and the preceding steps are repeated. The *arithmetic/logic unit* contains the circuitry necessary to perform the arithmetic and logical operations of the computer. The arithmetic/logic unit normally includes a limited amount of high-speed storage, called *registers,** for holding the values used during computer operations.

Input and output devices are necessarily related to a specific recording medium. The most frequently used input and output devices are briefly summarized:

1. *Card readers* and *card punches* are used to read punched cards and to punch cards, respectively.
2. *Magnetic* and *punched tape units* are used to read and write magnetic and punched tape, respectively. (Tape is used for both mass storage and conventional input and output.)

*Registers are analogous to the accumulator in a desk calculator or adding machine.

3. *Direct-access devices,* such as magnetic disk or drum, are used for mass storage and allow data to be accessed directly, without having to pass over preceding information as is the case with tape or card devices.
4. *Terminal devices* are used to communicate with the computer via telecommunications facilities. Terminal devices are usually similar to an ordinary typewriter or utilize a visual display along with a suitable keyboard.

To summarize briefly, what we have are: a processing unit for performing computer operations, a storage unit for holding instructions and data during computation, and input and output units for entering data into main storage so that it can be used by the processing unit, and for taking data from main storage and placing it on a recording medium for future use. One of the most obvious recording (output) media is the printed page, needed so that we can read the output. Two obvious input media are the punched card and the computer terminal. Computer terminals are also used for low-volume computer output.

STORAGE

The purpose of the main storage unit of a computer is to hold instructions, data, and computed results while a set of computations is being performed. Main storage is *not* used for long-term storage of instructions and data for several reasons:

1. Main storage is relatively expensive.
2. Only a limited amount of main storage can be attached to a computer.
3. Main storage is not portable.
4. Main storage is volatile, which means that when electric power is turned off, the information contained in main storage is lost.

For long-term storage of instructions and data, mass-storage devices such as tape or disk are used. Information is also stored on punched cards although the use of cards for storing large amounts of information is declining because of the sheer bulk involved. However, punched cards continue to be a primary input medium.

Conceptually, main storage is organized somewhat like a group of numbered mail boxes in a post office. Each box is identified and located by its number, which is termed a physical address. In the computer, main storage is organized in much the same manner into a set of locations. Each location can be used to hold a specific unit of data—such as a character, a digit, a series of characters, or a number, depending on the system. To insert or remove data at a location, the address must be known.

When data enters a location, it replaces the previous contents of that location. When data is taken from a location, however, the contents of the location remain unchanged so that the same data may be used many times.

REGISTERS

A *register* is a high-speed storage location that is used by the processing unit. Different computers have different registers. For example, some computers have several accumulators and others have a single accumulator. The question of "How many?" is one of basic design philosophy and is governed, to some extent, by the applications for which the computer is intended. Three registers are usually found in every computer and are briefly covered here:

1. The *accumulator register*. The accumulator register is used for performing arithmetic. Temporary results are frequently left in the accumulator for the next arithmetic operation. When more than one accumulator is used, they are usually identified by number.
2. The *current address register*. The current address register contains the address in main storage of the instruction currently being executed. (The significance of this register will become obvious later.)
3. The *instruction register*. The instruction register holds the current instruction during execution.

Of the three registers, the only register that is used explicitly is the accumulator.

INSTRUCTIONS AND DATA

One of the reasons that modern computers utilize the concept of a stored program is that the processing unit has access to instructions and data at electronic speeds, rather than having to retrieve each instruction and data item individually for processing from an electromechanical input/output device. What this means is that both instructions and data are held in main storage and that care must be taken not to interchange the two. Instructions and data are usually coded in the same form—usually binary—and are both regarded as a series of bits.* However, it is important to note that instruc-

*The term *bit* is an abbreviation for *binary digit*.

tions and data differ both in format and meaning even though each is a sequence of bits as seen in main storage.

The format of a computer instruction varies between computers; however, all formats require, as a bare minimum, three items:

1. An *operation field* that denotes what operation the computer is to perform.
2. At least one *operand field* that denotes the data on which the computer should execute the operation (specified in the operation field).
3. *Modifier fields* that augment the operation field or the operand field.

A typical computer instruction might exist as follows:

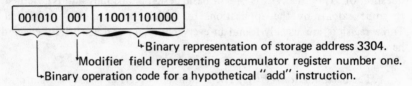

| 001010 | 001 | 110011101000 |

↳Binary representation of storage address 3304.
↳Modifier field representing accumulator register number one.
↳Binary operation code for a hypothetical "add" instruction.

For simplicity, this instruction is represented as follows:

| ADD | 1 | 3304 |

It is important to realize that an instruction occupies a storage location as does data.

The form of computer data is governed by a particular application, the nature of the information to be stored, and the computer involved. As an example, the "fixed-point" value* +37 might be stored as:

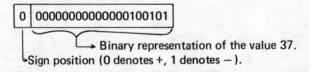

| 0 | 00000000000000100101 |

→ Binary representation of the value 37.
↳Sign position (0 denotes +, 1 denotes −).

For simplicity, again, the above number is represented as:

| + | 0000037 |

A numeric data item, like an instruction, occupies a location in main storage.

---

*The term "fixed point" refers to a format where the location of the decimal point in a storage location is fixed for a particular program.

COMPUTER OPERATION

The preceding discussion is leading up to a brief description of how the computer operates. We know, essentially, the general form of instructions and data and the fact that the instructions and data are held in main storage when the computer operates.

All computer instructions are executed in precise units of time that are governed by pulses emitted from an electronic clock. A fixed number of these pulses is termed a *machine cycle*. In a machine cycle, the computer can execute one or more micro instructions that are combined to form conventional computer instructions, such as ADD or MULTIPLY. The exact number of micro instructions that constitutes a given computer instruction is governed by the nature of the instruction itself and the data involved.

The processing unit operates in a prescribed sequence when executing instructions. Two cycles are involved: the "instruction" cycle and the "execution" cycle. The *instruction cycle* (referred to as the I-cycle) comes first and involves the fetching of the next instruction from main storage and the decoding of it to determine the operation to be executed. The following functions are performed during the I-cycle:

1. The address of the current instruction in main storage is obtained from the current address register.
2. The instruction is fetched from main storage and held in the central processing unit.
3. The instruction is decoded.
4. The current address register is updated to point to the next instruction.
5. Control signals are sent to the processing unit to have the specified operation executed.

The current address register is usually set initially to the first instruction in a prescribed set of instructions. Normally, instructions are executed sequentially so that the current address register is updated with the address of the next instruction during the I-cycle. Most computers incorporate a "branch" instruction that discontinues sequential execution and permits execution to continue from a specified location. Usually, a branch instruction simply alters the contents of the current address register.

The *execution cycle* (referred to as the E-cycle) follows the I-cycle and involves the execution of the prescribed operation. If an arithmetic operation is involved, the operand is fetched from main storage and the operation is performed using the specified operands. The length of the E-cycle depends on the instruction to be executed. Other computer instructions include input and output, loading, storing, branching, shifting, testing—to name only a few.

Figure 2.3 depicts the execution of three instructions in a hypothetical computer. The *first instruction* is located at main storage address 4050. This fact is denoted by the contents of the "before" current address register. The instruction on storage location 4050 is:

```
LOAD 1 7384
```

It tells the computer to load the "contents" of storage location 7384 into accumulator register number one. (The previous contents of accumulator register number one are simply replaced.) The current address register is updated to contain the address of the next sequential instruction (that is, 4051). The *second instruction,* located at main storage address 4051, is:

```
ADD 1 9123
```

It tells the computer to add the "contents" of storage location 9123 to the "contents" of accumulator register number one. Accumulator register number one contained +123 and storage location 9123 contains +14; the result is placed in accumulator register number one so that it now contains +137. The contents of storage location 9123 remain unchanged. The contents of the current address register are updated to contain 4052. The *third instruction* is located in the main storage location numbered 4052 and is:

```
STORE 1 7386
```

It denotes that the current "contents" of accumulator register number one should be placed (that is, should be "stored") in the main storage location numbered 7386. The contents of the accumulator remain unchanged.

The simplified example demonstrates three important points: (1) The computer executes discrete instructions; (2) both instructions and data are held in main storage; and (3) everything the computer does must be broken down into individual steps.

THE CONCEPT OF A COMPUTER PROGRAM

A meaningful sequence of computer instructions is referred to as a *program,* and the process of writing a program is called *programming.* People who program as an occupation are referred to as *programmers.* This section

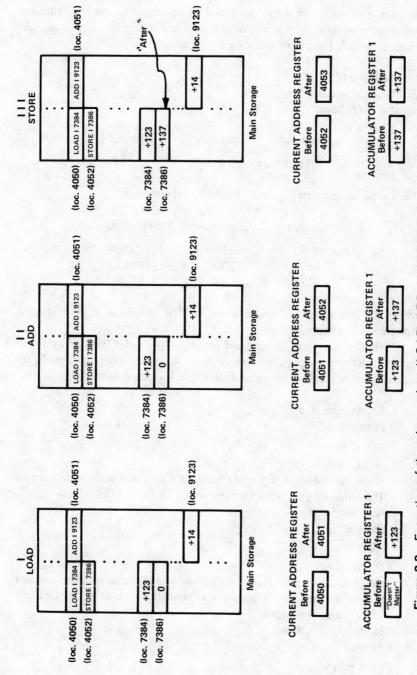

Figure 2.3 Execution of three instructions (LOAD, ADD, and STORE) in a hypothetical computer.

19

contains a computer program composed of computer instructions that are very similar to those found in most computers. For convenience, a symbolic notation is used. For example, the computer instruction:

```
ADD 1 9123
```

is written as follows:

Location	Operation	Operand
4051	ADD	1,9123

The sample program in Figure 2.3 would be expressed as:

Location	Operation	Operand
4050	LOAD	1,7384
4051	ADD	1,9123
4052	STORE	1,7386

where the "location" column denotes the address of the location the instruction is to occupy.

Obviously, the three instructions LOAD, ADD, and STORE are not sufficient to write a program and most computers contain a large number of different instructions. A set of useful instructions is defined as follows:

1. Load instruction
   Format:

   LOAD m,n

   Description:
   Place the contents of storage location n into accumulator register m. The contents of n remain unchanged.
2. Add instruction
   Format:

   ADD m,n

   Description:
   Add the contents of storage location n to the contents of accumulator register m; the result is placed in accumulator register m. The contents of n remain unchanged.
3. Multiply instruction
   Format:

   MULTIPLY m,n

Description:
Multiply the contents of accumulator register m by the contents of storage location n; the result is placed in accumulator m. The contents of n remain unchanged.

4. Subtract instruction
Format:

SUBTRACT m,n

Description:
Subtract the contents of storage location n from the contents of accumulator m; the result is placed in accumulator register m. The contents of n remain unchanged.

5. Divide instruction
Format:

DIVIDE m,n

Description:
Divide the contents of accumulator register m by the contents of storage location n; the result is placed in accumulator register m. The contents of n remain unchanged.

6. Store instruction
Format:

STORE m,n

Description:
The contents of accumulator register m are placed in storage location n. The previous contents of n are lost. The contents of accumulator m remain unchanged.

7. Branch instruction
Format:

BRANCH n

Description:
The computer takes the next instruction from storage location n and sequential execution continues from that point.

8. Test and branch instruction
Format:

BZERO m,n

Description:
The contents of accumulator register m are tested. If the value is less than or equal to zero, then the next instruction is taken from storage

location n and sequential execution continues from that point. Otherwise, the next sequential instruction is executed.

9. Read instruction
Format:

READ n

Description:
The next value is read from the input unit and placed in storage location n. The previous contents of n are lost.

10. Write instruction
Format:

WRITE n

Description:
The contents of storage location n are written to the output unit. The contents of n remain unchanged.

11. Stop instruction
Format:

STOP

Description:
The execution of the program terminates.

12. End instruction
Format:

END

Description:
The END card denotes the physical end of the program. (The computer does not contain an END instruction.)

13. Constant instruction
Format:

CONST v

Description:
The constant value v is placed in the storage location specified in the "location" column when the program is "loaded" into the computer.

Next, assume the computer contains three accumulator registers, numbered one through three, and also contains a main storage unit with 100 locations. The program may not be placed before location 10 because locations one through nine are used for special control purposes by the computer.

A program is given to solve the following problem:

Given: 3 numbers
Compute: The average sum of the squares of these numbers, that is,

$$\frac{1}{N} \sum_{i=1}^{3} A_i{}^2$$

Considerations: If $A_i = 0$, skip it and do not count it in the average; the counter is N and it is not increased in this case.

There are several ways of writing the program. A straightforward program to perform the above calculations is given in Figure 2.4. The program does the job and if a suitable computer existed, the program would work.* A key question is, "What would happen if there were 100 numbers?" The technique would result in a fairly long program. The solution to the problem is to use a program "loop." A *loop* is a series of instructions that are executed repeatedly—each time with different data.

To demonstrate a loop, let us modify the problem slightly. Suppose that in this case, we wish to compute the average of several values—the exact number of values is not known when the program is written. All we know is that the last number is zero. The problem is stated as follows:

Given: *n* numbers
Compute: The average sum of squares of these numbers, that is,

$$\frac{1}{N} \sum_{i=1}^{N} A_i{}^2$$

Considerations: The exact number of values is not known beforehand. The *last* number is zero.

A short program to perform these calculations, using a program loop, is given in Figure 2.5. The program would work for any number of input values, even though the program requires only 29 storage locations.

The concept of using the same instructions with different data, as demonstrated in Figure 2.5, is a frequently used technique in computing. It reduces the storage requirements of a program and allows a program to be developed that can operate on different sets of data.

AN IMPORTANT NOTE ON PROGRAMMING

The reader has probably wondered about those fantastic programming languages that make computer programming so easy that anyone can do it. Do they really exist? The answer is that they certainly do exist and they are "almost" as easy to use as they are claimed to be. In fact, two of these

---

*This comment is for the computer experts. The program is written as it is to prove a point. It is acknowledged that the program makes inefficient use of main storage.

Location	Operation	Operand	Comment
10	READ	41	Read and store A_1
11	READ	42	Read and store A_2
12	READ	43	Read and store A_3
13	LOAD	1,41	Load register 1 with A_1
14	MULT	1,41	Mult register 1 by A_1
15	STORE	1,44	Store A_1^2
16	LOAD	1,42	Load register 1 with A_2
17	MULT	1,42	Mult by A_2
18	STORE	1,45	Store by A_2^2
19	LOAD	1,43	Load A_3
20	MULT	1,43	Mult by A_3
21	STORE	1,46	Store A_3^2
22	LOAD	1,47	Sum (initially zero)
23	LOAD	2,47	Count
24	LOAD	3,44	A_1^2
25	BZERO	3,28	Test A_1^2
26	ADD	1,44	Add A_1^2 to Sum
27	ADD	2,48	Add 1 to count
28	LOAD	3,45	A_2^2
29	BZERO	3,32	Test A_2^2
30	ADD	1,45	Add A_2^2 to Sum
31	ADD	2,48	Add 1 to count
32	LOAD	3,46	A_3^2
33	BZERO	3,	Test A_3^2
34	ADD	1,46	Add A_3^2 to Sum
35	ADD	2,48	Add 1 to count
36	STORE	2,49	Store count
37	DIVIDE	1,49	Divide Sum by Count
38	STORE	1,50	Store Result
39	WRITE	50	Print result
40	STOP	0	Stop program
41	CONST	0	A_1
42	CONST	0	A_2
43	CONST	0	A_3
44	CONST	0	A_1^2
45	CONST	0	A_2^2
46	CONST	0	A_3^2
47	CONST	0	Zero value
48	CONST	1	Value 1
49	CONST	0	Count
50	CONST	0	Result
	END		

Figure 2.4 A straightforward program that computes $\dfrac{1}{N}\displaystyle\sum_{i=1}^{3} A_i^2$ for a maximum of 3 values. (See Figure 2.5)

Location	Operation	Operand	Comment
10	LOAD	1,25	Sum (initially zero)
11	LOAD	2,25	Count (initially zero)
12	READ	27	Read A_i
13	LOAD	3,27	Load A_i
14	BZERO	3,20	Test and branch (if zero) to compute average
15	MULT	3,27	Compute $A_i{}^2$
16	STORE	3,27	Store $A_i{}^2$
17	ADD	1,27	Add $A_i{}^2$ to Sum
18	ADD	2,26	Add one to Count
19	BRANCH	12	Loop to read another value
20	STORE	2,28	Store Count for DIVIDE
21	DIVIDE	1,28	Compute Average
22	STORE	1,29	Store result
23	WRITE	29	Print result
24	STOP		Stop program
25	CONST	0	Constant zero
26	CONST	1	Constant one
27	CONST	0	Storage for A_i and $A_i{}^2$
28	CONST	0	Temp storage for Const
29	CONST	0	Result
	END		

Figure 2.5 Program demonstrating a loop that computes: $\dfrac{1}{N} \displaystyle\sum_{i=1}^{N} A_i{}^2$ for n values.

languages, BASIC and FORTRAN, are introduced in this book. It is equally important, however, to have an idea of what goes on inside the computer. This chapter is intended to serve this need.

QUESTION SET

1. The investigation of historical computing devices offers opportunity for library study. Most devices have an interesting history. Select one of the following devices and prepare a short report on it:

Chinese abacus
Antikythera device
Pascal adding machine
Leibniz calculator
Babbage difference engine

Babbage analytical engine
Jacquard loom
Hollerith tabulating machine
Harvard Mark I computer
ENIAC

2. To some degree, the chapter treats the units of a computer system as though they were "black" boxes. Try to name 10 other devices and/or units that are usually treated in a similar manner.

3. A well-known biologist once conjectured that man's creativity is governed by his own self-image. Does this conjecture apply to computers? In what way?

4. Distinguish between a main storage location and a register.

5. Here is a brief but interesting research problem. Most computers store and process information in binary form. Why is this so? (Ask any computer scientist or electrical engineer.)

6. Using the computer instructions given in the chapter, write computer programs to do the following:

   (a)   Read three numbers a,b,c. Find the largest value; that is,

   $$r = \text{maximum } (a,b,c)$$

   Print the result r.

   (b)   Read two numbers a and b. Divide a by b; that is,

   $$r = a/b$$

   Print the result r.
   Easy? Not quite. Check for division by zero since the computer, like a desk calculator, does not permit it.

   (c)   Read two numbers a and n. Compute a to the nth power; that is,

   $$r = a^n$$

   Print the result. (Note: $a^0 = 1$)

   (d)   Read two numbers $hours$ and $rate$. Compute $totalpay$ as follows: If $hours$ is less than or equal to 40, then compute the total pay as

   $$totalpay = hours \times rate$$

   However, if $hours$ is greater than 40, then also pay overtime as follows:

$$totalpay = 40 \times rate + (hours - 40) \times rate \times 1.5$$

(That is, time and one-half for overtime.)

Print *totalpay*.

Loop back to read two more values. If *hours* is equal to zero, stop the program.

(e) Modify the preceding program to include an employee number as identification. The calculations are the same. For output, print employee number, hours, rate, and total pay.

7. Have you had enough programming? Well, you can take pleasure in knowing that you have just been though the most difficult part of computer programming. Here's the question. If you could do anything in the whole world to make computer programming easier. what would it be? Obviously, there is no right or wrong answer to this question, so let your imagination wander.

8. How does the computer, as described here, relate to information, as you know it?

9. Some computer scientists have discussed the possibility of a "household" computer to help around the house. What tasks could it perform? Would it be as useful as a robot? What about in the year 2000?

10. Now that you have an idea of what a computer is all about, why do you think that some people are afraid of them, in the sense that they will replace people or take over the world? Or, do you think this fear is a myth?

11. By the way, what is a myth? A *myth* is an untrue story of ostensibly historical events that partially explains the viewpoint of a person or a group of persons or that serves to give a practical lesson (that is, a moral). (This definition is due partly to the author and partly to Webster's dictionary.) Myths usually arise when phenomena cannot be explained by ordinary (that is, rational) methods. Develop a short (less than one page) myth about one aspect of computers and people. Beware, you might be able to have it published in a magazine.

CHAPTER 3

Solution by Computer

THE CONCEPT OF AN ALGORITHM

One of the most important aspects of using the computer as an aid in problem solving is that a precise description of the problem must exist. (Actually this is a good practice, in general. It would be difficult to estimate the time and effort that has been spent attempting to solve the wrong problem.) Normally, the problem description is followed by a list of the procedures that must be followed to solve the given problem. Many sets of procedures exist in everyday life; however, computer procedures are a little different.

Consider a simple recipe for brownies:

Ingredients

1 cup sugar	1 teaspoon vanilla
1/4 cup cocoa	1 teaspoon salt
1/2 cup melted butter	3/4 cup sifted flour
2 eggs	1/4 to 1/2 cup chopped nuts

Directions

Mix sugar, cocoa, and butter (margarine will do) until fluffy.
Add eggs, vanilla, and beat well.
Add sifted flour, salt, and mix well.
Add nuts and pour into a greased 8″ square pan.
Bake at 375° for about 25 minutes.

The recipe does indeed state a procedure. It has several characteristics:

1. It describes how to make one product—brownies. If the ingredients change, then the procedure produces an inedible product.
2. The recipe is not precise. What kind of nuts? Brown sugar or white sugar? What sized eggs? (Small, medium, or large.)
3. The directions are ambiguous. What is fluffy? How long is "about 25 minutes"?

With this recipe, a person experienced at baking would probably obtain good results. A novice might have some difficulty. Unfortunately, modern day computers do not have the built-in experience of an experienced baker, for example, so that a computer procedure must be more specific. In fact, it is important to state that a computer is a deterministic system in the sense that the dynamic behavior of a computer in response to input conditions can be predicted. The computer is controlled by a program comprised of a series of instructions, and the program tells the computer exactly what to do during each step of a computation. The old cliché "a computer only does what it's told to do" is very appropriate here.

A specific procedure that gives the solution to a problem is termed an "algorithm." More specifically:

An *algorithm* is a list of instructions specifying a sequence of operations that give the answer to any problem of a given type.

The notion of an algorithm has been known since antiquity, even though in modern times the term is most frequently used with computers. As an example of an algorithm, consider a simple procedure for adding two signed numbers, a and b (that is, $a + b$):

1. If a and b have the same sign, add the magnitude (absolute value) of b to the magnitude of a and affix the sign of either a or b.
2. If a and b have different signs, subtract the smaller magnitude from the larger magnitude and affix the sign of the larger magnitude.

(Thus, for example, $(-3) + (-2) = -5$, $(-3) + (+2) = -1$, $(+3) + (-2) = +1$, and so on.) Before we discuss the properties (or characteristics) of an algorithm, it is well to note that the simple procedure just given is slightly more general than is ordinarily used for computer solution. The following algorithm for the same procedure is more detailed:

1. If a and b have the same sign, go to step 5. (Otherwise continue with step 2.)

2. (By default, *a* and *b* must have different signs.) Subtract the smaller magnitude from the larger magnitude. (Continue with step 3.)
3. Affix the sign of the larger magnitude to the result. (Continue with step 4.)
4. Stop.
5. Add the magnitude of *b* to the magnitude of *a*. (Continue with step 6.)
6. Affix the sign of *a* to the result. (Continue with step 7.)
7. Stop.

Now, several of the characteristics of this algorithm (and algorithms in general) can be given:

1. The algorithm consists of a finite number of steps.
2. The instructions are precise.
3. The instructions are unambiguous.
4. The procedure will work for any two numbers, *a* and *b*.

The fourth characteristic is significant, and it must be stated that some people never quite get the hang of it. An algorithm to operate on any two numbers is different (and usually more complicated) than a procedure to operate on two specific numbers. For example, a procedure to compute $(-3) + (+2)$ is given as:

1. Subtract 2 from 3.
2. Affix a minus sign to the result.

In fact, the latter procedure usually is not even referred to as an algorithm.
As another example, consider the Euclidean algorithm stated as follows:

Given two positive integers *a* and *b*, find their greatest common divisor.

In light of the above discussion, there are as many problems of this type as there are pairs of positive integers *a* and *b*. The algorithm involves the construction of a descending sequence of numbers: The first is the larger of the two numbers; the second is the smaller; the third is the remainder from dividing the first by the second; the fourth is the remainder from dividing the second by the third; and so forth. The process ends when there is a zero remainder. The greatest common divisor is the last divisor in the sequence. For example, the descending sequence of numbers for the greatest common divisor of 44 and 28 is written as: 44 28 16 12 4 0. The last divisor is 4, which is the result. The algorithm can be summarized in the following list of instructions:

1. Write down *a* and *b*.
2. If *b* is greater than *a,* exchange them.
3. Divide *a* by *b* giving the remainder *r.*
4. If *r* is equal to zero, stop; *b* is the greatest common divisor.
5. Replace *a* by *b*; (i.e., $b \to a$).
6. Replace *b* by *r*; (i.e., $r \to b$).
7. Go to step 3.

The actual calculations can be listed as follows:

	GCD of 44 and 28:				*GCD of 10 and 8:*	
a	*b*	*r*		*a*	*b*	*r*
44	28	16		10	8	2
28	16	12		8	2	0
16	12	4				
12	4	0			Result is 2.	

Result is 4.

The Euclidean algorithm demonstrates another important characteristic of an algorithm. The number of operations that are actually performed in solving a particular problem is not known beforehand; it depends on the input data and is discovered only during the course of computation. This may appear to be a contradiction, but it is not. The number of instructions in an algorithm *is* finite; however, some instructions may be executed more than once and others may not be executed at all.

The concept of an algorithm can be summarized with two defining characteristics[1]

The deterministic nature of an algorithm. An algorithm must be given in the form of a finite list of instructions giving the exact procedure to be followed at each step of the calculation. Thus, the calculation does not depend on the calculator; it is a deterministic process that can be repeated successfully at any time and by anyone.

The generality of an algorithm. An algorithm is a single list of instructions defining a calculation that may be carried out on any initial data (in its domain) and which, in each case, gives the correct result. In other words, an algorithm tells how to solve not just one particular problem, but a whole class of similar problems.

[1]H. Katzan, *APL Programming and Computer Techniques,* New York: Van Nostrand Reinhold Company, 1970, p. 23.

PROBLEM DESCRIPTION

When algorithms are complex, a list of instructions, such as those given in the preceding section, is hard to follow. A similar situation is encountered when one is asking for directions in a strange city. If only a few directions are involved, such as:

1. go to the second traffic light and turn left;
2. go four blocks and turn right;
3. the building is on the left;

then a simple list is usually sufficient. When the directions get much more complicated, a map is usually preferred. This is the key point! The list of instructions is just as good (if they can be remembered or are written down), but a map is much more convenient and enables the onlooker to grasp a substantial amount of information at a glance. (A picture is worth a thousand words.)

In the computer field, people use flow diagrams (or flowcharts, as they are usually called) to describe a complex process. A *flowchart* is a graphical picture of the steps that must be performed to accomplish a given job; it is used for planning a program or system, for development, and for documentation. Figure 3.1 gives a simple flowchart of the algorithm for adding two signed numbers given earlier. In general, a flowchart can take *any* form and a bad flowchart is better than no flowchart at all. However, the computer industry has adopted standard flowcharting symbols to facilitate the exchange of information. The following conventions have been established (see Figure 3.2):

The *flow direction* symbol represents the direction of processing flow. The usual flow is top to bottom and left to right. Flow lines should not cross each other and arrowheads are usually used on all lines; an arrowhead should be placed at the point of entry to a connector or function symbol. (In actual practice, the conventions on the use of the flow direction symbol are relaxed and flow lines occasionally cross each other and flow sometimes goes right to left and bottom to top, depending on the algorithm being depicted.)

The *process* symbol is used to represent a computer operation or a group of computer operations. The process symbol is also used to represent computer operations not represented by other flowcharting symbols.

The *input/output* symbol is used to denote any input or output operation. Making information available for processing is an input function (that is, the read operation). The recording of processed information is an output function (that is, the write operation). The input/output symbol is also used

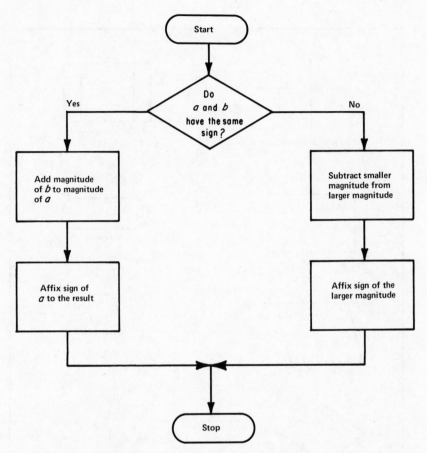

Figure 3.1 Flowchart of the algorithm for adding two signed numbers.

to represent input/output control operations, such as backspacing or rewinding a tape, positioning of a disk device, and so on.

The *decision* symbol is used to specify a point in an algorithm at which a branch to one of two (or more) alternate paths is possible. The basis on which the choice is made (that is, the test) should be clearly indicated.

The *predefined process* symbol represents a function not outlined in detail on the flowchart. (A typical predefined process is a library subprogram, such as a square root routine.)

A *terminal* symbol denotes any point that an algorithm originates or terminates.

A *connector* symbol specifies an entry to or an exit from the flowchart.

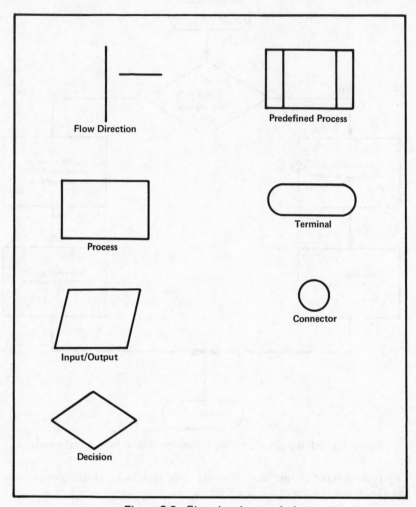

Figure 3.2 Flowcharting symbols.

A set of two connector symbols is used to indicate continued flow when the use of a flow direction symbol would not be practical.

Computer specialists use other flowcharting symbols; however, the symbols given here suffice for most applications.

Figure 3.3 depicts a flowchart for the Euclidean algorithm. It is slightly more complicated than the addition algorithm and includes a loop, wherein the same steps in the algorithm are executed more than once depending on the input data.

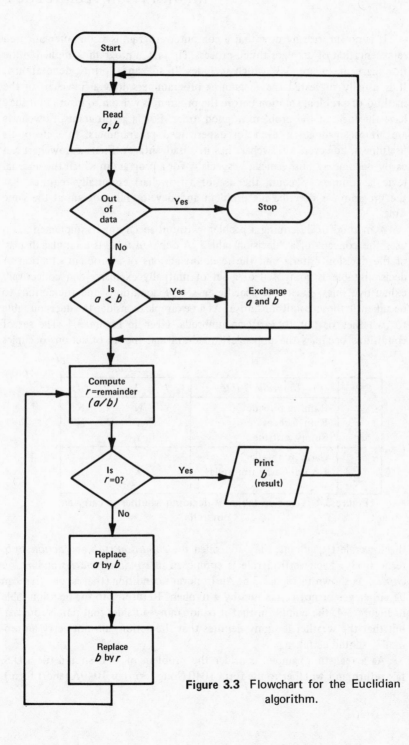

Figure 3.3 Flowchart for the Euclidian algorithm.

It is no surprise by now that a computer program is a computer-oriented representation of an algorithmic process. (In fact, a program is implied in the flowchart of Figure 3.3, which includes "read" and "print" denotations.) It is usually suggested that beginning programmers draw a flowchart of the method of problem solution before the program is written to insure that they have the logic of the problem in good order. For large programs, flowcharts are almost mandatory—even for experienced programmers. In spite of its usefulness, however, a flowchart has its disadvantages. First, a flowchart can easily become a "bushy mess," especially for a program in which the internal logic is complex. Second, the use of a flowchart essentially requires that the programmer describe his problem and develop his program at the same time.

A method of describing a problem without specifying its implementation uses the concept of a "decision table." A *decision table* is a tabular display of the decision criteria and the resultant actions of a problem situation. A decision table is composed of a set of mutually exclusive and collectively exhaustive rules. Each rule specifies a set of conditions and the actions to be taken if those conditions arise. As an example, consider the decision table for whether or not to carry an umbrella, given in Figure 3.4. The set of conditions occupies the upper left quadrant and the set of actions occupies

| | | *Rule* | | | |
	Umbrella Table	*1*	*2*	*3*	*4*
Conditions	Raining outside	Y	N	N	N
	Rain forecast	-	Y	Y	N
	Sunny outside	-	Y	N	-
Action	Carry umbrella	X		X	
	Do not carry umbrella		X		X

Figure 3.4 Decision table for deciding whether to carry an umbrella.

the lower left quadrant; they are called the *condition stub* and *action stub,* respectively. Each vertical rule is composed of *condition entries* and *action entries,* as shown in Figure 3.5. An irrelevant condition (that is, one that can be either yes or no) is denoted by a hyphen. Returning to the decision table in Figure 3.4, the condition that it is not rainy outside, that rain is forecast, but that the weather is sunny denotes that the action "do not carry an umbrella" should be taken.

As a realistic example, consider the problem of who should file a U.S. tax return and whether to use form 1040 (long form) or 1040A (short form).

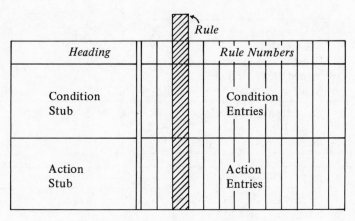

Figure 3.5 Format of a decision table.

An individual must file a return if one or more of the following conditions hold:

1. Citizen a resident of the U.S.
2. Earned $600 or more if under 65 years of age.
3. Earned $1200 or more if 65 years of age or older.
4. A tax refund is desired.

An individual is permitted to use the short form (1040A) if the following conditions hold:

1. Income is less than $10,000; *and*
2. Income consists of wages subject to withholding and not more than $200 total of other wages, interest, and dividends; *and*
3. The taxpayer wishes to use the tax table or take the standard deduction instead of itemizing deductions.

This problem is conveniently described (see Figure 3.6) in two decision tables: the first to determine if a return should be filed and the second to determine which form should be used.

The use of decision tables is particularly appropriate when it is necessary to insure that all possible conditions that can occur have been accounted for. In fact, many students have commented that a decision table would be useful in many legal contracts and make more sense than the legal jargon.

	Return Table	1	2	3	4	5	6	7
Conditions	Citizen or resident of U.S.	Y	Y	Y	Y	Y	Y	N
	Age less than 65	Y	Y	Y	N	N	N	-
	Earned $600 or more	Y	N	N	-	-	-	-
	Earned $1200 or more	-	-	-	Y	N	N	-
	Refund desired	-	Y	N	-	Y	N	Y
Action	File return (go to form table)	X	X		X	X		X
	Do not file return			X			X	

	Form Table	1	2	3	4
Conditions	Income less than $10,000	Y	Y	Y	N
	Not more than $200 of other wages, interest, etc.	Y	Y	N	-
	Tax table or standard deductions	Y	N	-	-
Action	Use Form 1040 (long)		X	X	X
	Use Form 1040A (short)	X			

Figure 3.6 A set of decision tables for filing income tax.

COMPUTER PROGRAMS

There is a certain similarity between an algorithm, as defined in this chapter, and a list of computer instructions, as presented in Chapter 2. The similarity is not a coincidence, and most, but not all, computer programs originate as algorithmic processes. In the short history* of computers, hundreds of thousands of algorithms have been developed by mathematicians, engineers, analysts, researchers, and students. Most of these algorithms have resulted in computer programs. Actually, anyone with a problem that lends itself to computer solution, in one way or another, can develop an algorithm and a corresponding computer program. This would not be possible, however, if all programs had to be written in the detailed machine-oriented format used in Chapter 2.

There was a time, in the early 1950s, when programs were actually written in internal form (that is, binary or whatever the representation was)

*It is only a little over 20 years since computers have been applied to practical problems.

and the programmer had to use actual operation codes and real computer addresses instead of symbolic equivalents, such as ADD or STORE. It is sufficient to say that there were a lot of problems involved with writing programs this way and programming was a costly and time-consuming business. Then, someone thought of the idea of using symbolic operation codes and symbolic names for data (as we used in Chapter 2), somewhat as follows:

Location	Operation	Operand	Comment
	LOAD	1,ZERO	Sum (initially zero)
	LOAD	2,ZERO	Count (initially zero)
LOOP	READ	A	Read A_i
	LOAD	3,A	Load A_i in register 3.
	BZERO	3,AVER	Test and branch (if zero) to compute average.
	MULT	3,A	Compute $A_i{}^2$
	STORE	3,A	Store $A_i{}^2$
	ADD	1,A	Add $A_i{}^2$ to Sum
	ADD	2,ONE	Add one to COUNT
	BRANCH	LOOP	Loop to read another value
AVER	STORE	2,COUNT	Store Count for DIVIDE
	DIVIDE	1,COUNT	Compute Average
	STORE	1,RESULT	Store Result
	WRITE	RESULT	Print Result
	STOP		Stop program
ZERO	CONST	0	Constant zero
ONE	CONST	1	Constant one
A	CONST	0	Storage for A_i and $A_i{}^2$
COUNT	CONST	0	Temporary storage for count
RESULT	CONST	0	Result
	END		

(By the way, this symbolic program computes $\dfrac{1}{N} \sum\limits_{i=1}^{N} A_i{}^2$.) The program looks like a program, but is not in an internal form. It is punched onto cards—one line per card—and read as input into a computer and processed by a program called an *assembler program*. The assembler program essentially translates the symbolic form of the program into a corresponding internal form. Thus, the computer is used as an aid in preparing its own program. A set of conventions for programming in this way is referred to as assembler language—a language close to the language of the machine—or symbolic machine language.

This form of symbolic programming was a substantial improvement over the old method, but it was not good enough. Most people who programmed in assembler language were professional programmers who had to be trained to utilize the computer effectively. A typical problem-solving sequence, at that time, existed somewhat as follows:

1. A scientist, engineer, or analyst has an idea that a particular computer program might be useful for a problem of some kind that he is involved with.
2. The problem originator meets with a programming manager to discuss the feasibility of having a program written.
3. If a computer program seems desirable, a professional programmer is called in and he meets with the problem originator and the programming manager to discuss the scope of the project.
4. The problem originator and the programmer decide on the details (such as input and output specifications) of the program, as well as the main processing requirements.
5. The programmer writes the program, as specified.
6 The problem originator verifies that the program satisfies requirements and that results are correct. (Frequently, specifications are changed at this point and steps 5 and 6 are repeated.)

Obviously, there are serious disadvantages to this way of doing business. First, the process is cumbersome and communication problems frequently arise. Second, the process is time-consuming and many programs that need to be developed are never written because of the time factor. Last, the growth of the computer field *and* the computer industry is limited by the supply of professional programmers.

As a result of these problems, it seemed desirable to develop a language, of some kind or another, that could be used to communicate with the computer. The English language was ruled out because of its verbosity and because of ambiguities that arise in everyday usage. One of the characteristics of a language that would facilitate programming is that it should be meaningful to the intended user. Thus, a language for engineers and scientists should be mathematically oriented, and so forth. The main idea was that a mathematician, engineer, analyst, or student could develop his own programs and both the computer industry and the users would benefit.

After several pilot projects and research efforts by various computer groups, IBM finally made the first commercial programming language available to customers in 1957. It was named FORTRAN, which is an acronym for FORmula TRANslation. FORTRAN was designed for scientific computer programming and it caught on very quickly because many computer applications involve numerical calculations of a scientific nature. With the use of FORTRAN, a person could write his own programs since a notation familiar to his kind of work is involved. For example, a simple FORTRAN program to compute $r = \dfrac{-b + \sqrt{b^2 - 4ac}}{2a}$ for several values a, b, and c is given as Figure 3.7. A program in the FORTRAN language is converted to internal computer language with a computer program known as a *compiler*.

```
2   READ (5,8)A,B,C
    IF (A .EQ. 0.0) GOTO 3
    ROOT = (−B+SQRT(B**2-4.*A*C))/2.*A
    WRITE (6,9)A,B,C,ROOT
    GOTO 2
3   STOP
8   FORMAT(3F6.2)
9   FORMAT(1X,3F6.2,F9.3)
    END
```

Figure 3.7 FORTRAN program to compute $\dfrac{-b + \sqrt{b^2 - 4ac}}{2a}$ for several values of a, b, and c.

The popularity and success of FORTRAN gave rise to other programming languages. Some well-known programming languages are:

1. The algorithmic language ALGOL for scientific computing.
2. The business-oriented language COBOL for data processing applications.
3. The multipurpose programming language PL/I for scientific and business applications and for applications that include characteristics of both areas.
4. The easy-to-use language BASIC for problem solving in a time-sharing environment.*

The bibliography at the end of the book contains several references to publications on programming languages and the reader can pursue the subject at his leisure.

The exception to the preceding remark concerns the BASIC language, developed at Dartmouth College to enable students and faculty to utilize the computer for problem solving and research work without having to make

*Time sharing refers to the remote use of the computer via telecommunications facilities and computer terminals. It is discussed later.

a significant investment in learning time. BASIC has been extremely popular and is now used in a large number of business concerns for small- to medium-scale problem solving, the kind of thing an analyst or statistician might do. The BASIC language as well as FORTRAN are introduced in Part II of the book. A BASIC version of the "root" program of Figure 3.7 is given in Figure 3.8. In fact, the BASIC program in Figure 3.8 can be simplified further as shown in Figure 3.9.

```
10   READ A,B,C
20   IF A=0 THEN 60
30   R=(−B+SQR(B↑2−4*A*C))/2*A
40   PRINT A,B,C,R
50   GOTO 10
60   STOP
70   DATA 1, −1, −6, 8, −2, −3, 0, 0, 0
80   END
```

Output:

```
1  −1  −6  3
8  −2  −3  0.75
```

Figure 3.8 BASIC program to compute

$$\frac{-b + \sqrt{b^2 - 4ac}}{2a}$$ for several values of a, b,

and c.

```
10   READ A,B,C
20   PRINT A,B,C,(−B+SQR(B↑2−4*A*C))/2*A
30   GOTO 10
40   DATA 1,−1,−6,8,−2,−3
50   END
```

Output:

```
1  −1  −6  3
8  −2  −3  0.75
OUT OF DATA IN 10
```

Figure 3.9 Simplified form of the BASIC program
given in Figure 3.8.

How and why are programming languages so effective? The answer is inherent in the following discussion. Consider a computation that involves multiplying $(A - B)$ by C and storing the result in the location that is given the symbolic name D. In assembler language, suitable machine instructions would be:

```
LOAD   1,A
SUB    1,B
MULT   1,C
STORE  1,D
```

and a statement in a programming language would be:

D=(A−B)*C

(where * denotes multiplication and = denotes replacement). In this case, the programming language is only slightly more convenient than assembler language. Next, consider a more complicated computation such as the calculation of

$$\frac{a}{\dfrac{b}{c-d}+e}$$

and the replacement of w with the result. In assembler language, a suitable set of machine instructions would be:

```
LOAD   1,C
SUB    1,C
STORE  1,TEMP
LOAD   1,B
DIV    1,TEMP
ADD    1,E
STORE  1,TEMP
LOAD   1,A
DIV    1,TEMP
STORE  1,W
```

and a corresponding statement in a programming language would be

W=A/(B/(C−D)+E)

(where / denotes division). The convenience of a programming language in this example is more obvious. Another important advantage of a programming language is that it reduces the number of errors that arise, since it uses a notation similar to mathematics and is easy for a human being to use.

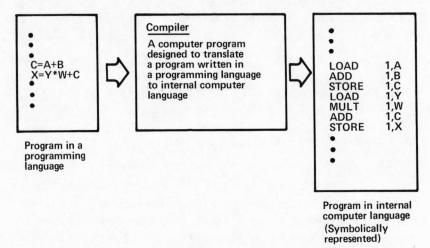

Figure 3.10 Conceptual view of the translation of a program written in a programming language to internal computer language using a compiler program.

Assembler language, on the other hand, is generally unfamiliar, in addition to being more detailed; the use of assembler language is more likely to result in programming errors that have to be identified and corrected.

To sum up, the use of a programming language subordinates the details of "machine-level" programming to a computer program called a compiler, as summarized in Figure 3.10. Another important advantage of most programming languages is that they can be machine independent. This means that a program written for one computer, let's say an IBM machine, can be used with another computer, for example, a UNIVAC machine. All a user needs do is to recompile the program on the second computer. This is a very significant concept. All we need to learn is a single programming language, such as FORTRAN. We can use this programming language with any computer that has a FORTRAN compiler. In a sense, therefore, the compiler provides the key link between the programming language and the computer.*
Computer manufacturers usually provide compilers for "standardized" programming languages, such as BASIC, COBOL, and FORTRAN.

Programming languages have become the key link between man and the computer, and the topic of programming languages has become a bona fide field of study. To a great extent, the growth of the computer industry is

---

*It is important to recognize that computers differ. They have different system configurations and they have different instruction repertoires. Moreover, operating conventions and basic design philosophy also differ between computer manufacturers and between distinct computer models from the same manufacturer.

dependent on programming languages, since they provide for machine independence, they facilitate programming, and they provide a means of describing a computational process so that the information contained in it can be passed from generation to generation.

PROGRAM PREPARATION

All of the necessary tasks in program preparation have been covered: problem definition and analysis, algorithm development and description, and programming. Sounds easy, doesn't it? Actually, program preparation is a relatively straightforward process, provided that each task is clearly understood. Each of the tasks just given, however, is relatively broad and should be expanded into its component parts. The various steps in preparing a program, therefore, are usually listed as follows:

Problem definition
Systems analysis
Algorithm development
Programming
Compilation or assembly
Debugging and testing
Documentation
Systems implementation or production

Each step is discussed separately.

At first glance, *problem definition* would hardly seem to be worth considering. (This is especially true of students who have programs assigned by an instructor.) In the real world, however, a problem is manifested by a need of some sort. Examples are the need to process test data within 24 hours or the need to test a hypothesis or theory on an extensive set of test cases. On a larger scale, a banking need might be the keeping of up-to-date banking records through a network of teller terminals. Frequently, the person recognizing the need and who is in a position to do something about it is limited in several ways:

1. He is not exactly sure of what he wants.
2. He is not certain that his needs can be satisfied.
3. He does not know how his needs can be fulfilled.
4. He is not certain that he can justify the computer application.
5 He is uncertain of how a system satisfying his needs would fit in the total organization.

Usually, the person or group originating the computer application is advised to state the proposed idea clearly, giving all relevant facts that might require further study. The key point is that the problem originator may not be experienced in computer technology.

The proposed computer application then goes through a *systems analysis* cycle in which a person experienced in both computer applications and computer technology studies the problem to determine the following:

1. Whether the proposed application can be done.
2. The "general" methodology to be employed.
3. If the proposed application can be effectively integrated into the operational structure of the organization.

For cases in which a proposed application is considered to be a viable project for the organization involved, the systems analysis cycle continues with a detailed flow analysis of the program or system, and a precise specification of inputs and outputs. This is the stage at which flowcharts and decision tables are used.

Depending on the computer application, *algorithm development* may be a part of systems analysis, programming, or a separate phase of the development cycle. Algorithm development involves the precise specification of the procedures the computer is to follow and may require mathematical analysis, heuristic reasoning, or the simple formulation of a list of steps. For example, if the computer application is to compute the trajectory a space vehicle should follow to a distant planet, then algorithm development would involve the specification and solution to complicated mathematical equations. Similarly, if the application is to perform a statistical analysis of experimental test data, then algorithm development involves the selection of appropriate statistical formulas and a specification of how they should be applied. For a payroll program, algorithm development would involve the methods for computing overtime, withholding tax, FICA, insurance, pension contributions, and so on. For a chess-playing program, algorithm development would involve a means of representing board positions in the computer and a procedure for move selection.

Programming is the process of writing the statements that comprise the computer program. Sometimes, the selection of an appropriate programming language is done during systems analysis or algorithm development. In other cases, the programmer chooses the programming language to be used. The same holds true for the development of the flowchart that describes the program. Sometimes the programmer develops it and sometimes he does not. When assembler language is used, programming is a complicated process. When a programming language is used, programming is easier but it is never a trivial process. Assembler language is used when a suitable programming language is not available for the given program or when special circumstances prevent the use of a programming language.

Compilation or *assembly* involves the conversion of a program written in a programming language or in assembler language to machine language for execution on the computer. (Recall here that compilers and assemblers are also computer programs.) A program is usually written on a "coding form" or simply a sheet of paper and then punched on cards or entered at a computer terminal on a line-by-line basis. Not all programs compile or assemble correctly the first time; in fact, most of them do not. The process of removing errors from programs is referred to as "debugging and testing," which is covered next. The manner in which a program is actually executed is covered in Chapter 6.

Errors can occur in programs in several ways:

1. The algorithm is incorrect or inappropriate.
2. One or more statements of the program have syntax errors in them—that is, they are written incorrectly.
3. The logic of the program is incorrect.
4. The program is correct but applies only to a limited subset of data that must be processed.
5. The systems analysis is faulty and the program does not serve its intended purpose.

The recognition and removal of program errors is referred to as *debugging*. The process of insuring that the program computes correctly is referred to as *testing*. Debugging and testing can occur at several stages as follows:

1. The correctness of the algorithm can be determined by applying it to test cases, manually.
2. The program can be desk checked to locate syntactical errors and detect obvious logic errors.
3. During compilation or assembly, the computer checks for syntactical errors and a "clean" compilation or assembly is not obtained until errors of this type have been removed. The program cannot be executed until it is syntactically correct. However, the compiler or assembler does not verify the logical correctness of a program.
4. The logic of the program is tested by running it against a set of test data—frequently referred to as a test deck.
5. Lastly, the program is run with actual data, which may involve running in parallel with the "old" method.

An important consideration is this. When a program error in uncovered in any of the above stages, except obviously the first, a change is made to the program and it must be recompiled or reassembled. Sometimes, the process of correcting one error creates others. When a program is modified, therefore, it must be retested to insure it is correct. The practice of retesting a program after modification is frequently referred to as *regression testing*.

Documentation has two meanings. It refers to the process of describing a program or a data processing system and it refers to the description itself. There are three major forms of documentation: a system or program document, an operator's document, and a user's document. The *system* or *program document* includes introductory and descriptive material, decision tables, flowcharts, and a listing of the programs. For most student assignments, this level of documentation is sufficient. For nonacademic programs or systems, programs are frequently developed for use by several people. Therefore, an *operator's manual* tells the computer operator how to run the program and the *user's manual* tells a prospective user what the program does and how he can use it. In the latter case, a precise description of the required input data is mandatory.

Documentation is very important, especially in business and governmental organizations that make a substantial investment in computer programming. Personnel are transferred, or promoted, or they resign, and a new person frequently has to work with another person's programs. In cases such as these, adequate documentation is an absolute necessity.

Systems implementation or *production* refers to what happens to programs after they are written. Many programs are "one-shot" jobs. Student, scientific, or engineering programs frequently, but not always, fall into this category. The name "one shot" implies that the program is written, tested, debugged, documented, and answers are obtained. Afterward, the program is very likely to remain unused. At the opposite extreme are programs, such as a company payroll program, that are used for many years—often going through change cycles to meet the needs of the times. Sets of programs that are useful to a wide range of users are called *applications packages,* and are now sold like any other commodity. In the last few years, companies have emerged that deal exclusively in the development of applications packages.

Computer programs are frequently a component in a larger system, such as a billing system, an accounts receivable system, or an inventory control system. Programs used in this way sometimes replace similar procedures done manually and require a high level of testing and verification. Similarly, computer-based systems require verification to insure that all conditions that can arise are accounted for in the systems design. Many of the difficulties that ordinary citizens have with computer-based systems, as with billing procedures with charge accounts and up-to-date record keeping, are the result of a poor systems design rather than an incorrect computer program. The systems analysis neglected to take cognizance of a possible case that could occur.

QUESTION SET

1. Prepare a flowchart to input five numbers and find the maximum value.
2 Prepare a flowchart of the procedure necessary for dropping or adding a course at your school.
3. Prepare a flowchart of the logic for "making change."
4. Prepare a decision table of the procedure for "making change."
5. Write a flowchart to tell a robot how to find a door in an L-shaped room and open it. The starting point and the position of the door(s) are not known. Initially, the robot faces parallel to some wall. The doors slide open to the left. The computer in the robot has a stored program. The robot can accept the following commands:

    a. *Move* straight ahead until you either bump something or sense the crack on the right of a door. The crack cannot be sensed unless the wall is directly to the robot's right, and the sensing mechanism is unreliable and should be given three chances to find a crack.
    b. *Turn* 90° to the left.
    c. *Insert* hand in crack.
    d. *Ring* buzzer—to be done if crack cannot be found.

The computer receives the following feedback:

    a. Whether the robot has stopped moving.
    b. Whether it was stopped by a wall or a crack.
    c. Whether there is a wall on the robot's right.

CHAPTER 4

Computer Hardware

INTRODUCTION

One of the most irritating things to computer people is to have someone call a computer an IBM machine. While it is true that a great many computers are built by the International Business Machines Corporation, many computers are not built by IBM, in fact, IBM's product line is not limited to computers. Something similar to this happened to the author while this book was being written. A call was made to a high-level administrator of a prestigious governmental agency requesting information on a technical, but not computer-related, subject. The author introduced himself as a professor of computer science at Pratt Institute. The administrator called to one of his administrative assistants, "There's an IBM man on the phone; see if you can supply the information he wants."

The point has been made. Computers differ. Sometimes the difference is obvious, as in the case of a Mercedes Benz and a Cadillac. Other times, the difference is more subtle, as in the case of a 707 and a DC8. As far as computers are concerned, obvious differences between computers involve the major components that comprise a computer system and how they are utilized. Subtle differences involve the manner in which data is represented and is used internally to the components of the computer system. Another difference between computers is the "software" available for using the computer. *Computer software* is collectively defined as the programs required to use a computer; a familiar example is the compiler, mentioned previously, for translating a program written in a programming language to machine language. Computer software is presented as a separate topic in a later chapter.

DATA REPRESENTATION

Like the human brain, the computer is a symbol processor. What does this mean? The most obvious answer goes somewhat as follows: When we think about a house or a train, we do not have a house or train in our brain. We have a mental image of a house or a train stored in our brain, and our thinking process uses that mental image. One might say, therefore, that a mental image is a symbolic representation of an object. (Obviously, the human brain goes further and we frequently deal in abstract concepts.)

The computer operates in a similar manner and is designed to process symbols. However, a computer is not a natural phenomenon; it is a man-made physical machine and the symbols processed must be something physical that a computer designer can work with. Modern computers use binary symbols, representing "on" and "off" conditions, for two reasons:

1. Binary symbols can easily be represented physically, as depicted in Figure 4.1.
2. Binary symbols are the most efficient means of recording an amount of information.[1]

Each binary device must be in either of the two states. It is convenient to ignore the type of device and to represent the two states by the symbols 1 and 0. (Note that any two other symbols, such as + and −, would be equally useful.*) The symbols 1 and 0, used in this manner, are not to be regarded as numerals but as marks representing the two states of a binary system.

A single binary device is capable of representing only two symbols and is insufficient for building or describing a computer. Thus, binary devices are used in combination to represent a larger number of symbols. For example, two binary devices can be used to represent four distinct symbols as follows:

---

[1]N. Weiner, *Cybernetics: or Control and Communication in the Animal and the Machine* (2nd ed.), Cambridge, Mass.: The M.I.T. Press, 1961, pp. 116–118.

*Morse code is another example of a binary system. A short electrical signal (represented by • and pronounced "dit") and a long electrical signal (represented by - and pronounced "dah") are used to represent characters of an alphabet. For example, the distress signal SOS is represented by: ··· - - - ···.

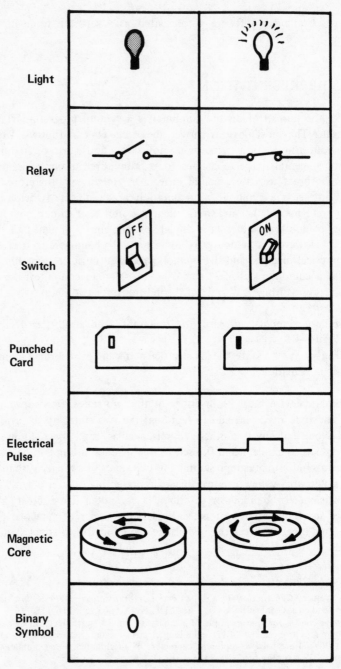

Figure 4.1 Representation of binary symbols.

Device

1	2	
0	0	Symbol represented by 00
0	1	Symbol represented by 01
1	0	Symbol represented by 10
1	1	Symbol represented by 11

A single 1 or 0 is referred to as a *bit,* so we can say that two bits can be used to represent four symbols. Similarly, three bits can be used to represent eight symbols, that is, 000, 001, 010, 011, 100, 101, 110, 111. It follows that *n* bits can be used to represent 2^n symbols, that is $\dfrac{n}{2 \times 2 \times 2 \ldots \times 2}$. One of the major differences between computers is the manner in which bits are combined for the storage of information.

WORDS VERSUS BYTES

Recall that in Chapter 2, it was mentioned that main storage consists of "locations" used to hold information and that each location is identified by and referenced with an address, usually taken to be numeric in nature. The question is, "How much information should a location hold?" Two basic philosophies, or schools of thought, are widely used. The first school says that a location should be capable of storing a relatively large number of bits—say 36. A computer that employs this philosophy is referred to as a *word-oriented computer* and each group of 36 bits is referred to as a *word.* We will see in the next section that a word can represent a number, a computer instruction, or several characters of information. The second school says that a location should be capable of storing a relatively small number of bits—say eight. A computer that employs this philosophy is referred to as a *byte-oriented computer* and each group of eight bits is referred to as a *byte.* A byte can represent a single character of information; successive bytes are used to represent numbers and computer instructions.

It is important to note than in a word-oriented computer, a word in main storage is directly addressable and in a byte-oriented computer, a byte in main storage is directly addressable.

CHARACTERS AND NUMBERS

After all this, we still have not discussed how information is stored. Well, here it is. Information in the computer is interpreted according to conventions established by computer designers and users. In other words, a series of bits, such as 010001, has an agreed-upon meaning.* It is important to note, however, that a series of bits may have a different meaning, depending on how it is used. Thus, more than one convention exists, depending on how the information is used. Table 4.1 gives commonly used 6-bit and 8-bit character representations. Using the 6-bit representations, the characters UNITED STATES OF AMERICA would be stored in a word-oriented computer, with 36-bit words, as depicted in Figure 4.2. Using the 8-bit representa-

Word _n_

| 110100 | 100101 | 011001 | 110011 | 010101 | 010100 |

"UNITED"

Word _n_+1

| 110000 | 110010 | 110011 | 010001 | 110011 | 010101 |

" STATE"

Word _n_+2

| 110010 | 110000 | 100110 | 010110 | 110000 | 010001 |

"S OF A"

Word _n_+3

| 100100 | 010101 | 101001 | 011001 | 010011 | 010001 |

"MERICA"

Figure 4.2 Storage of the characters UNITED STATES OF AMERICA using 6-bit representation with 36-bit computer words.

tion, the characters OMAR KHAYYAM would be stored in a byte-oriented computer, with 8-bit bytes, as depicted in Figure 4.3. There are advantages to both methods that are discussed after the representation of numbers is presented.

*In six-bit character code, 010001 is a representation for the letter A.

TABLE 4.1   REPRESENTATIVE 6-BIT AND 8-BIT CODES.

Character	6-bit code	8-bit code
0	000000	11110000
1	000001	11110001
2	000010	11110010
3	000011	11110011
4	000100	11110100
5	000101	11110101
6	000110	11110110
7	000111	11110111
8	001000	11111000
9	001001	11111001
A	010001	11000001
B	010010	11000010
C	010011	11000011
D	010100	11000100
E	010101	11000101
F	010110	11000110
G	010111	11000111
H	011000	11001000
I	011001	11001001
J	100001	11010001
K	100010	11010010
L	100011	11010011
M	100100	11010100
N	100101	11010101
O	100110	11010110
P	100111	11010111
Q	101000	11011000
R	101001	11011001
S	110010	11100010
T	110011	11100011
U	110100	11100100
V	110101	11100101
W	110110	11100110
X	110111	11100111
Y	111000	11101000
Z	111001	11101001
blank character	110000	01000000
=	001011	01111110
+	010000	01001110
−	100000	01100000
*	101100	01011100
/	110001	01100001
(	111100	01001101
)	011100	01011101
, (comma)	111011	01101011
. (period or dec. pt.)	011011	01001011
$	101011	01011011
' (quote)	001100	01111101

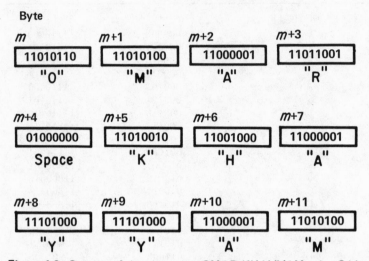

Figure 4.3 Storage of the characters OMAR KHAYYAM using 8-bit representation in a byte-oriented computer with 8-bit bytes.

Numbers are stored as computer words using the binary number system. First, recall that in the decimal number system, the number 123 is defined as follows:

$$1 \times 10^2 + 2 \times 10^1 + 3 \times 10^0$$

which is evaluated as 100+20+3=123. It is called a *positional number system* and uses the digits 0 through 9. A positional number that uses the digits 0 and 1 is called the *binary number system,* so that the binary number 101 is defined as:

$$1 \times 2^2 + 0 \times 2^1 + 1 \times 2^0$$

which is evaluated as 4+0+1=5. Similarly, the binary number 1011 is defined as:

$$1 \times 2^3 + 0 \times 2^2 + 1 \times 2^1 + 1 \times 2^0$$

which is evaluated as 8+0+2+1=11. The reader probably has guessed what comes next. The 1 bits in a binary number correspond to "on" conditions of a binary device and the 0 bits in a binary number correspond to an "off" condition.

In a word-oriented computer, the bits of the word correspond to the bits in a binary number. For example, the binary word:

| 000000 000000 000000 000000 000101 010001 |

represents the number:*

$$0 \times 2^{34} + \ldots + 0 \times 2^{11} + 0 \times 2^{10} + 0 \times 2^9 + 1 \times 2^8 + 0 \times 2^7 + 1 \times 2^6 + 0 \times 2^5 + 1 \times 2^4$$
$$+ 0 \times 2^3 + 0 \times 2^2 + 0 \times 2^1 + 1 \times 2^0$$

which is evaluated as

$$0 + \ldots + 0 + 0 + 0 + 256 + 0 + 64 + 0 + 16 + 0 + 0 + 0 + 1 = 337$$

It is also important to note that the same word can represent the characters "00005A" using the 6-bit codes in Table 4.1.

In a byte-oriented computer, words are comprised of two or more bytes, depending on the precision desired by a particular computer application. Standard word signs are established by the computer manufacturer. For example, one well-known computer allows 2-byte, 4-byte, and 8-byte words. For example, the two-byte word:

| 01001101 11000010 |

represents the number:†

$$1 \times 2^{14} + 0 \times 2^{13} + 0 \times 2^{12} + 1 \times 2^{11} + 1 \times 2^{10} + 0 \times 2^9 + 1 \times 2^8 + 1 \times 2^7 + 1 \times 2^6 + 0 \times 2^5 + 0 \times 2^4$$
$$+ 0 \times 2^3 + 0 \times 2^2 + 1 \times 2^1 + 0 \times 2^0$$

which is evaluated as 16384+0+0+2048+1024+0+256+128+64+0+0+0+0+2= 19906. The same two bytes also represent the characters "(B" using the 8-bit codes in Table 4.1.

In both of the above examples, the information stored as words or bytes could be interpreted as character data or as binary numeric data. The precise meaning is dependent on the instructions that process the data. If an in-

---

*The first bit gives the sign: 0 for plus and 1 for minus.
† Again, the first bit represents the sign: 0 for plus and 1 for minus.

struction designed for character data references the data then it is interpreted as character data. Similarly, if an instruction designed for numeric
data references the data, then it is interpreted as numeric data. The computer
is a precise instrument that does not allow any ambiguity.

The relative merits of 6-bit characters and 8-bit bytes are discussed later.
So far as this section is concerned, it is important to note that a 6-bit
character allows 2^6 (or 64) possible different characters and an 8-bit byte
allows 2^8 (or 256) possible different characters. Eight-bit bytes are characteristic of some modern computers and one of the reasons they were adopted
is that 64 different characters is insufficient for some applications.

COMPUTER INSTRUCTIONS

The basic parts of a computer instruction are the operation code, modifier, and the instruction operands. In a word-oriented computer, the length
of a computer instruction is usually fixed and takes the following general
form:

Operation Code	Modifiers	Operand Address

Each of the three fields exists as a series of bits that represents a specific
computer instruction. It is composed of an operation code that specifies
the operation to be performed, a modifier that augments the instruction in
some fashion, and an operand address. The operand address is the address of
the location in main storage of data to be used in the instruction. The bits,
comprising the address field, are interpreted as a positive number that denotes the relative location of the data word used as an operand. Thus, the
number of bits in the operand field implicitly specifies the number of locations there can be in main storage. As a trivial example, if the operand address field were comprised of four bits, then main storage could contain 2^4 or
16 locations numbered 0000, 0001, 0010, 0011, 0100, 0101, 0110, 0111,
1000, 1001, 1010, 1011, 1100, 1101, 1110, and 1111. If the operand address field contained 15 bits, then main storage could have 2^{15} or 32,768
locations. Similarly, if the operation code field contained five bits, then 2^5 or
32 different computer instructions could be possible.

In a byte-oriented computer, different sized instructions are permitted.
Thus, some instructions can utilize registers only, as in the following 2-byte
instruction:*

*The instructions given are hypothetical but representative of several modern com-
puters.

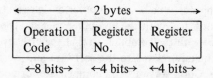

(A sample instruction might be: add the contents of register 1 to the contents of register 2.) A typical 4-byte instruction might be:

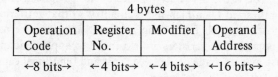

(A sample instruction might be: Subtract the contents of the specified main storage location from the contents of the specified register.) A typical 6-byte instruction would be:

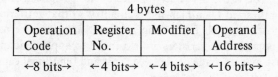

(A sample instruction might be: Move the bytes starting at operand address 2 to byte locations beginning in operand address 1. The length of the move is specified in the modifier field.) In all cases, the *length in bytes of the instruction* is implied in the operation code.

Although this discussion of computer instructions has indeed been simplified, it demonstrates several important points:

1. The format of the instructions for a particular computer determines the range of main storage addresses that can be addressed and the number of different operation codes that can be used.
2. The word- versus byte-oriented storage question does make a difference in the types of instructions (for example, one operand versus two operands) that can be used.

Clearly, the difference between word- and byte-oriented computers does not matter for some computer applications, such as those that deal primarily with numerical calculations. When a substantial amount of character handling is involved, however, then there seems to be some advantage to a byte-oriented computer over a word-oriented computer. But basic computer design can be misleading because most users do not deal with the computer, per se. They use "computer software" to interface with the computer so that the effectiveness of the computer system is ultimately related to the software and is not completely dependent on hardware. Good software can compensate for poor hardware, and vice versa. The current trend is to integrate the design of the hardware and the software.

Another difference between computers was briefly discussed in Chapter 2: the number of arithmetic registers (or accumulators). Recall here that an arithmetic register is synthesized from high-speed circuitry so that retrieving an operand from a register is much faster than retrieving an operand from main storage. The key point is that registers are expensive to implement and computer designers must make a trade-off between cost and functional capability. Consider the calculation of the statement:

A= B*C+D*E

which means: multiply B by C; multiply D by E; add the results of the two multiplications; and replace the value of A with the result of the addition. In a computer with one accumulator, the computations might exist as follows:

```
LOAD     B
MULT     C
STORE    TEMP1
LOAD     D
MULT     E
STORE    TEMP2
LOAD     TEMP1
ADD      TEMP2
STORE    A
```

In a computer with two registers, numbered 1 and 2, the calculations might be:

```
LOAD     1,B
MULT     ' C
LOAD     2,D
MULT     2,E
ADD      1,2
STORE    1,A
```

The number of instructions is reduced by 33 percent, which may be significant depending on the calculations being performed.

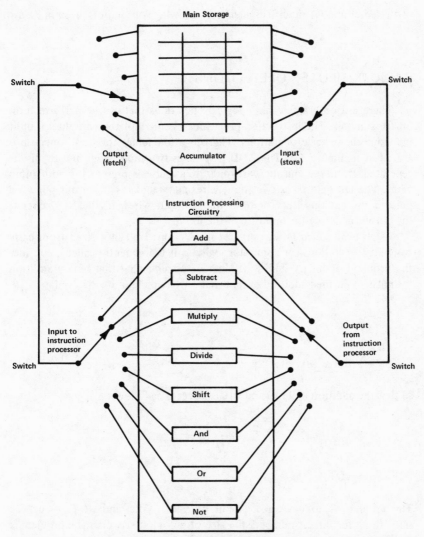

Figure 4.4 Simplified diagram of the relationship between main storage and instruction-processing circuitry.

Thomas H. Crowley,[2] Director of the Computing Science Research Center at Bell Telephone Laboratories, has developed a useful diagram that depicts the relationship between main storage and the instruction-processing circuitry

[2]T. H. Crowley, *Understanding Computers,* New York: McGraw-Hill Book Company, 1967, p. 58.

of the computer. A modified version of Crowley's diagram is given in Figure 4.4.

BASIC COMPUTER OPERATIONS

There are only a few basic logical operations that can be performed on binary symbols. The instruction-processing circuitry of the computer is built up from these basic operations. The operation tables for these operations are given in Figure 4.5. The AND gate takes two input wires and a pulse is generated from the output wire only if a pulse is present on both input wires. The OR gate takes two input wires and generates an output pulse if a pulse is present on either or both of the input wires. In the NOT circuit, the output is simply the opposite of the input.

As an example of how computer instructions are synthesized from basic computer operations (or computer logic, as it is frequently called), consider the problem of binary addition. Most of us remember that binary addition is similar to decimal addition except that only two digits are involved:

$0+0=0$
$0+1=1$
$1+0=1$
$1+1=0$ with a carry of 1

so that the addition of 1110 and 0101 proceeds as follows:

$$
\begin{array}{r}
1110 \\
+0101 \\
\hline
\end{array}
$$
Carry 11
Sum 10011

The problem is to develop a circuit of ANDs, ORs, and NOTs to do the same thing for binary numbers the size of a computer word. The problem is depicted in Figure 4.6.

First, it is important to note that two kinds of addition are involved. When A_0 is added to B_0, the addition takes two inputs—A_0 and B_0. When A_1 is added to B_1, the addition takes three inputs—A_1, B_1, and C_0. An adder circuit that takes two inputs is referred to as a *half-adder,* depicted as follows:

(Input) A_i → | Half | → S_i (Sum)
(Input) B_i → | Adder | → C_i (Carry)

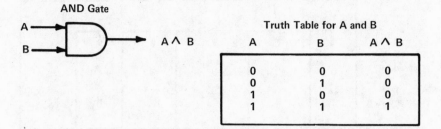

AND Gate

Truth Table for A and B

A	B	A ∧ B
0	0	0
0	1	0
1	0	0
1	1	1

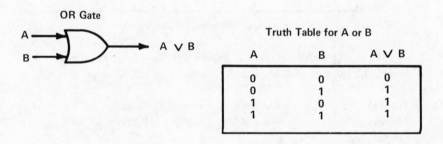

OR Gate

Truth Table for A or B

A	B	A ∨ B
0	0	0
0	1	1
1	0	1
1	1	1

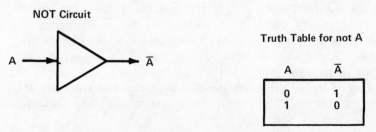

NOT Circuit

Truth Table for not A

A	Ā
0	1
1	0

Figure 4.5 Basic computer operations and their corresponding truth tables.

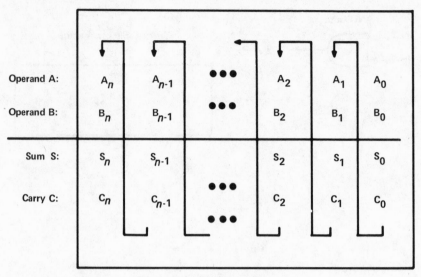

Figure 4.6 Binary addition.

The logic of a half-adder is given in Figure 4.7. An adder circuit that takes three inputs is referred to as a *full adder*, depicted as follows:

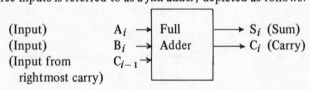

A full adder can be constructed from two half-adders and an OR gate, as depicted in Figure 4.8.

So far as the complete addition is concerned, the circuitry for the add instruction is constructed from $n - 1$ full adders and one half-adder—that is, when the word to be added contains n bits. Computer designers synthesize computer circuits, such as the one just described, from electronic components such as transistors or vacuum tubes.

Most of the other arithmetic operations use the addition circuitry. For example, the subtraction operation is implemented by taking the negative of the subtrahend and adding it to the minuend; that is, the subtraction operation $A - B$ is computed as $A + (-B)$. In a somewhat analogous fashion, multiplication is performed as repeated additions and division is performed as repeated subtractions.

There are obviously other operations in the instruction repertoire of a computer; for example, all computers include load, store, shifting, branching,

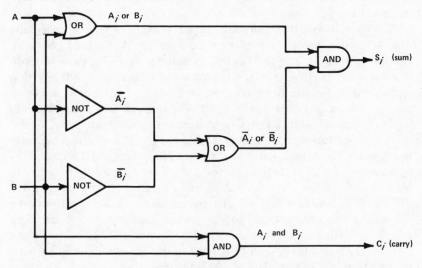

Figure 4.7 Logic design of a half-adder.

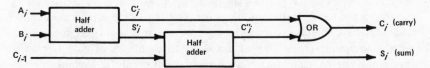

Figure 4.8 A full adder constructed from two half-adders and an OR gate.

and input/output instructions. The circuitry for these instructions as well as the instruction-decoding circuitry, the control circuitry, and the circuitry for referencing main storage would be synthesized from basic computer operations—just as the add operation was synthesized above. The key point, however, has been made: The computer is a complex device built up from a collection of relatively simple components.

MAIN STORAGE

Main storage is one of the critical components in a computer system because large amounts of it are costly. Two technologies for implementing main storage are generally used: passive and active. *Passive* memory devices possess two states, and energy (that is, electricity) is not needed to maintain a given state. Energy is only needed to change the state. Passive devices are also nonvolatile in the sense that the information is not destroyed when the power is turned off. *Active* memory devices require energy to maintain the state of the device.

The most frequently used main-storage technology uses ferromagnetic cores–a passive device, referred to as core storage. A magnetic core is an "iron doughnut" about 1/16 of an inch in diameter with wires strung through it, as depicted in Figure 4.9(*a*). The presence of a bit (that is, a 0 or a 1) is represented by the fact that a core can be magnetized in either of two directions, as shown in Figure 4.9(*b*). Cores are organized into planes and into stacks (see Figures 4.9(*c*) and 4.9(*d*)) to represent bytes or words.

A core is selected for reading by sending one-half of the current necessary for "sensing it" through the X and Y wires. Note that only the core at the intersection of the two wires receives the full current; other cores receive only one-half of the current. As depicted in Figure 4.10, the presence of a "1" bit is detected by the fact that current in the X and Y wires causes the state of the core to "flip" so that current flows in the sense wire. This process is referred to as "destructive read out" since a "1" bit is cleared to a "0" bit. The core must be reset by sending current through the X and Y wires in the opposite direction. This is where the *inhibit wire* is used (see Figure 4.9); current is sent through the inhibit wire to prevent the core from being reset if it was originally "0." The process of writing a magnetic core is essentially the same as the procedure for resetting a core after a destructive readout. The primary advantage of core storage is that it is relatively inexpensive to manufacture. One of the main disadvantages of core storage is that as the size of main storage is increased, its physical size becomes a limiting factor on its speed–remembering that modern computers operate at speeds measured in billionths of seconds (nanoseconds).

One means of implementing main storage with very high speeds is to use electronic components, such as transistors. Figure 4.11 depicts a schematic of a basic storage cell that utilizes two transistors collectively to represent the on and off states. The storage cell, referred to as a "flip flop," is read by raising the word-line voltage causing the flip-flop current to transfer to one of the bit lines and be detected by a current-sensing amplifier. Writing is accomplished by varying the voltage on the bit lines and thereby forcing the flip-flop into the specified state. This is an example of an "active" memory device. The primary advantage of using circuitry for main storage is that many memory circuits can be etched into chips, frequently made of silicon, so that physical size becomes less of a limiting factor. (In the IBM System/ 370 Model 145, for example, a silicon chip approximately 1/8 inch square has 1,434 circuit elements etched in it. These circuit elements form 128 bits

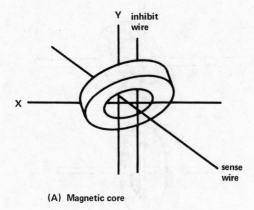

(A) Magnetic core

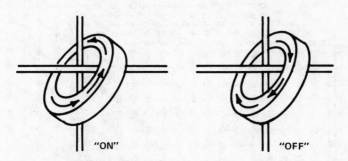

"ON" "OFF"

(B) Two states of a magnetic core

Figure 4.9 Magnetic core storage.

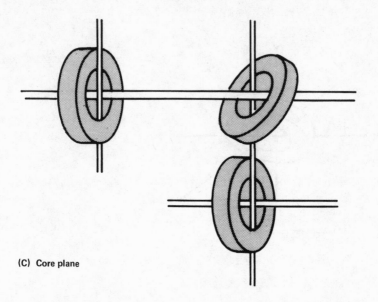

(C) Core plane

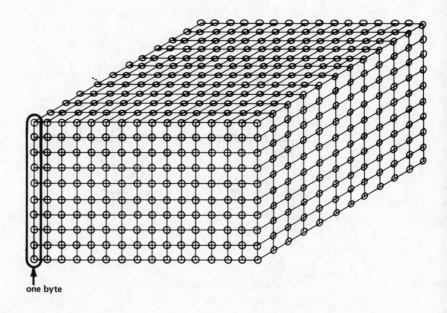

one byte

(D) Core Stack

Figure 4.9 (cont.)

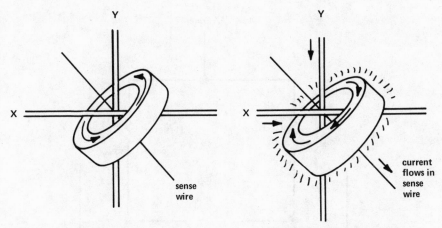

(A) Representation of "1" bit

(B) Current is applied to X and Y to "select" the core. The core is flipped (magnetism is reversed) causing current to flow in sense wire denoting presence of bit.

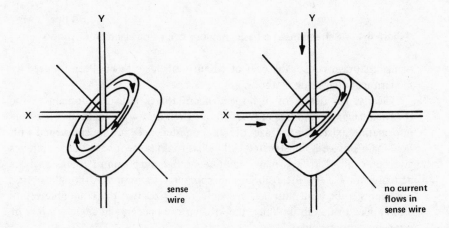

(C) Representation of "0" bit

(D) Current is applied to X and Y to "select" the core. The core is not flipped and no current flows in the sense wire.

Figure 4.10 Operation of core storage.

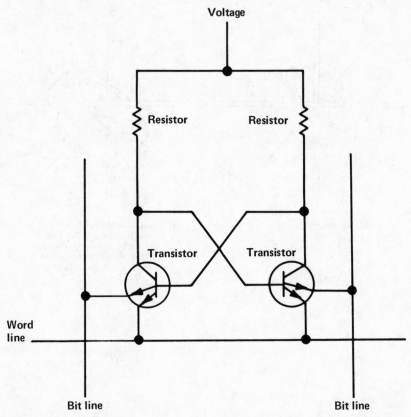

Figure 4.11 Schematic of a basic memory cell using electronic components.

of main storage.) Also, the cost of circuitry of this type has been reduced by modern manufacturing methods.

Clearly, the design of high-speed main storage is in the domain of the electrical engineer and it is only fair to mention that other methods of storing information exist. The average user of computers need not be concerned with how main storage is constructed. All he has to do is use it with the techniques given previously. In fact, many computer programmers and systems analysts actually know very little about the computer hardware. Although at first this seems to be a bit unusual, one quickly realizes that the same philosophy also applies to the automobile, the kitchen can opener, and a wide variety of other modern machines.

THE COMPUTER AS A SYSTEM

Now that we have a reasonably good idea of the internal structure of the computer, it is useful to put the pieces together. First, let us review what we already know:

1. The computer is constructed from electronic components that are synthesized in a logical fashion.
2. The computer operates under control of instructions that perform well-defined operations; the instructions along with data are held in main storage.
3. The central processing unit controls the operation of the computer.
4. Before a computer can be used, a computer program must be written.
5. Computer languages and other descriptive techniques are used in program preparation.
6. Computer programs, called language processors, are used to translate programs written in a computer language into internal machine language.

This section is concerned with how the instructions and data are stored on computer storage media and how they are transferred between the computer and the storage media.

Figure 4.12 depicts a typical computer system. Units shown are the central processing unit and main storage, the control panel (placed on the face of the central processor), disk storage, magnetic tape unit, a card reader/punch, and a line printer. A schematic of a similar computer system including associated control units is given in Figure 4.13. A schematic is more useful for discussion because the interconnections are shown; in most computer systems, components are housed in separate cabinets and are connected by cables placed under a specially raised floor.

It is important to emphasize that programs and data are not stored in the central processing unit and main storage. They are read into main storage from an external storage medium when they are to be used by the central processing unit. This is why the additional equipment is required.

The central processing unit and main storage are electronic devices. Input and output devices are both electronic and mechanical, and since electronic devices are inherently faster than mechanical devices, the central processing unit is faster than input and output devices. For example, it takes approximately one hundred milliseconds for a card reader to read one punched card. In that time, an average computer can execute approximately 50,000 instructions. Therefore, the central processing unit, which is an expensive com-

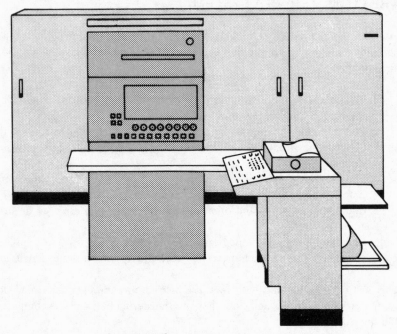

Figure 4.12 Typical computer system.

ponent, should not be kept waiting for input and output. This is where the "data channel" comes in. A *data channel* is essentially a small hard-wired computer connected to main storage; it receives control from the central processing unit. A sample input/output subsystem is depicted in Fig. 4.14. The central processing unit, under control of a computer program, tells a data channel to transfer data between main storage and an external device. (It also gives the amount and location of the data.) Then the central processing unit continues to operate. The data channel signals to the input/output device and manages the data transfer operation. Let us take a read operation as an example. The data channel accepts information from an input device (perhaps a card reader) one character at a time at a relatively low speed. The characters are put into a temporary storage area in the data channel called a buffer. When enough characters are accumulated, the central processing unit is interrupted and the information is placed in main storage by the data channel. This process is depicted in Figure 4.15. Two important concepts are involved. First, the connection between an input/output device and the data channel is standard (called the *standard interface*), so that devices other than

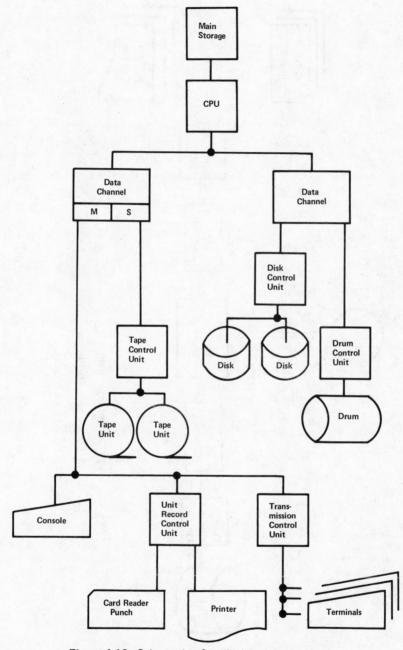

Figure 4.13 Schematic of typical computer system.

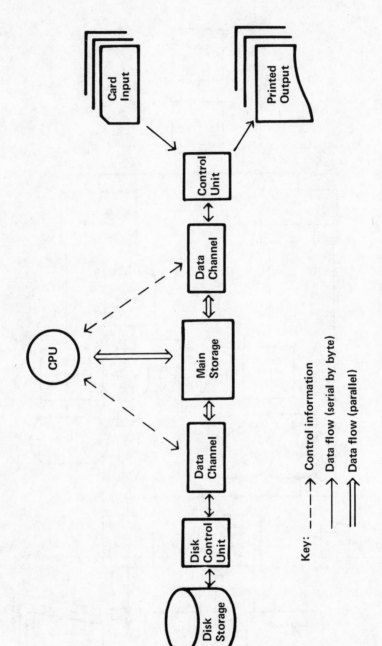

Figure 4.14   Sample input/output subsystems.

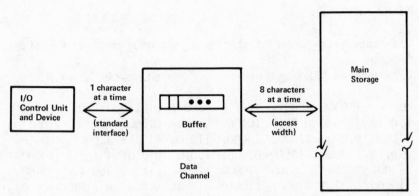

Figure 4.15 Data transfer between an input/output device and main storage.

those manufactured by the computer manufacturer can be connected.* Second, the number of times the central processing unit is interrupted by the data channel is significant. The amount of data transferred between a data channel and main storage at one time is referred to as *access width*. Some large computers have an access width of 128 bytes. On small computers, the access width is in the neighborhood of two bytes. This is another difference between computers and a contributing factor to the speed of the overall system.

The exact status of data channels differs between computer systems. In some systems, a data channel is a stand-alone unit. In other systems, a data channel is integrated into the central processing unit and housed in the same cabinet. In these systems, circuitry is occasionally shared between the two components.

A *control unit* controls an input/output device by handling data transfer operations and by initiating nondata operations such as a tape rewind. Similar to the data channel, a control unit can be stand-alone or integrated with the input/output device.

The organization of computer system components is significant for several reasons. Effective organization promotes effective computer utilization and provides for flexibility and reliability. Organization also affects system cost and the "foreign" devices that can be attached. Last, organization has been used by some computer manufacturers to prevent their competitor's input/output devices from being attached to their computers.

The next chapter covers input and output devices and their respective media.

---

*Incidentally, this has given rise to the widely publicized "plug-compatible computer peripherals" industry.

QUESTION SET

1. Describe five devices (other than those given in Figure 4.1) that are binary in nature.
2. Decipher the following quotation using the 6-bit codes in Table 4.1:

```
010001  110000  100011  100110  010001  010110  110000  100110
010110  110000  010010  101001  010101  010001  010100  110011
110000  010001  110000  100001  110100  010111  110000  100110
010110  110000  110110  011001  100101  010101  111011  110000
010001  100101  010100  110000  110011  011000  100110  110100
110000  010010  010101  110010  011001  010100  010101  110000
100100  010101  110000  011001  100101  110000  110011  011000
010101  110000  110110  011001  100011  010100  010101  101001
100101  010101  110010  110010  011011
```

3. Convert the following numbers from the binary positional number system to the decimal positional number system:

```
    10       1  1000000   1010
   110   10101      1000  10100
 10111    1111       100  11110
```

4. Given a computer with the following instruction format:

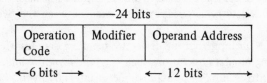

Compute the maximum size of main storage and the total number of operation codes permitted.

5 Try to develop a rationale for determining how many arithmetic registers a computer should have.

6. Draw logic circuits for the following expressions:

$$S = (A \wedge B) \vee C$$

$$S = (\bar{A} \wedge \bar{B} \wedge C) \vee (\bar{A} \wedge B \wedge \bar{C}) \vee (A \wedge \bar{B} \wedge \bar{C}) \vee (A \wedge B \wedge C)$$

7. The chapter mentions that many machines (or devices) exist in our everyday lives about which the user actually knows very little. Other than the automobile and the kitchen can opener, try to name 12 others.

8. The concurrent operation of the central processing unit and a data channel is often referred to as "input and output" overlap. From what we have discussed previously, what kinds of applications would this feature be most appropriate for?

9. Try to think up the pros and cons of having a standard interface. (This is a good question for class discussion.)

CHAPTER 5

Input and Output – Media and Devices

INTRODUCTION

Almost anyone who has registered at a college, paid a telephone bill, or made a purchase at a large department store has dealt with computer media of some kind. The average person, however, is exposed to only a limited subset of the media that are currently available. Obviously, not all media and devices can be covered in a book of this type. The objective here is to cover the most widely used media and associated devices and also those with the greatest educational value.

It is important to distinguish between the medium and the device used to read or write it. For example, a punched card is a medium for recording information; a card reader or a card punch is a device.

Four media and associated devices are presented in detail: punched cards, magnetic tape, magnetic disk, and the line printer. A variety of other devices is covered briefly to acquaint the reader with the current thinking with regard to input and output devices. Telecommunications facilities are widely used these days and much of the concern over large data banks is related to the manner in which they can be accessed via ordinary telephone lines and a terminal device. Telecommunications and terminal devices are also covered in this chapter.

PUNCHED CARDS

The punched card as we know it today was invented by Herman Hollerith in the 1880s for work on the U.S. census. In fact, card code is frequently

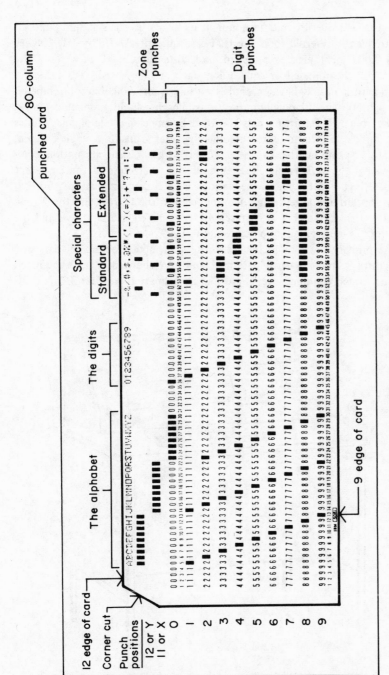

Figure 5.1 Hollerith card code.

79

referred to as Hollerith code in honor of its inventor. The standard punched card, frequently referred to as the IBM card, measures 7 3/8 by 3 1/4 inches and is 0.007 inch thick. A punched card costs about 1/10 of a cent. The corners may be rounded or square and one corner is usually cut to detect when a card is upside-down. A card is organized into 80 columns, numbered 1 through 80, with 12 punching positions in each column, numbered 12, 11, and 0 through 9. Information is recorded by punching "rectangular" holes in the card; one column represents one character. Thus, in a single column, there are 12 positions that can be punched. By established convention, combinations of the various punches represent the characters of the computer alphabet. Figure 5.1 depicts the various card code combinations. For example, the letter B is represented by punches in the 12 row and the 2 row. Similarly, the character 7 is represented by a punch in the 7 row, and the character * is represented by punches in the 11, 8, and 4 rows.

The primary use of punched cards is as an input medium for data prepared through human participation. Figure 5.2 shows a typical keypunch machine, which contains a keyboard like an ordinary typewriter. Blank cards

Figure 5.2 Typical keypunch machine for punching cards.

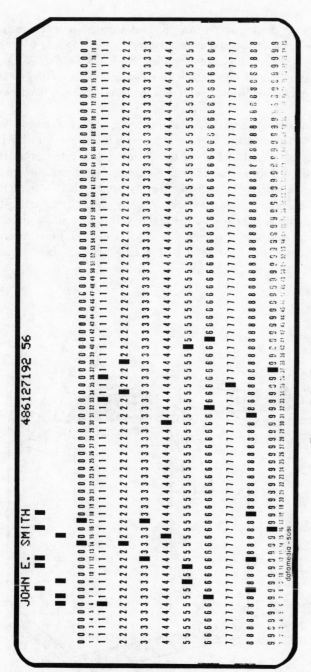

Figure 5.3 Typical input card.

81

are entered into the keypunch machine and appropriate holes are punched
when a given key is depressed. Figure 5.3 gives a typical input card. It contains
three fields: name, social security number, and hours. (A *field* is a group of
columns that represent one data item.) Punched cards are convenient for
human use because individual cards can easily be added, deleted, replaced,
and sorted.

Most computer systems include a card reader and a card punch, depicted
in Figure 5.4. The objective of the card reader is to detect (that is, recognize)
the contents of a card and place the corresponding information in main
storage. Figure 5.5 shows the internal workings of an automatic card reader/
punch. Holes in the card are sensed either by brushes that protrude through
the card and make an electrical connection, or by photoelectric cells. Reading
is performed on the right side of the unit. Cards to be read are placed in the
read hopper; a card is read when a read signal is received from the computer,
via the data channel and control unit. The card passes through two read sta-

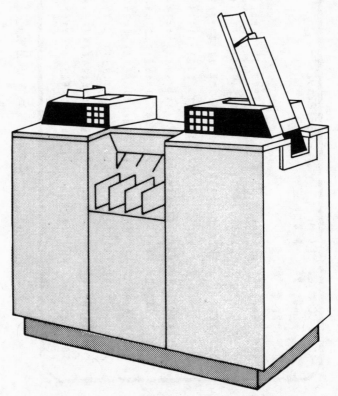

Figure 5.4   Combined card reader/punch unit.

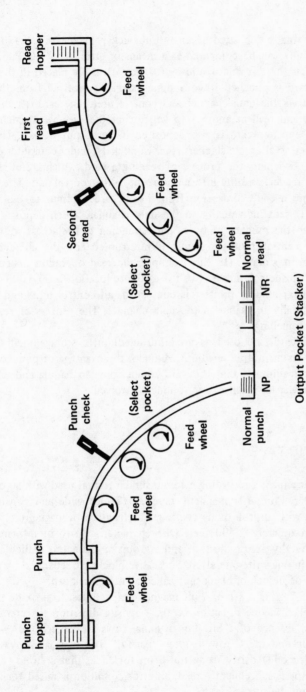

Figure 5.5 Internal mechanism of the card reader/punch.

83

tions and is finally deposited in an output stacker. Each card is read twice so that the results can be compared as a means of error checking. Punching is performed on the left side of the unit. Blank cards are placed in the punch hopper; a card is punched when a punch signal is received from the computer—again via the data channel and control unit. The card is punched at one station and read at another to verify that the card was punched correctly. The punched card is also deposited in an output stacker. The cards may be routed to alternate stackers (that is, pockets) under computer control.

Figure 5.6 depicts the process of reading a card, which is initially read by the card reader, and the information sent to the control unit. The control unit performs a code conversion from 12-bit card columns to 8-bit bytes. Each byte is sent individually to the data channel, which deposits it in a buffer. When the number of bytes corresponding to the access width is received, the central processing unit is interrupted and the characters are placed in main storage. (In this example, the read operation instructs the computer to place columns 1–4 of the card into location 1000–1003 of main storage.) As far as data transfer is concerned, all control units and devices appear essentially the same to the data channel. The process of reading is reversed for punching.

Punched cards are used as an input medium, a storage medium, and occasionally as an output medium. A major disadvantage of punched cards as a storage medium is that they are cumbersome to handle and occupy a relatively large space when a large volume is involved.

MAGNETIC TAPE

Magnetic tape is a recording medium similar to that used with an ordinary tape recorder. Computer magnetic tape is 1/2 inch wide and consists of a plastic base with an iron oxide coating. The length of a magnetic tape varies up to approximately 2,400 feet. One character's worth of information is recorded laterally across the tape and a group of characters (called a block) is recorded in one write operation. Successive blocks are separated by approximately 3/4 of an inch of blank tape called an interblock gap.

Figure 5.7 gives a set of 7-bit magnetic tape codes. Iron oxide particles are magnetized in one direction or the opposite direction to represent the presence or absence of a bit. Longitudinal rows are labeled CBA8421 for identification and the C row denotes "parity." The tape is always written with even (or odd) parity using the C bit for codes that are odd (or even). When the tape is subsequently read, an error condition is raised for all characters without the correct parity.

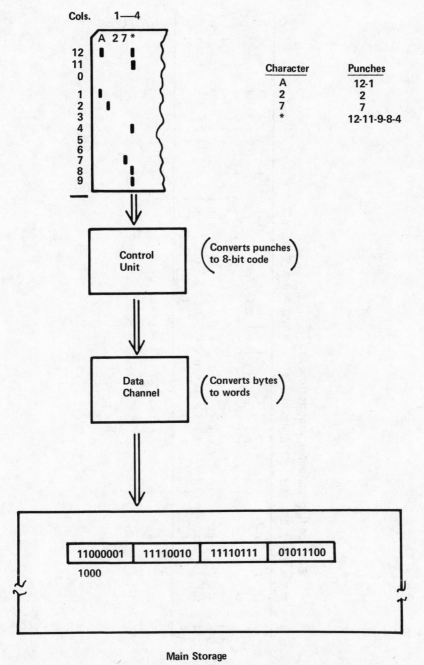

Figure 5.6 The code conversion process in reading a punched card.

85

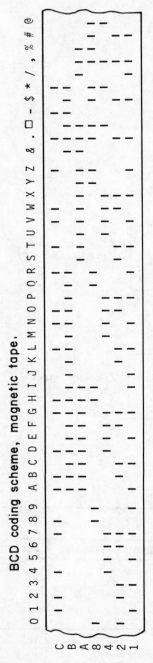

Figure 5.7 Magnetic tape codes.

86

Figure 5.8 Magnetic tape units.

Magnetic tape is read and written by a magnetic tape unit, such as the one depicted in Figure 5.8. One reel serves as the supply reel and the other serves as the take-up reel. The tape is written or read as it passes over a magnetic read-write head, as depicted in Figure 5.9.

The process of reading a magnetic tape is similar in concept to that of reading a punched card. (See Figure 5.10.) The control unit performs a code conversion from 6-bit code (7 bits including the parity) to 8-bit bytes.* Magnetic tape is a "sequential" device in the sense that the tape unit must pass over the $(i - 1)$th data item before the ith data item can be accessed. In the example of Figure 5.10, the "next" information on tape (A27* in this case) is read into locations 1000–1003. Again, the conversion process is reversed for writing.

Magnetic tape is characterized by the width of the tape, the recording density, and the tape speed. As mentioned above, magnetic tape with a width of one-half inch is the most widely used. However, tape up to one inch has been used to increase the data transfer rate. *Density* refers to the number of bytes that are recorded per inch. Typical values range from 200 bytes per

---

*Nine-channel (that is, one parity bit and eight data bits) magnetic tape is also in widespread use, so that with 8-bit bytes, no code conversion is necessary.

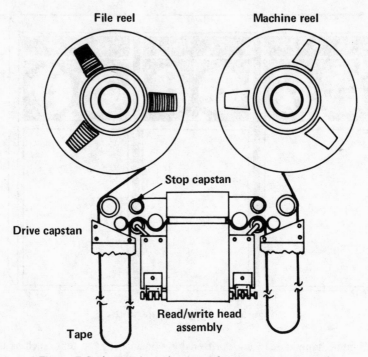

Figure 5.9 Internal mechanism of a magnetic tape unit.

inch (BPI) to 1600 BPI. Tape speed varies from 37.5 inches per second to 200 inches per second. Overall, the data rate of magnetic tape varies from 7,500 bytes per second to 320,000 bytes per second.

The primary advantages of magnetic tape are that it is inexpensive (the average 2,400 foot reel costs about $12) and that it can store a large amount of information for its size. A tape reel ranges from 8 to 12 inches in diameter and can hold from 1 to 20 million bytes. Magnetic tape, unlike punched cards, can be reused by simply writing over previously stored information.

Magnetic tape is useful for storing large amounts of data that can be accessed sequentially. Typical applications that lend themselves to the use of magnetic tape involve the processing of large data files, such as those that might be found in payroll, personnel management, customer billing, and inventory control.

MAGNETIC DISK

Although magnetic tape provides reasonably high data transfer rates and is a relatively inexpensive storage medium, it is ineffective when data must

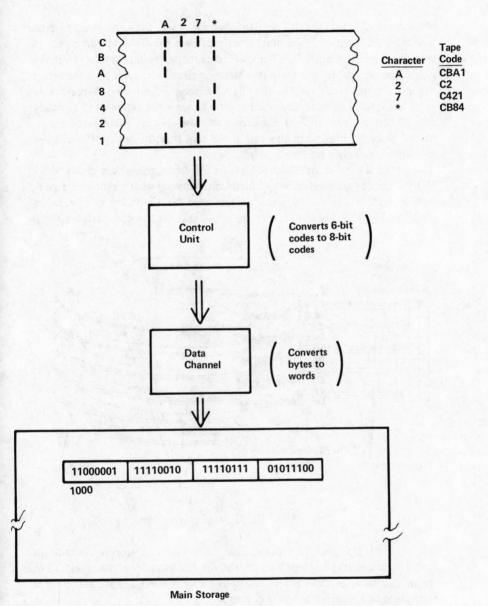

Figure 5.10 The code conversion process in reading a magnetic tape.

89

be accessed directly. Recall that with magnetic tape, the computer (or more precisely, the magnetic tape unit) must pass over the $(i - 1)$th data item to be able to access the ith data item, unless perhaps, the tape unit was initially positioned at the $(i - 1)$th item. Many applications, such as information storage and retrieval, require that data be accessed directly. A reasonably good example is an insurance company that uses a computer to store policy data. When a policy holder inquires about his policy, his records are retrieved directly. Implied in this case is the fact that the policy files of most insurance companies are usually large.

One of the most widely used devices for direct access is magnetic disk. The recording medium is a set of metal disks coated with magnetic material, such as ferrous oxide. The disks are mounted on a rotating spindle, as depicted in Figure 5.11. Data is recorded on tracks on the disk surfaces and is

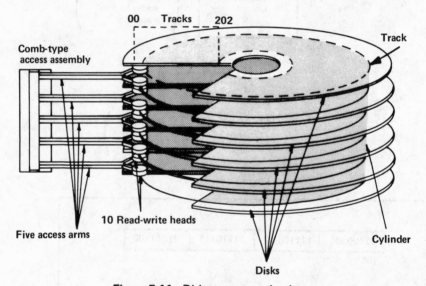

Figure 5.11   Disk storage mechanism.

read or written as the disks rotate. The concept of disk storage is similar to that of a phonograph record except that the tracks are concentric instead of spiral. The stack of disks is referred to as a *disk volume,* and if the volume is removable, it is referred to as a *disk pack.*

Data is recorded on both surfaces of a disk (except perhaps the top and bottom surfaces of a volume that are used for protection) and a single access arm controls two read/write heads—one for the upper surface and one for the lower surface. The access arms form a comb-type assembly that moves in and out together. A single read/write head is used to access a single surface.

Each track can store the same number of bits* and is identified by a track address. Typically, track addresses range from 000–199. Each surface is also identified by a head address (that is, the read/write head used to read the surface); the implication is that the heads are switched electronically when a given surface is to be read. Thus, a particular track is identified by (and located by) a track number and a head number. A magnetic disk is read or written by first moving the access arms to the proper track address prior to the input or output operation and by then switching on the desired read/write head. The process of moving the read/write head to the proper place is referred to as the *disk seek*. The time necessary to retrieve information from disk storage is therefore a function of three variables: seek time, the time necessary for the disk to rotate to the desired position on a track, and data transfer time. Rotation speed is about 2,400 revolutions per minute and recording density varies from 3,500 to 15,000 bytes per track. As a result, the data transfer rate of disk storage varies from 300,000 bytes per second to 1,500,000 bytes per second. Average seek time varies from 25 to 60 milliseconds.

A disk storage module has three major components: the disk volume, the access arms and read/write heads, and the disk mechanism that causes the recording surfaces to rotate and works in conjunction with the access arms and read/write heads to record and retrieve data. A disk storage unit is usually classed by several factors:

1. The number of disk storage modules per unit.
2. The number of recording surfaces per module.
3. The capacity of each track and the number of tracks per surface.
4. Seek time and rotation speed.
5. Whether the disk volume is removable or not.

Figure 5.12 depicts two disk storage units, one that contains a single disk module and the other that contains eight disk modules. Both utilize disk packs, such as the one shown in the same figure. The major advantage of removable disk packs is that they can be removed from the disk storage unit, so that the total disk capacity of a computer system is not limited by the number of disk units. Disk packs range in capacity from approximately 7 million bytes to approximately 100 million bytes. Therefore, a single storage facility, such as the eight-disk module of Figure 5.12, can hold as many as 800 million bytes.

Not all disk volumes are removable. Nonremovable disk volumes generally provide faster access but have a smaller capacity.

*Since inner circumference is shorter than outer circumference, bits on outer tracks are more spread out.

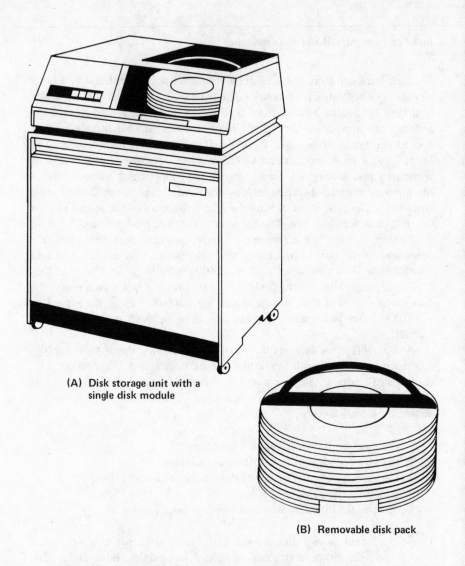

(A) Disk storage unit with a
single disk module

(B) Removable disk pack

(C) Disk storage facility with 8 disk modules

Figure 5.12.   Disk storage.

Data that is stored on magnetic disk can be stored and retrieved sequentially or directly, depending on the needs of a particular application. However, the cost of magnetic disk is approximately 20 times that of magnetic tape, all factors considered. (For example, the cost of a small disk pack with 10 recording surfaces that can hold about 7 million characters ranges from $350 to $500. The "average" 2,400 foot magnetic tape also holds about 7 million characters. These figures obviously depend on how the respective media are used.) For computer applications that require direct-access capability, there is no alternative. For applications that require only sequential access, the choice between magnetic tape and magnetic disk is a matter of input/output time and cost.

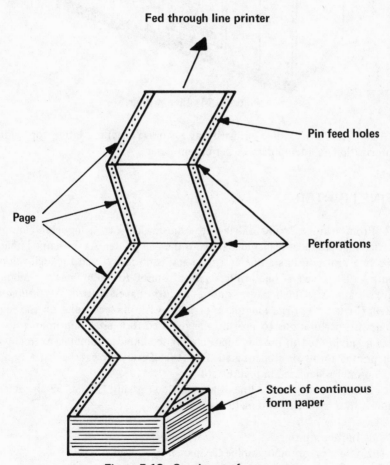

Figure 5.13 Continuous form paper.

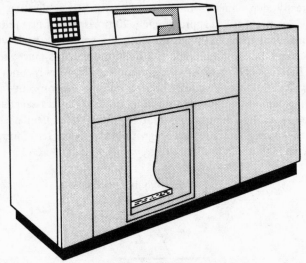

Figure 5.14   Line printer.

Magnetic disk is used primarily as a storage medium, either for storing information on a temporary or permanent basis.

LINE PRINTER

From a human point of view, the most widely used input and output device that produces readable material is the line printer. As the name implies, the line printer prints a line at a time and is normally used for high-volume output. The speed of line printers varies from 60 to 5,000 lines per minute. To sustain these high rates, continuous form paper is used. A *continuous form* (Figure 5.13) is a long piece of paper with pin-feed holes on the edges and with perforations to provide the required form size. Continuous forms can be preprinted to provide reports of various kinds. Common examples of preprinted forms are student grade reports and everyday paychecks. A typical line printer is depicted in Figure 5.14.

A line printer prints a line of information (usually 120 or 132 characters) at one time by one of two methods:

1. Impact printing
2. Chemical or photographic techniques

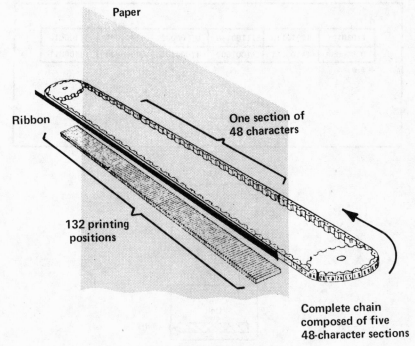

Figure 5.15 Print chain.

The impact technique is more widely used because it generally produces better quality printing at a lower line speed. Impact printing uses a print chain, a print wheel, or a print drum and involves impacting the paper (and the ribbon) with the printing mechanism or vice versa. Figure 5.15 shows a print chain that contains several sets of print characters mounted on a chain that moves horizontally in front of the paper. An electro-mechanically controlled hammer behind the paper forces the paper against the type face as the character to be printed passes in front of the proper position on the paper. The speed of line printers usually varies between 500 and 3,500 lines per minute. Line speeds less than 500 lines per minute are used for small computers or special purposes.

Chemical or photographic techniques generally are used in printers with ultra-high speed in the range of 3,000 to 5,000 lines per minute. Nonimpact techniques usually result in lower printing quality; however, this comment is more of an observation on the past and it is expected that the use of nonimpact printers may surpass the use of impact printers as the quality of the former improves.

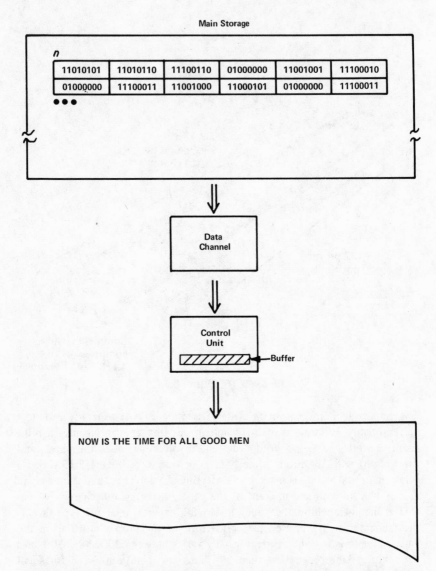

Figure 5.16 The code conversion process in printing a line on the line printer.

Figure 5.16 depicts the process of printing a line. As in previous cases, data is sent from main storage to the data channel and then on to the control unit through the standard interface on a byte basis. Information is collected in a buffer in the control unit until a complete line is formed; then, the print mechanism is activated to print the line.

The line printer is the primary output device for printed material because there is usually a large amount of printing to be done. Typewriter-like devices that print on a character-by-character basis are frequently used for low-volume output. The printed page is also a storage medium, of a sort, but it is difficult to read the information back into the computer without rekey-punching the information. Optical readers are occasionally used for this purpose.

MISCELLANEOUS INPUT AND OUTPUT DEVICES

Because of the standard interface mentioned earlier in the previous chapter, a wide variety of devices have been developed that provide input, storage, and output facilities. The market for peripheral devices of this type is large and engineers have been known to develop input and output devices in their basement prior to embarking on a new business venture. This section summarizes a variety of well-known devices.

Keytape and Keydisk

Punched cards are the primary means of entering original data into the computer; however, card reading is relatively slow. An alternative approach to data entry is to use a *keytape device,* where the data is placed directly on magnetic tape. The data is entered via a keyboard and placed into a small memory by the keytape unit. The data is also displayed on a CRT* display so the operator can inspect the input data for accuracy. When the operator has finished typing a line, it is entered directly on magnetic tape. A variation to the keytape approach is to use a *keydisk system,* where the data is placed directly on magnetic disk. A limiting factor with keydisk systems is that disk storage units are expensive and it is difficult to justify stand-alone units for the data-entry operation. A recent technique is to connect several keydisk entry stations to a minicomputer that writes the entered data on a few disk units. Thus, the disk units are shared among many keydisk stations.

Optical and Magnetic Character Readers

An *optical reader* is a device that reads letters, numbers, and special characters from printed, typed, or handwritten documents. The optical reader scans the document, compares the result with prestored images, and enters appropriate data into the computer. Documents with invalid characters are rejected.

*CRT is an acronym for cathode ray tube, which is a display device similar in concept to a home television.

A *magnetic ink character reader* reads characters printed with ink containing metallic materials. The most common examples of magnetic ink characters are found at the bottom of bank checks. These characters can be read visually and by a magnetic ink character reader. Special magnetic ink character readers have been developed for the banking industry.

Paper Tape

A medium that is used for input, storage, and output is punched paper tape. Punched paper tape is similar to magnetic tape, in concept, except that data is recorded by actually punching holes in the tape. The advantage of paper tape over cards is that paper tape does not have an 80-character limit on data records. The major disadvantages of paper tape are that errors are difficult to correct and readers and punches are relatively slow, operating at approximately 500 and 300 characters per minute, respectively. Some types of computer terminals permit punched paper tapes to be prepared "off-line" prior to entry to the computer, minimizing errors when the user is connected to the computer.

Magnetic Drum

Magnetic drum is a mass-storage device that uses a metal cylinder coated with a magnetizable material as a storage medium. Data is stored in circular tracks, referred to as *bands*, that are generally analogous to tracks on a disk. The magnetic drum is housed in an upright cabinet and frequently contains its own control unit. Data transfer rates are generally faster than disk storage and range from 300,000 to 1,500,000 bytes per second. Access time is somewhat lower (that is, it is faster) than disk, as is storage capacity. The drum, per se, is not removable and a drum storage unit is generally more expensive than disk storage. Magnetic drum storage is usually used to store programs and tables.

Magnetic Strip and Card Devices

Magnetic strip and *magnetic card* devices are high capacity electromechanical devices. A magnetic strip consists of a plastic strip coated with iron oxide—similar to magnetic tape. A magnetic card consists of a card coated with iron oxide. Both devices consist of several storage media (that is, strips or cards) mounted in a removable cartridge holder. When an instruction from the computer is received, a strip or card drops from the holder and is moved under a read/write head. Each strip or card can be addressed directly. The cost of magnetic strip and magnetic card storage is less than disk storage. Because of the mechanical access mechanism, access times are high. Devices of this type are used for applications that require immediate access to high-volume data.

Graphic Devices

Two types of graphic display units are graph plotters and drafting machines. Units of this type are either on-line or off-line. On-line devices are connected directly to the computer. Off-line devices use a magnetic tape as input; the magnetic tape is written by a computer program as a separate operation.

Graphic devices operate under control of instructions, such as "move the pen to point (10,5)." By synthesizing sequences of instructions, such as this, the device can be made to prepare a desired figure. *Graph plotters* usually operate by drawing straight lines from point to point. *Drafting machines* allow a variety of plane curves to be drawn.

One of the advantages of using graphic display units is that a figure can be redrawn as many times as necessary by simply rerunning the program, whereas a skilled artist or draftsman would invariably include differences between two copies of the same figure.

Microfilm

Printed output from the computer can be voluminous, and a means of solving the volume problem is to write the output directly on microfilm. The process is referred to as "computer output microfilm" and is abbreviated as COM. Computer output microfilm operates as follows:

1. The data is converted to a form that can be displayed on a CRT tube;
2. The pictures appear on a CRT tube;
3. The face of the CRT tube is photographed; and
4. The film is processed and developed.

Steps 2-4 are performed by a COM device, available as an ordinary peripheral device. COM output can be produced in one of the well-known forms of microfilm technology, that is 16, 35, 70, or 105 mm film, microfiche, or aperture cards (punched cards with microfilm windows).

COM devices operate at very high speeds up to 1,000 lines per second, which is approximately 50 times faster than the average line printer. One of the primary advantages of COM output is that printed and graphic output can be conveniently incorporated on the same report.

Other Devices

Several other well-known devices exist ranging from CRT devices to audio response units. Devices such as these, which are normally used with data communications facilities, are covered in the next section. It should be emphasized that not all input and output devices known to man have been covered—only the devices that the reader is most likely to encounter. The reader is directed to the references given at the end of the book for additional information on input and output devices.

DATA COMMUNICATIONS FACILITIES

Data communications refers to the use of teleprocessing facilities, such as ordinary telephone lines, for the transmission of data between remote locations. Technologically, data communications is not new and has been used with military/defense systems since the early 1950s. With the widespread use of computers in nonmilitary/defense organizations, the use of data communications facilities is a natural technical extension. Data communications is glamorous, fun, cost effective, very useful in a business environment, indispensable in the space program, but lastly, is a relatively cumbersome process. Data communications has given rise to a "popular" set of computer applications, such as time sharing, computer networks, message transmission and switching, and information-based systems, such as airline reservation and brokerage information systems. Data communications is a cumbersome process because interfacing two different types of equipment invariably leads to problems and because many of the "privacy and security" issues relate to data communications. As a problem, privacy and security would exist without data communications (or even computers, as a matter of fact); however, the widespread use of data communications simply makes the problem worse. Nevertheless, the benefits to be derived from the use of data communications greatly outweigh the difficulties, and this means of communication is here to stay.

Data communications facilities are used for three major reasons:

1. To provide computational facilities to a user at a remote location.
2. To permit information to be entered or retrieved from a data management system on a dynamic basis from a remote location.
3. To transfer data between locations at a high rate of speed.

On the surface, the three areas appear to be diverse, but from a technical point of view, they are essentially the same and can be generally categorized as "communications systems."

A *communications system* has five components:

1. A message source
2. An encoder

3. A signal channel
4. A decoder
5. A message destination

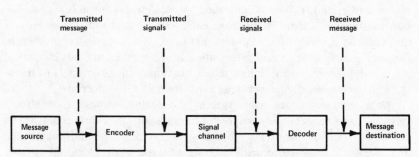

Figure 5.17 Conceptual model of a communications system.

A conceptual model of a communications system is given in Figure 5.17. In a computer communications system, the source or the destination is a computer system and the channel is either telegraph or ordinary telephone. Telegraph and telephone facilities usually are designed as open wires, coaxial cable circuits, and microwave systems.

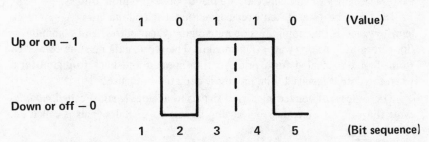

Figure 5.18 Data can be represented as a train of bits for data transmission.

As depicted in Figure 5.18, data is represented as a train of bits for data transmission. Successive bits represent a character, as covered previously with respect to computer codes. Data can be transmitted in one of three modes: asynchronous start-stop, synchronous, and parallel. When *asynchronous transmission* is used, one character at a time is transmitted between source and destination and start and stop codes are used to achieve calibration between transmitter and receiver. Asynchronous transmission is almost always used when a human being is involved in the communications process. When *synchronous transmission* is used, an entire block of characters is transmitted between source and destination without employing start and stop codes. The block is accumulated in a buffer prior to transmission and the synchronization of transmitter and receiver is controlled by oscillators. Obviously, synchronous transmission is more efficient since there are no start and stop codes and no pauses as a result of human response time. Synchronous transmission is frequently used when human intervention is not required in the transmission process. *Parallel transmission* uses several communications channels to transmit a character—usually, one channel exists for each bit in the code.

Data communications lines (that is, the communications channel) are classified as to the data rate—or speed of transmission—they can sustain. Three classes are usually identified: subvoice grade, voice grade, and wide band. *Subvoice-grade lines,* customarily used for teletype service, transmit at rates from 45 to 180 bits per second. *Voice-grade lines,* used for ordinary telephone, transmit at rates from 600 to 1,200 bits per second. *Wide-band lines* are used for high-volume data and transmit at rates of 19,200 to 50,000 bits per second. The most significant characteristic of data communications lines is whether they are switched or private. *Switched lines* go through public exchanges and are located practically everywhere. Telegraph and public telephone lines fall into this category. *Private* (or leased) *lines* avoid the public switching network and are frequently used for high-volume traffic. Private lines are normally available in the three grades given previously. Many companies lease lines when many calls are made between remote offices.

Data can be transmitted over conventional telephone lines. A key problem, however, is that computers operate digitally (in pulses) and communications lines use analog (wave) transmission. Therefore, data must be converted from digital to analog form prior to transmission and back to digital form when the data is received. The process is depicted in Figure 5.19.

The process of converting digital signals to analog signals is called *modulation*; the process of converting analog signals to digital signals is called *de-*

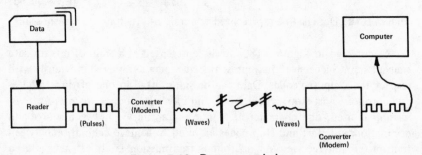

Figure 5.19 Data transmission.

modulation. A hardware device that performs modulation/demodulation is called a *modem*; it must be attached to both ends of the communications lines. Two types of modem are widely used: a dataset and an acoustical coupler. A *dataset* is a fixed connection between the telephone line and a unit of computer equipment and is supplied by the telephone company. An *acoustical coupler* is attached to a computer terminal device and converts digital signals to audible tones. Since the acoustical coupler is not attached to a communications line, the terminal device can be portable. The acoustical coupler mechanism allows the receiver of an ordinary telephone to be clamped into it to establish the line connection.

Use of an acoustical coupler has great advantages. A salesman can have a computer terminal with an acoustical coupler in his car. All he need do to access the computer is to stop at a telephone booth, dial the number of the computer, clamp the receiver into his acoustical coupler, and he is ready to use the computer.

Data communications systems can take several forms: computer to computer, input/output device to computer, terminal device to computer, and so on. Figure 5.20 depicts sample data communications systems. From the "computer's" point of view, a data communications line is essentially treated as an ordinary input/output device—such as a card reader or printer.

There are a variety of terminal devices ranging from keyboard/typewriter-type devices to audio response units. Figure 5.21 shows five major devices: a keyboard/typewriter unit, a CRT device, an audio response unit, a data collection station, and an intelligent terminal (see below).

A *keyboard/typewriter terminal device* resembles an ordinary typewriter in all respects, except that the terminal device is connected to the computer via data communications lines. The unit serves for both input and output. For input, the user types the information he wants sent to the computer. As each character is typed, it is printed at the terminal and sent to the computer. When the line is complete, the user presses RETURN to return the carriage and to send a special code to the computer indicating "end of line." Output is under control of a computer program. As each character is sent to the terminal device, it is handled immediately. Printable characters are typed. Control characters tell the terminal to "carriage return," "double space," and so on.

A *CRT terminal device* contains a display device that resembles a portable television set and a keyboard. The display device essentially replaces the carriage and paper of the previous device. As each character is typed for input, it is displayed on the screen. As above, pressing RETURN completes the line and returns a position indicator to the beginning of the next line. As lines are displayed, preceding lines are successively "rolled up" until the top line disappears at the top of the screen. The output lines are displayed in

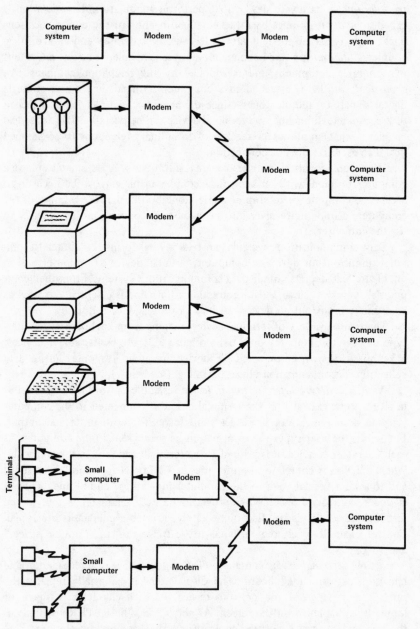

Figure 5.20 Sample data communications systems.

CRT Device

Data Collection Terminal

Audio Response Unit

Intellegent Terminal

Keyboard/Printer

Figure 5.21 A variety of terminal devices.

a similar manner. CRT-type devices are more costly than keyboard/type-writer devices and provide no "hard copy"; however, CRT-type devices allow faster display speeds.

An *audio response unit* is used to provide convenient low-volume output. A device of this type consists of a small magnetic drum and an audio speaker unit. The drum contains a small number of prerecorded syllables, words, or phrases. To generate a particular message, the computer sends an appropriate sequence of codes to the audio response unit, which selects the corresponding sounds from the drum and outputs them through the speaker unit. Audio response units are commonly used with stock quotation or credit verification systems.

A *data collection station* is an input device located in a remote location—such as an assembly plant or a medical ward of a hospital. Normally, data is entered through keys, dials, or switches. The data is stored at the computer on a recording medium such as tape or disk for subsequent processing.

An *intelligent terminal* is a terminal device that can be programmed to perform relatively minor data verification and editing functions. The use of an intelligent terminal, when appropriate, provides better service to the user and reduces the work load on the main computer. Intelligent terminals are commonly used in data-entry systems to verify input data. Another interesting use of intelligent terminals is for computer consoles designed for use by executives. The terminal is programmed to dial the computer automatically when the executive turns the device on for use.

The above devices are only a few of the devices that can and have been used with data communications facilities. Remote tape units, card readers, and line printers are also in widespread use.

One of the more exotic uses of data communications facilities involves computer-to-computer communications without human intervention. Systems of this type are referred to as computer networks. (Again, computer programs are necessary for instructing the computer when and what to do.) One computer is simply programmed to dial the telephone number of the other computer to establish a data communications link. Once the link is established, appropriate programs are designed to make requests for information or respond to requests for information, as the case may be.

QUESTION SET

1. The chapter emphasized the difference between a device and a medium. Give as many analogous "combinations" as you can that exist in the non-computer world. Example: pencil and paper. What about pen, ink, and paper?
2. Interpreting a punched card is known as the process of determining the recorded information. Interpret the card on the facing page.

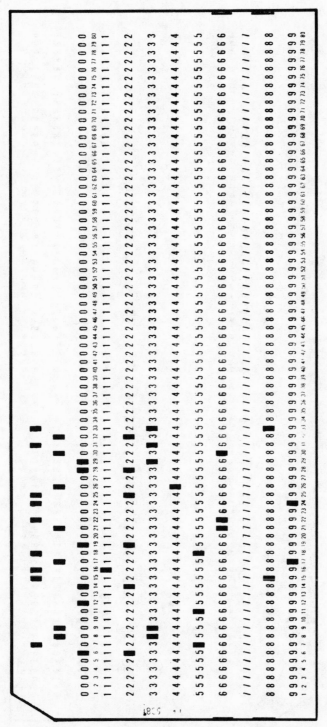

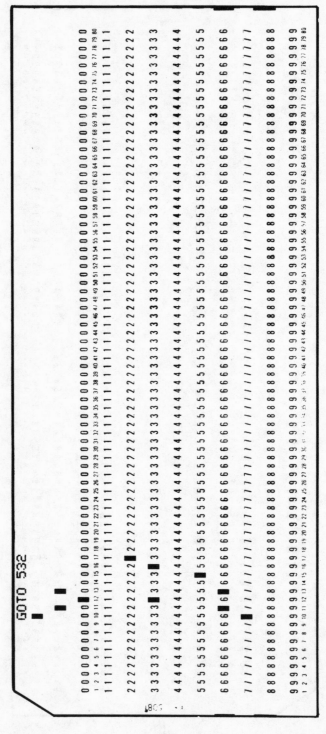

GOTO 532

3. Suppose columns 10-17 of the card on page 108 were read into computer storage, byte locations 5320-5327. Give the contents in binary of those byte locations.

4. The contents of byte location 5320-5327, from question 3, are written on magnetic tape. Give a picture of that segment of tape showing the recorded information.

5. Given a magnetic tape unit that records at 800 BPI and moves at 75 inches per second, compute the data rate of that unit.

6. Data is recorded on magnetic tape in blocks of 80 characters with 3/4 inch gaps between blocks. The recording density is 800 BPI. What percentage of the tape is blank (that is, contains gaps) and what percentage contains recorded information?

7. What is the storage capacity of the following disk pack?

    recording surfaces: 10
    tracks per surface: 200
    bytes per track: 3620

8. Why is continuous form paper used?

9. Prepare a short but in-depth report on one of the following devices:

    Keytape or keydisk device
    Optical or magnetic character reader
    Paper tape (including codes)
    Magnetic drum
    Magnetic strip or card device
    Graph plotter device
    COM

References are given at the end of the book.

10. Your instructor will give you the telephone number of a computer data communications line. Dial the number and describe what happens.

11. Visit the computer center or a terminal room. Prepare a short report on a dataset or an acoustical coupler.

CHAPTER 6

The Computer Operating Environment

INTRODUCTION

The fact has been well established that once we load a program into the computer and get it started executing, it continues to operate automatically. There are several steps involved:

1. The computer program to be compiled is punched on cards or placed on another storage medium.
2. The compiler* program is loaded into the computer.
3. The compiler program reads the program to be compiled and produces a machine language program; it is punched onto cards or placed on another storage medium.
4. The machine language program is loaded into the computer; it reads the user's data and produces computed results, as programmed.

The process of loading a program (of any kind) into main storage for execution is performed by a small self-loading utility program that is designed first to load itself into the computer and then to load an accompanying program.

Even though computer programs such as compilers and even loaders do a considerable amount of work, execution time is usually short by human standards. Thus, if each of the above steps were initiated manually, an inordinate amount of computer time would be wasted while people were

---

*Recall that a compiler is a program that translates a user written program to computer (machine) language. The process is referred to as "compiling" or "compilation."

"fiddling around," as they say. Modern computer systems use a set of sophisticated programs called an *operating system* to schedule how the computer is used and to pass between the various steps automatically without human intervention. In fact, an operating system is also designed to pass between the steps of successive users without human intervention. The end result of course is that the computer essentially runs itself. All we have to do is to get it started and tell it what we want done.

THE CONCEPT OF A JOB

Although it would be convenient to give instructions to the computer system with some means of verbal input,* it is not feasible using today's technology; therefore, we must enter instructions through one of the input devices. In this section, punched cards are used to illustrate how programs and instructions are entered into the operating system.

The work performed by the computer for one user in one time span is referred to as a "job." Stated in another manner, a *job* is a single run on the computer. The operating system needs the following information to run a job:

1. The identity of the user
2. Control information
3. Program(s)
4. Data

Essentially, the control information tells the operating system what the user wants the computer to do. The operating system reads the control information and initiates the execution of programs that perform the required functions.

Figure 6.1 shows the deck setup for a hypothetical operating system. The $JOB card identifies the users and provides accounting information on whom to charge for the execution of the job. The $FORTRAN card tells the operating system to read in the FORTRAN compiler from magnetic tape or disk. The statements of the FORTRAN program are read by the FORTRAN compiler and the machine language program, resulting from the compilation, is placed on disk or magnetic tape for subsequent loading and execution. A print out of the program is produced as a by-product so the user has a record of his program. The print out is also used for testing and debugging the pro-

---

*Verbal input to the computer has been accomplished for limited cases on an experimental basis. Widespread use of this capability, if at all, is many years off.

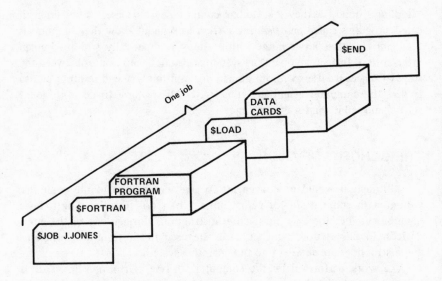

One job

$END

DATA
CARDS

$LOAD

FORTRAN
PROGRAM

$FORTRAN

$JOB J.JONES

Figure 6.1 Sample deck setup showing representative control cards.

gram. Normally, a program such as the compiler passes control back to the operating system to read the next "control" card. In this case, the next card is the $LOAD card that causes the loader program to be read in. The loader program loads the machine language program, previously placed on magnetic tape or disk, into main storage and turns program control over to it for execution. Now the user program has control of the computer. It reads its own data and produces computer results, as mentioned previously. When the user program has completed its execution, it exits to the operating system for the next job, and the above process is repeated.

Each computer center has its own operational procedures, and how a user actually submits a job differs widely. For example, in some centers, card decks are placed on a table outside the computer room. In others, the user submits his deck through a window established for that purpose. When the computer is in a remote location, a messenger is used to pick up jobs at a central station and transport them to the computer. Results are normally returned in the same manner.

In the computer room, a computer operator collects a set of jobs and enters them into the computer as a "batch of jobs," and the entire process is referred to as *batch processing*. In most modern computer installations, jobs are read in and placed on disk storage. When the operating system needs the next job, it goes to disk to get it.

The control cards demonstrated here are hypothetical. If you run a computer program using batch processing, you will use control cards established by your computer installation.

THE OPERATING SYSTEM

The *operating system* is a set of programs designed to manage the resources of the computer system and to provide job-to-job transition. These programs are frequently referred to as *control programs,* since they control the operation of the entire computer system.

Although operating systems also vary widely between installations and computer vendors, there are four types of facilities (or routines) that are usually provided:

1. *System management* routines control the operation of the computer system and provide a logical interface between the hardware and the other routines of the operating system. System management routines monitor hardware functions, perform actual input/output operations, schedule jobs for execution, control peripheral input/output devices, allocate main storage, and handle abnormal conditions that arise during computation.

2. *Job management* routines provide a logical interface between a job (processing program) and the system management routines. Job management routines control and monitor the execution of a job, read control cards, and handle job terminations.

3. *Data management* routines provide a software interface between processing programs and external storage. Data management routines control data transfer operations, maintain catalogs and libraries, manage input/output device assignment, and allocate space on mass-storage devices. Even though data management is generally concerned with input and output, it uses system management functions for that purpose so that all input and output is managed on a system-wide basis.

4. *User service* routines comprise utility programs, necessary for using a computer system, and service programs that facilitate the programming process. Utility programs include disk initialization, core dumps, card-to-tape, diagnostics, and so on. Service programs perform sort/merge, editing, loading, and many other similar functions.

Early operating systems were characterized by the fact that jobs were loaded into main storage and executed on a sequential basis. In spite of automatic job-to-job transition, input/output systems, and so forth, normal delays in the processing of a job caused the CPU to "wait" for short periods of time

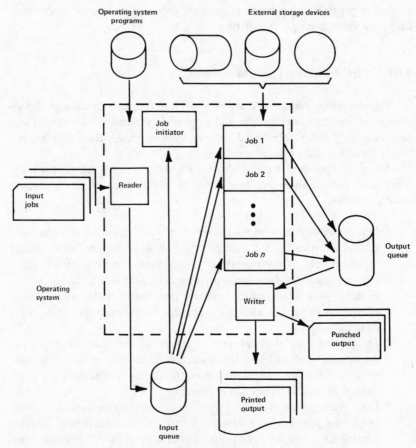

Figure 6.2 Modern operating system environment.

on an intermittent basis and resulted in ineffective use of main storage. Modern operating systems (see Figure 6.2) utilize a technique known as *multiprogramming* to allow several jobs to share the resources of the computer system and to allow card reading, printing, and punching to proceed concurrently with system operation. In a multiprogramming system, a scheduler routine is designed to give control of the central processing unit to another program when the executing program encounters a *natural wait*—such as when waiting for an input operation. Thus, the more expensive units in the system are fully utilized. Input jobs are maintained in a queue on direct-access storage and output is maintained in a similar queue on the same or another device. When the operating system needs another job to process, it is selected from the input queue on either a sequential or priority basis.

REMOTE JOB ENTRY/REMOTE JOB OUTPUT

By definition batch processing causes delays. First, a user's job must be transported to the central computer and entered into the system. Next, the job must wait in the input queue until its turn for processing. Last, the output queue must be printed or punched and the results are then sent back to the originator. A recent technique known as *remote job entry* allows a job to be transported from a remote location to the central computer over ordinary telephone lines. An analogous facility, known as *remote job output,* provides a means of sending results back to the originator over telephone lines. The user (or originator) in this case must have an appropriate terminal device in his work area to send and receive information from the central computer.

When using remote job entry, a job enters the input queue directly and "people" delays are avoided. This technique is frequently employed when a centralized computer is used to provide service to offices in different locations.

TIME SHARING

Although remote job entry/remote job output solves, in some cases, the problem of transporting programs and data to and from the central computer, the scheduling bottleneck at the computer still causes delays—especially when small one-shot programs are involved. Another technique, known as *time sharing,* allows the user at a remote location to enter into a conversation with the computer (figuratively speaking) using, again, a terminal device and telephone lines. In a time-sharing system, however, computer time is scheduled differently. When time sharing, each user is given a short burst (called a *time slice*) of computer time on a periodic basis. The switching between programs, by the computer, is sufficiently fast that the user is given the illusion that he has the computer to himself—whereas, in reality, he is sharing with many other users. Time sharing is most frequently used during program development, by professional programmers and problem solvers, such as analysts, scientists, or engineers, or to enter or retrieve information from the system on a demand basis. Time sharing is particularly useful in an academic environment. A student can sit at a terminal and, within a short period of time, solve an assigned problem using the computer. The greatest benefit of time sharing is that when an error is encountered, it can be corrected immediately and progress on the problem can continue. When using batch processing, an error is discovered only when a completed job is returned to the user. If an error does occur, at least one more run must be made to correct the error.

[User dials computer and makes line connection.]

```
HELLO
GOOD MORNING ON AT 9:13 MON.          Sign-on and user identification pro-
  06-11-73                             cedure
USER NUMBER? 08520
SYSTEM? BASIC                          User chooses BASIC language and a
NEW OR OLD? NEW                        new program named FACT.
NAME? FACT
READY                                  Computer is ready to accept
                                       program

100  PRINT "ENTER K"
110  INPUT K
120  LET F=1
130  FOR I=1 TO K
140     LET F=F*I
150  NEXT I
160  PRINT K; "FACTORIAL="; F          Program to compute K factorial,
170  PRINT                             entered by user.
180  GO TO 100
190  END
RUN

FACT 9:30 MON. 06-11-73
ENTER K                                User enters data
?4
  4 FACTORIAL=24                       Result
ENTER K
?6
  6 FACTORIAL=720
ENTER K
?0
  0 FACTORIAL=1
ENTER K                                User terminates input loop
?STOP

TIME 1 SEC.                            Central processing unit time
```

Figure 6.3 Sample terminal session for a time-sharing system.

Figure 6.3 shows the terminal printout for a typical time-sharing session. Four major steps are involved:

1. *Sign-on,* where the user establishes a data connection to the computer and identifies himself to the system.
2. *Program initiation,* where the user specifies that he wants to use an old program or prepare a new one. The user also gives the name of the program so that it may be retrieved from or stored in a library (on direct-access storage) for easy access.
3. *Program preparation,* where the user enters a new program on a statement-by-statement basis, or enters modifications or corrections to an old program.
4. *Program execution,* where the program is actually executed by the computer.

In time sharing, a user may run one program or several programs—in other words, his needs may change depending on the results he obtains. The concept of a job does not apply and the notion of a terminal session is used. A *terminal session* is the time between when a user first signs on to the computer and when he finally logs off. A terminal session may extend from minutes to hours. A key point is that the computer is not idly waiting while a user is thinking about what he wants to do next; it is doing work for other users. This is what is known as time sharing—people are sharing time on the computer.

THE TIME-SHARING SYSTEM

A time-sharing system is similar in concept to the operating system mentioned earlier in this chapter. System management routines manage the resources of the computer system and determine which user programs use the central processing unit and when they use it. Job management routines read and interpret control information supplied by people from terminals. Data management routines manage input and output operations and maintain libraries of programs on direct-access storage. When a person desires to use one of his programs, all he need do is supply its name and data management routines can make the program available for use. However, the basic objective is different. In an operating system, the objective is to keep the computer busy and to get as much work done (by the computer) as possible. With time sharing, the objective is to keep the user busy and the time-sharing system is designed to provide that service. A time-sharing system is definitely more people-oriented, but this service is costly because computer resources are used to switch between users.

There are normally many users of a time-sharing system. A distinction must be made, however, between the users who *can* use the system and the users who *are* using the system at any point in time. The time-sharing system contains a list (or a table) of the identification codes of people who can use the system. The number of identification codes may be as large as 2,000. At any point in time, however, only a small subset of these people can be actively using the computer. Large time-sharing systems allow as many as 200 active users. A small time-sharing system may limit the number of active users to between five and 10.

For purposes of demonstration, assume a time-sharing system with 100 active users. The number 50 would work just as well. Obviously, the programs of 100 users could not possibly occupy main storage at one time. What this means is that system management routines must manage main storage on a dynamic basis, and programs and data must be moved back and forth between main storage and direct-access storage. This process is referred to as *swapping.* When a person requests the services of the computer, his programs and data must be "swapped in." When main storage space is needed for another user, programs and data must be "swapped out." Swapping takes computer time and requires space on direct-access storage media.

Another function that must be performed by system management routines is that of scheduling. Active users can be placed into three groups:

1. *Active*–this user's program is currently being executed.
2. *Ready*–programs for these users are waiting to use the computer.
3. *Waiting*–these programs are "inactive" in the sense that the computer is waiting for the user to respond.

Obviously, active and ready programs can use the central processing unit. Normally, a program is placed in the "waiting" group when the computer issues a "read" instruction to a user's terminal. In the time it takes a user to read and react to a message from the computer, several programs can be serviced. There are several methods of scheduling in time-sharing systems. A straightforward method is given here. "Ready" programs are given control of the central processing unit on a round-robin basis. The technique operates as follows: A small value, such as 100 milliseconds, is put into a computer timer. Then the central processing unit is turned over to a program. The program executes and the timer counts down. When the timer reaches zero or the program needs input data, the program's time slice is over and the central processing unit is given to the next program on the ready list. As depicted in Figure 6.4, several activities are taking place at any point in time in a time-sharing system:

1. A program that has finished its time slice is being swapped out.
2. A program is currently going through a time slice.
3. A program is being swapped in for its next time slice.

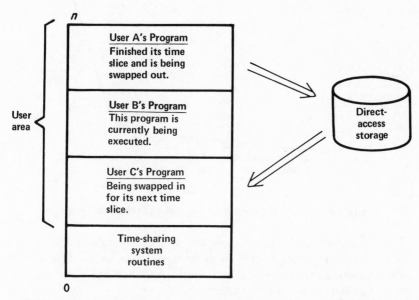

Figure 6.4 Simplified diagram of main storage in a time-sharing system.

Normally, the computer goes through the above procedure so rapidly that there is no appreciable delay in response time, that is, the time it takes the computer to respond to a person's input. There is a saturation point, however, and when the number of users passes the saturation point, response time increases markedly. A typical response-time curve of a time-sharing system is shown in Figure 6.5.

Time-sharing systems are classed as being closed or open. A *closed system* provides computer service exclusively through one or two programming languages. An *open* system allows the user at a remote terminal to utilize all facilities of the computer system—including assembler language, a variety of input/output devices, and data management capabilities. Most time-sharing facilities provide closed service since the intended audience is the general user, such as the engineer, analyst, or student mentioned previously. The use of an open system is slightly more complicated and is intended for the professional programmer.

Many organizations employ large-scale computers for data processing applications and continually strive to use them as efficiently. The bread-and-butter jobs, such as payroll and inventory control, are run on these computers in a multiprogramming mode of operation. Time-sharing service for technical problem solving and for program development is normally provided in one of three ways: (1) in conjunction with multiprogramming on the same com-

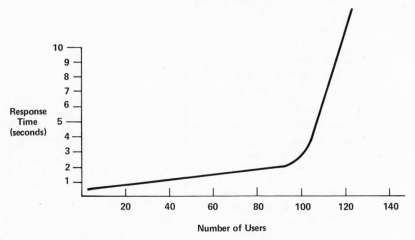

Figure 6.5 Response-time curve for a typical time-sharing system.

puter; (2) through an "in-house" computer system dedicated to time sharing; and (3) from an outside vendor providing time-sharing service. In the latter case, time-sharing service companies frequently offer relatively low rates because of a competitive market situation.

ON-LINE SYSTEMS

An *on-line system* allows a user in a remote location to access the computer via data communications facilities without necessarily resorting to the time-sharing mode of operation. A common example is a bank teller system used to assist in the making of banking transactions by banking personnel. Generally speaking, a bank teller program runs as a conventional job in an operating system environment; however, the job never terminates and is put into a dormant state when no transactions need to be processed. In fact, a single bank teller program has been known to service several hundred tellers. This is possible only because the volume of transactions is low, from the computers' point of view, and the computer processing involves straightforward record keeping.

INFORMATION SYSTEMS

An *information system* stores large amounts of information on a large-capacity storage medium for access by people through batch-processing facilities or through an on-line data communication system. This area of computer utilization is commonly known as *information storage and retrieval* and relates to library services, literature and abstract search, market research, medical and academic record keeping, and a wide variety of other informational services.

Information systems are usually characterized by a large bank of data organized for fast retrieval and by a query language that enables a user to easily pose a question that can be answered by the information system. Most information systems are implemented as on-line systems where a single job can provide informational services to a large number of people on a dynamic basis.

THE COMPUTER INSTALLATION

It is probably unnecessary to state that people are needed to utilize computers effectively, and as in any other occupation, there are "divisions of labor," job classifications, specialists, clerks, and so on. In fact, many well-thought-out computer applications, such as magazine subscription systems, are turned into chaotic situations by the conflicts and misunderstandings of the people involved. Even in the simplest case where an engineer, analyst, or student prepares his own program, a computer operator is needed to actually run the program on the computer. At the completely opposite extreme, a person, for example, the manager of accounts receivable in the accounting department, may come to the computer department with the intuitive feeling that a well-designed program would help him in performing the work for which he is responsible. This person needs much more than an operator. He needs someone to determine what should be done, someone to prepare and debug the program, someone to prepare the data for his program, and someone to run the program on a periodic basis. It is true that most computer applications fall somewhere in between and most college graduates these days have some exposure to the computer, so they can appreciate what has to be done.

Computers and data processing are regarded as a high technology area in the sense that a person has to know something about the subject to get something done. There are areas in modern society where an unknowledgeable person can stumble along with the hope that everything will eventually turn out all right. In the area of computers, the opposite result is very likely to take place. Another important point is that, sooner or later, difficulty is encountered with most computer applications. The operator goofs and mounts the wrong tape or drops a deck of cards. The program has a logic error that is not detected until the program is in production for two years. A clerical person prepares the data incorrectly. A systems analyst, through a misunderstanding with the problem originator, inadvertently omits one of the cases that can arise. When a program "bombs out," as they call it, everyone involved has a tendency to blame someone else. The programmer blames the operator; the systems analyst blames the programmer; the problem originator blames the systems analyst; and everyone blames the clerk. The solution, naturally, is an organization chart and precise job descriptions.

Figure 6.6 gives an organization chart for a typical data processing installation. The *data processing manager* is responsible for the personnel and equipment in his department. This is typically a management position, and the data processing manager spends much of his time with budgets, planning, and personnel responsibilities. However, the data processing department primarily performs a service function for the organization and the data processing manager owes his allegiance to the total organization. Departments such as finance, marketing, and engineering are the customers of the data processing department and the data processing manager serves as an administrative link between these departments and cost/effective computer utilization. The data processing manager normally uses administrative and planning assistants at the staff level for tasks that range from ordering supplies to producing five-year plans for the department. The data processing department is typically organized into four areas: systems programming, systems analysis, programming, and operations.

Systems programming is responsible for the following technical functions:

1. Equipment analysis and selection.
2. Development, acquisition, and effective utilization of programming languages, compilers, and applications systems.
3. Selecting and maintaining operating systems and time-sharing facilities.
4. Development of technical specifications for future computers, systems, and applications.
5. Establishment of programming standards.

Systems programming is primarily a technical area and the most experienced programmers and systems analysts tend to be "promoted into" the systems programming group. Normally, the work in the systems programming group is computer-oriented and the personnel are regarded as computer specialists.

Systems analysis is responsible for computer-based systems that support the activities of other departments. For example, in the billing department, a systems analysis would analyze and describe the flow of information from a credit purchase to payment, which might include the following steps:

1. Purchase
2. Entry of purchase record to computer
3. Collection of charges for each customer
4. Preparation of bill
5. Stuffing and mailing
6. Recording of payment

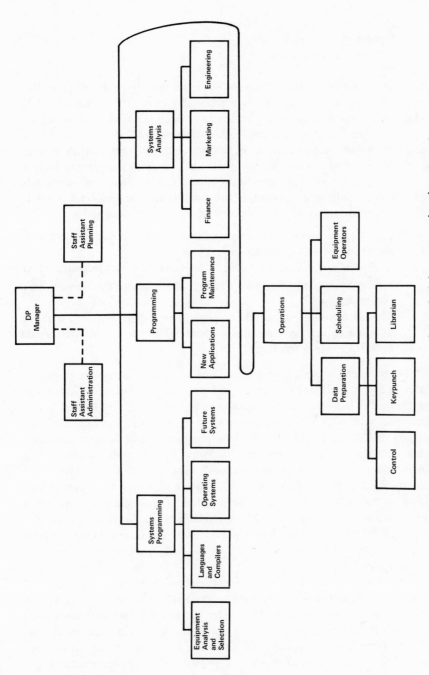

Figure 6.6 Organization chart of a typical data processing department.

123

7. Computer entry of payment record
8. Update of customer's record
9. Summary and reporting

The systems analyst would develop the optimum flow for an operation of this type and attempt to apply the data processing capability of the computer whenever its use would be cost-effective from the point of view of the organization. Systems analysts are applications-oriented and are not necessarily computer experts. However, systems analysts tend to be specialists in the area of the organization to which they apply their talents. The systems analyst normally prepares program specifications and forms layouts and serves as a communications channel between the programmer and the problem originator. The systems analyst usually obtains his work in either of three ways:

1. The D.P. manager discovers an area that might lend itself to computer processing and has a systems analyst look into it.
2. A department manager intuitively feels that a computer program or system might improve his operation and requests the services of a systems analyst.
3. The systems analyst, because of experience and interest, feels that one or more of the "systems and procedures" of the organization would benefit from in-depth study.

Programming is concerned with the development of computer programs. Although practically anyone can prepare a simple program, complicated programs require the services of programming specialists who are trained to prepare programs with a minimum of wasted effort. The programmer is concerned with detailed specification of the program, coding, debugging, testing, and documentation. A programmer may work directly with a problem originator, such as an engineer, or with the systems analyst when many people are involved in the application, such as the billing procedure given above. Once the validity of a program has been verified, the programmer turns a program over to operations personnel for production use. For example, consider a payroll program. Once the program is complete and is turned over to operations, the programmer is not involved in day-to-day running of the program unless something goes wrong.

Operations is organized into data preparation, scheduling, and equipment operators. *Data preparation personnel* are concerned with the paperwork both into and out of the computer. Data entry and keypunching are normal functions. Most data preparation sections also utilize a librarian who records the status of production programs and data files. *Scheduling personnel* are concerned with the running of production programs. In most organizations, certain programs must be run on a regular basis; obvious examples are payroll, billing, and inventory control programs. *Equipment operators* physically operate the computer equipment. Normal functions performed by an operator are:

1. Starting the computer and loading of systems programs.
2. Mounting tapes and disk packs.
3. Responding to informational requests from the operating system.
4. Entering jobs into the computer.
5. Recognizing when the computer is malfunctioning and calling repair personnel.

Each of the areas mentioned has a hierarchy. For example, there are junior programmers, associate programmers, lead programmers, senior programmers, and programming managers. In many large organizations, a college degree is required for programming, systems analysis, or management. This requirement has been relaxed in some small organizations because of a lack of qualified personnel. Many organizations, however, feel the requirement is good since it allows a career path to be established for an individual and he is not "dead ended."

In most organizations and in most fields (engineering, accounting, and so on), the normal progression is upward through the ranks of management. This normal sequence, if it can be called that, does not necessarily hold in the computer field. When it does hold, many problems exist. First, many qualified computer people decline to move into management and prefer to pursue a technical career in systems programming or systems analysis. Although many people have conjectured as to why this is so, the only reason that holds water is that the computer field has progressed and is progressing very rapidly and that many people find the technical aspects interesting and challenging. Another problem is that technological obsolescence occurs very quickly—in a time span as short as five to seven years. Thus, many people who have moved into management positions find their technological knowledge obsolete in just a few years and are severely threatened by younger men with up-to-date technical knowledge. This, of course, is a pretty good reason why many technical people are reluctant to move into management positions. This phenomenon will probably continue to some extent until the pace of technological advancement in the computer field begins to show signs of slowing down.

The computer people mentioned here reflect a typical computer installation, which represents one group of people in the computer field. There is a multitude of people also that design, produce, and sell computers, input and output devices, computer programs, and computer supplies. There are service bureaus that sell time-sharing service and do contract programming. The computer field also uses consultants and requires auditors. There are computer magazines, computer newspapers, and companies that specialize in used computers. Other companies produce computer furniture, computer floors, and computer security devices. There are companies that lease computers and others that will come in and run your computer installation for you. Finally, there are companies that will come and analyze how well you are running your computer.

Another means of classifying a computer installation is whether it is an "open" shop or a "closed" shop. The terminology actually applies to two areas: computer operations and computer programming. Applied to computer operations, closed shop means that only people assigned the position can operate the computers, and open shop means that any user can operate the computers. In large computer installations, the closed shop is used because of data security, efficiency, and the fact that modern computers and associated operating systems are too complicated to be run by the ordinary computer user. An open shop is frequently used with small business computers and minicomputers where only a handful of people are involved with the total computer facility.

Applied to computer programming, closed or open shop refers to who can write programs in an organization. Closed shop means that only people in the programming section can write programs; an engineer or analyst who wants a program written must communicate his needs to a programmer who subsequently prepares the needed program. In an open shop, any qualified employee can prepare a program. There is no simple answer to the latter problem and any philosophy depends on the organization and the kinds of programs being written. For complicated systems, professional programmers are needed. For fairly short "one-shot" programs, the communications process becomes time-consuming and cumbersome and many programs that objectively need to be written are not, because answers are needed before the program can be prepared. This is where time sharing is useful. The engineer or analyst can be provided time-sharing service so that he can do his own programming for the short "one-shot" jobs. As a result, professional programmers are free to work on larger, more demanding programs.

QUESTION SET

1. Distinguish between a job and a terminal session.
2. An operating system is organized into system management, job management, data management, and user service. Generalize and try to apply the same type of structure to an organization with which you are familiar. Is the structure a "management structure" or an "operational structure"?
3. Why are sign-on procedures needed in a time-sharing system?
4. Based on the preceding discussion, what "kind" of people would be good as:

    Data processing managers
    Systems analysts
    Programmers
    Computer operators

Are different personalities needed? What about overtraining?
5. Give advantages and disadvantages of open and closed programming departments.

PART II

PROGRAMMING LANGUAGES

CHAPTER 7

Introduction to Programming Languages

INTRODUCTION

In Part I of this book, an overview of basic computing concepts was presented; it is computer systems oriented in the sense that aspects of the computer and the computer environment are emphasized. This chapter is on programming languages and related topics. Knowledge of the material contained in this chapter is assumed in Chapters 8 and 9.

This part of the book covers two programming languages: BASIC and FORTRAN. The objective regarding both languages is the same—the preparation of programs for execution on the computer. BASIC is intended for the time-sharing environment and FORTRAN is intended for a batch-processing mode of operation.

A program is composed of statements that are executed sequentially until either a statement, such as the GOTO, is executed that transfers control to another point in the program or the program terminates. The material presented here is concerned with how statements are constructed and numerous examples are given to demonstrate the concepts.

Neither language is covered completely since the treatment is intended as an overview. Several good references are given at the end of the book and the interested reader is encouraged to pursue either or both languages further. The area of programming languages is actually a field of study in its own right, and many computer scientists classify themselves as specialists on the subject matter. Programming languages are important. Communicating with the computer is something of a problem and the effective use of programming languages facilitates the process considerably.

A VIEW OF PROGRAMMING

Some fiction writers have likened the computer to the brain and have "made hay" out of such notions as, "Can computers think?" Other writers, leaning toward the dramatic, have written about computers that take over the world. Promulgating ideas of this sort has actually done society a disservice, and has frightened people without due cause. There are bona fide questions over which we should be concerned, but computers taking over the world is definitely not one of them. (In fact, one computer scientist has stated that computers, as we know them today, are not reliable enough to take over anything, much less the world.)

There is, however, one useful analogy. The preparation of a program can be viewed as the development of knowledge and the entering of a program into the computer is regarded as teaching the computer. Thus, the computer can perform any task that we have metaphorically taught it to perform.

STATEMENTS AND PROGRAMS

The characters that can be used to construct statements are termed the *alphabet* of the language (being used). Although there is some similarity between the alphabets of different languages, significant differences exist. It is important to recall that the user is actually dealing with codes when, for example, he enters the statement:

A=B+C

The binary information that is transferred to the computer (via a punched card, via a terminal device, or whatever) is used by the language processor, and the manner in which it is displayed on a program listing is an operational convenience and not a requirement of the input process. Effectively, then, the user and the language processor enter into an "implicit agreement" as to the meaning of the various codes. In most cases, the characters are meaningful; for example, the + symbol usually denotes "plus," and so forth. Occasionally, a person has to transliterate characters when his data-entry device does not have a needed character. For example, many keypunch machines used for commercial applications do not have the characters (and), but have ¤ and % instead. The codes are the same; only the printed characters are different.

Most programming languages use an alphabet that includes at least 48 characters. The characters that comprise the alphabet are grouped into letters (such as A, B, and so forth), digits (such as 1, 2, and so forth), and special characters (such as +, *, %, and so forth). The size of the alphabet has very little to do with the computer since a six-bit character permits 64 combinations (that is, 2^6) and an eight-bit byte permits 256 combinations (that is, 2^8). In many cases, however, the size of the alphabet is related to the number of printable characters on the card-punch machine, the terminal device, or the line printer.

It is necessary to emphasize another important point. A program is composed of statements; but what constitutes a statement? Statements are punched on cards or typed in at the computer terminal. Different statements must be separated (or delimited) in some way and a convenient means of doing that is to start each statement on a new card or a new line. In many programming languages, the end of a card (or line) denotes the end of a statement, that is, unless a continuation is specified in some way, and a program is thus composed of a collection of cards or lines.

A program can be short or long, depending on the work that has to be done. As an example of a short program, consider the following statements:

```
10  PRINT "MY NAME IS ASHER LEV"
20  PRINT 100+100
30  END
```

Output:

```
MY NAME IS ASHER LEV
   200
```

The program is composed of three statements—each beginning on a new line. The line numbers by 10s are used for ordering in case a person wants to insert a statement between two others (such as line 15). The END statement denotes the physical end of the program. When program control reaches the END statement, the execution of the program terminates. Statement number 10 tells the computer to print a message; information enclosed in quotation marks is always printed on a literal basis. Statement number 20 tells the computer to compute 100+100 and print the result. Most statements begin with a word identifying the function the statement is to perform.

In Chapters 8 and 9, much of the discussion concerns statements, statement structure, and actual examples, and very little is presented on the precise manner in which a statement is entered. This is the case because the statement is of prime concern and its means of representation is merely an operational convention.

DATA

In general, a computer program can process two types of data: numeric data and descriptive data. Numeric data are numbers, and descriptive data are names assigned to physical entities and usually exist as a string of characters. In the preceding example, the quotation "MY NAME IS ASHER LEV" is descriptive data while 100 is numeric data.

In ordinary arithmetic, calculations are performed on numbers represented as sequences of decimal digits, possibly a decimal point, and possibly an algebraic sign. A number of this type is called a *fixed-point* or a *decimal* number. Thus, a fixed-point number x can be represented by an expression of the form

$$x = n+0.d_1 d_2 d_3 ...$$

where n is a signed or unsigned whole number and the d_is are digits in the range 0-9. The following constants are regarded as fixed-point numbers:

7	.00138
-19	-93000
+54.137	

Obviously, it is not necessary that unneeded constituents be written—except as required by a particular programming language. A fixed-point number without a fraction is an *integer*. Integer arithmetic has some characteristic properties. When integers are added, subtracted, multiplied, or divided, the result is an integer (that is, a whole number). The same holds true for all arithmetic operations on integers. Thus, if the division of a by b is defined by:

$$a = q*b+r \text{ where } r < b$$

then the result is the quotient q and the remainder r is lost. Thus, when integer arithmetic is used, 5 divided by 2 (that is 5/2) gives the result 2 and (3/2)*4 gives a result of 4. (The asterisk in the preceding expression denotes multiplication.)

Working with fixed-point numbers is not always convenient. For example, the evaluation of the expression:

3000000 X 150000000

is hindered by having to keep track of a large number of decimal places. Values of this type occur frequently in quantitative analysis and in computer applications. As a result, scientists and engineers use a simplified form known as *floating point*.* The above example is expressed as

$$3\times10^6 \times 15\times10^7$$

which is easily evaluated to 45×10^{13} using simple rules of arithmetic. The following list gives several examples of floating-point numbers:

Fixed-Point Numbers	Equivalent Floating-Point Numbers
73	$.73\times.10^2$ or 7.3×10^1
3.413	$.3413\times10^1$
−3600.1	$-.36001\times10^4$
.00123	$.123\times10^{-2}$
−.0009	$-.9\times10^{-3}$

In a floating-point number, the position of the decimal point is determined by the value of the exponent. In computer storage, the space occupied by a given number is fixed in size. Thus, floating-point notation is convenient for storing values that vary in magnitude from large to small.

Input data to the computer is limited to a linear sequence of characters requiring that a means be established for recording the exponent of a floating-point number. The need is satisfied by the letter E, in a constant, which denotes a power of ten. Thus, the number $.83\times10^4$ would be keypunched .83E4 and 2.67×10^{-15} as 2.67E-15.

Computer specialists also identify several other kinds of data: complex data, logical data, label data, pointer data, character data, and so on. Of these other data types, we will use logical data resulting from a comparison operation. A logical datum can assume the values true or false, and this value can be used in a decision-making statement. An example of a comparison operation is:

A+B>10

which asks the question "Is A+B greater than 10?" If the answer is yes, then the value of the expression is true; otherwise, the value of the expression is false. We also will use character data in the form of description information, as mentioned previously.

*Also regarded as engineering or scientific notation.

THE CONCEPT OF A VARIABLE

In mathematics, the name given to an unknown quantity is a *variable*. For example, one might say, "Let x equal the. . . ." In actual practice, the concept is more general and enables principles to be developed independently of a particular problem. The term "variable," in contrast to the word "constant," implies a term that can assume a set of values; or in other words, that the value of a variable is not constant but is subject to change. A variable is also used as a symbolic name in everyday discourse. Thus, variables such as X or Y are frequently used to represent an unknown quantity or to help in explaining a complex idea for which ordinary language is inadequate.

In a programming language, a variable is the name given to a location in main storage. For example, in the expression

A+B

A and B are variables and the expression means: add the contents of B to the contents of A. Clearly, a variable must be assigned a value before it can be used and this need is performed by one of the statements in the programming language. An important point is that the value of a variable can change during the course of computation.

OPERATORS AND EXPRESSIONS

A computer can perform a variety of operational functions, known as computing or computation. Some of these functions are: (1) arithmetic and comparison operations, (2) data movement, (3) sequence and control functions, and (4) input and output. Normally, these operational functions are available to a user through statements in a programming language, and when the user desires to specify a particular type of operation, he uses the most appropriate statement for that purpose.

Assume that one desires to add the value of variable A to the value of variable B. This operation could be specified in several ways, such as

A+B   (1)

or

ADD A TO B.   (2)

Method 1 is similar to ordinary mathematical notation and is the most frequently used method in programming. Method 2, which is similar to a statement in the business language COBOL, is less convenient when several mathematical operations need to be performed or when it is desired to include mathematical operations in one of the other statements in a programming language. As a means of specifying a stand-alone operation, however, method 2 has the advantages of being convenient, straightforward, and readable. (The BASIC and FORTRAN languages utilize the first method.)

In a programming language, a symbol that denotes a computational operation is known as an *operator*. Thus, in the statement

A+1

for example, + is an operator; the variable A and the constant 1 are *operands* to the operator. If A has the value 7 then A+1 has the value 8. More specifically, an operand is a quantity upon which an operation is performed; it can be either a variable or a constant. Some operations, such as addition and subtraction, require two operands and are written with the operator symbol separating the operands. The expression A+B, to use an earlier example, denotes that the value of variable B should be added to the value of variable A. (The example is, of course, abbreviated since there is no indication of what to do with the result.) An operator of this type is referred to as a *binary operator*. Operators that require a single operand, such as negation, are referred to as *unary operators* and written with the operator preceding the operand. The expression –A, for example, computes the expression 0–A and is used to change the sign of A. If A=10, then –A equals –10.

The operators used here are classed into two general areas:

1. *Arithmetic operators* such as + (for addition and identity), – (for subtraction and negation), * (for multiplication), / (for division), and ↑ or ** (for exponentiation).

2. *Comparison operators* that compare two data items (also referred to as relational operators), that is,

   < for *less than*
   ≤ for *less than or equal to*
   = for *equal to*
   ≥ for *greater than or equal to*
   > for *greater than*
   ≠ for *not equal to*

The representations of some of these operators vary between programming languages; for example, the comparison operator "greater than" is represented by the symbol $>$ in BASIC and by .GT. in FORTRAN. However, the mathematical meaning of the operations is invariant. Table 7.1 gives a "semiformal" definition for each of the above operators.

TABLE 7.1 COMPUTATIONAL OPERATORS

	Operation	Type	Form	Definition (R=result)	Example ($\longleftrightarrow$ denotes equivalence)
Arithmetic Operators	Addition	Binary	A+B	R=A+B	$2+3\longleftrightarrow 5$
	Subtraction	Binary	A−B	R=A−B	$6-4\longleftrightarrow 2$
	Multiplication	Binary	A*B	R=A×B	$4*3\longleftrightarrow 12$
	Division	Binary	A/B	R=A÷B	$9/2\longleftrightarrow 4.5$
	Exponentiation	Binary	A**B	$R=A^B$	$3**2\longleftrightarrow 9$
	Negation	Unary	−A	R=0−A	$-A\longleftrightarrow -3$, where A=3
Comparison Operators	Less than	Binary	A<B	R is true if A is less than B and is false otherwise.	$3<2\longleftrightarrow$ false
	Less than or equal to	Binary	A≤B	R is true if A is less than or equal to B and is false otherwise.	$3\leq 3\longleftrightarrow$ true
	Equal to	Binary	A=B	R is true if A is equal to B and is false otherwise.	$3=2\longleftrightarrow$ false
	Not equal to	Binary	A≠B	R is true if A is not equal to B and false otherwise.	$3\neq 2\longleftrightarrow$ true
	Greater than or equal to	Binary	A≥B	R is true if A is greater than or equal to B and false otherwise.	$2\geq 3\longleftrightarrow$ false
	Greater than	Binary	A>B	R is true if A is greater than B and is false otherwise.	$3>2\longleftrightarrow$ true

As in mathematics, operators and operands can be combined to form an expression denoting that a sequence of operations is to be performed. For example, A+B*C means that the product of B and C is to be added to A. Implied here is that computational operations are executed in a prescribed sequence and that operators possess a priority that determines the order in which the operations are executed. A simple priority scheme is:

Priority	*Operator*
highest	**
↓	* or /
lowest	+ or −

which means that ** is executed before * or /, and so forth. Thus, the expression 2+3*4 has the value 14 rather than 20. The programmer can use the priority of operators to his advantage. For example, the mathematical expression ax^2+b can be written in a programming language as A*X**2+B while maintaining the intended order of operations. In other cases, such as $\frac{(a+1)^2}{a+b}$, it is necessary to depart from the established order of execution. This need is served with parentheses that can be used for grouping. Expressions within parentheses are executed before the operations of which they are a part. The above example can be written in a programming language as (A+1)**2/(A+B). Similarly, the expression (2+3)*4 has the value 20. The use of parentheses can be extended to as many levels of nesting as are required by a particular sequence of operations.

REPLACEMENT AND DATA MOVEMENT

Expressions are permitted in some statements in a programming language because a computed value is frequently needed. For example, the following statement in the BASIC language:

IF A+B>13.5 THEN 510

directs the flow of program control to the statement numbered 510 if the value of the expression A+B is greater than 13.5. However, the most frequent use of the expression is to specify that a set of computations is to be performed and that the value of a variable is to be replaced with the result. Thus in the statement

A=B+C

the value of A is replaced with the *value* of the expression B+C. The "equals sign (=)" denotes replacement but does imply equivalence since values and not expressions are involved. Thus if B contains the value 10 and C contains the value 20, then execution of the statement A=B+C causes A to be replaced with the value 30; B and C retain their original values.

In mathematics, an identity, such as

$$(a+1)(a+2) = a^2+3a+2$$

is commonly used. Statements of this type are strictly illegal in programming languages. The *assignment statement*, which is introduced above, takes the general form:

$v=e$

which means that the value of variable v is replaced with the value of expression e, evaluated at the point of reference. The precise forms that v and e can assume are discussed later with respect to each programming language. In general, an expression e can be a constant, a variable, or a meaningful combination of constants, variables, operations, and parentheses. All of the following are valid expressions:

P	2**ML
25	(A1+B2)*C3-D4
I*J	A*B**2-1
DOG+CAT	(A)

In general, the only way that a value of a variable can change is through the replacement statement or an input statement.* For example, the statement

A=B1

causes the value of A to be replaced by the value of B1, and the value of B1 remains the same. This is a simple replacement operation and no computation is performed. The expression to the right of the equals sign is evaluated first and then the replacement is made. Thus, in the statement

*A data initialization statement is also included in the FORTRAN language.

    B=B+A

the value of A is added to the current value of B and the current value of B
is replaced by the result of the addition. Thus, if A=1 and B=2, the statement
B=B+A causes B to be replaced by 3, and the old value of 2 is lost. If a person
wanted to preserve the original value, he would have to save it by assigning it
to another variable.

DATA ORGANIZATION

A single item of data is known as a *scalar*. Thus, a value like a person's
age, the name of a part, or the result of a comparison operation is considered to be a scalar regardless of its data type. It can be expressed as a
constant or as a variable. It follows that a variable that names a scalar is
known as a *scalar variable*.

In a great many cases, data take the form of a family of related data
items. For example, a measurement taken at different locations at successive
intervals might be recorded as follows:

Location–Date	*Temperature*
New York–Jan 1.	29°
Miami–Jan. 1	69°
Chicago–Jan. 1	26°
Los Angeles–Jan. 1	60°
New York–March 31	41°
Miami–March 31	79°
Chicago–March 31	38°
Los Angeles–March 31	67°
New York–June 1	75°
Miami–June 1	92°
Chicago–June 1	80°
Los Angeles–June 1	88°

Storing the information in the above form is indeed cumbersome and would
occupy an excessive amount of storage. In this case, an array, such as the
following:

| | Date | | |
| | Index | | |
TEMP	1	2	3
1	29	41	75
2	69	79	92
3	26	38	80
4	60	67	88

Location
Index

matrix

would be considerably more convenient. The temperature in Miami, which has a location index of 2, on March 31, which has a date index of 2, is easily retrieved as 79°. A key point is that only the array, as a whole, need be given a name—in this case TEMP. A one-dimensional array is used to store a *list* of values, or as mathematicians call it—a vector. A two-dimensional array is used to store a rectangular arrangement of scalar values called a *matrix*. In computing, the concept is extended to include *n* dimensions—hence the more general name *array*. The process of retrieving an element of an array, termed *selection*, uses the name of the array and the relative position of the desired element in the array. Indices used to select an element from an array are termed a subscript and can be expressed as constants, variables, or expressions. The established practice is to reduce an index to an integer before selection takes place. The number of indices in a subscript must equal the number of dimensions in the array. Thus, TEMP (3,2), in the above example, would select the value 38. When writing a subscript, the indices are separated by commas and the entire set of indices is enclosed in parentheses following the array name. The convention is used since subscripts or superscripts in the usual sense are cumbersome to enter into the computer.

An array has several properties of interest. The array A, defined as:

$$\begin{pmatrix} a_{11} & a_{12} & a_{13} \\ a_{21} & a_{22} & a_{23} \end{pmatrix}$$

is used as an example. The first property is the *number of dimensions*, of which A has two. Each dimension is further characterized by an extent. The *extent* is the number of elements in a dimension. A has a row extent of two and a column extent of three. Another characteristic is homogeneity. *Homogeneity* refers to the fact that the properties of each element of an array must be the same. Thus, for example, the array must contain all fixed- or all floating-point numbers. Obviously, distinct values may differ. The last property of an array is how it is stored. Two methods are in widespread use: row order and column order. *Row order*, also known as *index order* or *lexicographic order,* denotes that the elements of an array are stored in consecutive locations in computer main storage in a rowwise fashion. Row order is used in the BASIC language. *Column order* denotes that the elements of the array are stored in a columnwise fashion. Column order is used in the FORTRAN language. Examples of both techniques for the array A, given above, are listed as follows:

Row Order	*Index*	*Column Order*
A(1,1)	1	A(1,1)
A(1,2)	2	A(2,1)
A(1,3)	3	A(1,2)
A(2,1)	4	A(2,2)
A(2,2)	5	A(1,3)
A(2,3)	6	A(2,3)

It is necessary to know how an array is stored in a given language for the following reason. Consider the following statements in BASIC:

DIM A(13,4)   (1)

MAT READ A   (2)

Statement 1 defines a matrix with 13 rows and 4 columns. Statement 2 specifies that data is to be read from a data set into computer storage to occupy matrix A. Data must be placed in the data file in a prescribed sequence so that a value is placed in the intended matrix position. Therefore, the order in which the matrix elements are stored must be known or a specific "convention" must be established.

METALANGUAGES

Most programmers recognize the process of constructing a computer program is a creative act and that once a program is suitably encoded, it is as much a contribution to the world of knowledge as a poem, a mathematical formula, or an artist's sketch. In fact, computer programming is usually regarded as an art rather than a science. A computer program written in a programming language becomes a body of knowledge when a suitable description of that language is available that can be used to distinguish between a syntactically valid program and a syntactically invalid program and to determine the meaning of the program. A language that describes another language is called a *metalanguage*, and most programming languages utilize a descriptive technique of this kind.

The most frequent use of a metalanguage is to describe a statement in a programming language in such a way that the reader can construct a valid instance of a particular statement. Thus, the metalanguage should utilize a notation outside of the programming language being described and should lend itself to use in the construction of valid statements by a user of the language described.

A metalanguage that is particularly useful for describing BASIC and FORTRAN is known as Extended Backus Notation in honor of John Backus of the United States who developed one of the first metalanguages for programming languages.

Extended Backus Notation employs seven rules and appropriate symbols, given as follows:

1. A *notation variable* names a constituent of a programming language. It takes one of two forms: (1) Lower-case letters, digits, and hyphens— beginning with a letter; for example:

   constant
   arithmetic-variable
   array-dimension-specification

   or (2) Two or more words separated by hyphens where one word consists of lower-case letters and the others consist of upper-case letters; for example:

   DATA-statement
   MAT-READ-statement

   A notation variable represents information that must be supplied by the user and is defined formally or informally in preceding or adjacent text.

2. A *notation constant* stands for itself and is represented by capital letters or by special characters. A notation constant must be written as shown. For example, in the statement

   GOSUB statement-number
   NEXT arithmetic-variable

the words GOSUB and NEXT are notation constants and must be written as indicated.

3. A *syntactical unit* is regarded as a notation variable, a notation constant, or a collection of notation variables, notation constants, and notation symbols enclosed in braces and brackets.

4. The *vertical bar* | is read "or" and indicates that a choice must be made between the item to the left of the bar and the item to the right of the bar. For example:

    character-reference|arithmetic-reference
    &PI|*E|*SQR2

5. A set of *braces* { } is used for grouping or to indicate that a choice is to be made among the syntactical units contained in the braces. For example:

    {+|-}
    {integer-constant|fixed-point constant}

6. A set of *brackets* [] represents an option and the enclosed syntactical units can be omitted. For example:

    [+|-]
    alphabetic-character[numeric-character]

7. The *ellipsis* (a series of three periods) indicates that the preceding syntactic unit may be repeated one or more times. For example:

    DATA constant [,constant] . . .
    REM [string character] . . .

Extended Backus Notation is further described by giving some examples from the BASIC and FORTRAN languages. The *FOR statement* in BASIC has the form:

FOR arithmetic-variable=arithmetic-expression TO
    arithmetic-expression [STEP arithmetic-expression]

An example of this FOR statement is:

FOR I = J TO M/2 STEP 2

the *computed GOTO* statement in FORTRAN has the form:

GOTO (statement-number [statement-number]...),
    integer-scalar-variable

An example of the computed GOTO statement is:

GOTO (150,17,3000), I4B

The significance of the use of a metalanguage will become apparent in Chapters 8 and 9.

COMMENT

This chapter is intended to provide background material for either Chapter 8 or Chapter 9 or both. Similar concepts are grouped here to reduce the amount of duplicate material.

At this point, complete comprehension of each topic covered is not essential and only general concepts are required. However, the reader may find himself referring back to this chapter as he studies Chapters 8 and 9. This is the author's intent. Programming languages should be studied and understood; they are much too important to read over lightly.

QUESTION SET

1. Evaluate the following expression using integer arithmetic when A=5, B=3, C=2:

    A+B+1   −B   (A+B)/C
    A/B+C   A*B/2
    A+B/C   C*(A−B)

2. Evaluate the following expressions using floating-point arithmetic when D= $.2 \times 10^3$, G= $.5 \times 10^1$, and H= $.1 \times 10^2$:

    D+G   (D−H)*G
    D+.4E5
    .3E2*H

3. Evaluate the following comparison expressions when A=5, B=3, C=2:

     A>B   A≠C
     A>B+C   B=C+1
     B<C   3*A≤5*B

4. Indicate the value stored in the following statements, where A=5, B=3, C=2:

     T=A+B+C   B=B+C
     R1=(A+B)/C   A=A-B-C
     W=3*(A+B-C)

5. Assume the following statements are executed in sequence:

     TEMPY=M
     M=N
     N=TEMPY

Can you describe the "general" function being performed?

6. Given the array TEMP found in the chapter, evaluate the following expressions:

     TEMP (3,2)+1
     TEMP (1,2)+TEMP (4,1)

7. List the values of TEMP in row order.

8. Execute the following statements in order:

     TEMP (3,2)=6
     TEMP (2,1)=TEMP (4,3)
     TEMP (1,3)=TEMP (3,3)+1
     TEMP (4,1)=0

Print the matrix TEMP when you are finished.

9. Give an example of the following statement:

     DATA constant [,constant] . . .

CHAPTER 8

The Basic Language

BASIC LANGUAGE STRUCTURE

Introduction

The BASIC language achieves its greatest utility from the simple fact that it is easy to learn, easy to use, and easy to remember. (BASIC is an acronym for Beginner's All-purpose Symbolic Instruction Code.) BASIC is particularly appropriate for the student or the problem solver who wants to utilize the advantages of computer processing without becoming a computer expert.

BASIC was originally developed at Dartmouth College under the direction of Professors John G. Kemeny and Thomas E. Kurtz. BASIC has been under continuous development and several implementations of the language are currently available at universities, through computer service companies, and in business concerns. Enhancements have been made to the original concept of BASIC such that one frequently hears of an "extended BASIC," "super BASIC," "advanced BASIC," and so forth. Occasionally, one even hears of a "basic BASIC."

The BASIC language serves two purposes in this book:

1. It prepares the reader for writing programs in the BASIC language; and
2. It demonstrates a language that can be used with time-sharing facilities.

This part of the book covers the original Dartmouth version of BASIC plus many of the subsequent extensions to the language. As yet, a BASIC standard has not been established and therefore variations exist between different implementations of the language. Any person making extensive use of the language should consult the reference manual for the system he is using.

Fibonacci Numbers

As an example of the general appearance of a BASIC program, consider the Fibonacci sequence, depicted as follows:

1 1 2 3 5 8 13 21 34 ...

The pattern is obvious. After the first two numbers, each succeeding number is the sum of the previous two numbers. A BASIC program that generates Fibonacci numbers less than or equal to 50 is given as follows:*

```
 10  LET N1=0
 20  LET N2=1
 30  PRINT N2
 40  LET N3=N1+N2
 50  IF N3>50 THEN 100
 60  PRINT N3
 70  LET N1=N2
 80  LET N2=N3
 90  GOTO 40
100  END
```

Output

```
 1
 1
 2
 3
 5
 8
13
21
34
```

Amazing applications of Fibonacci numbers arise in the physical world. For example, Fibonacci numbers can be used to describe the arrangement of stems on a branch and the growth in rabbit population.

*This footnote is intended for the person being exposed to BASIC for the first time. It is not necessary that the first few programs be completely understood. Only general concepts are required since all topics are covered in later sections.

The above program is fairly obvious and is not discussed further. After the next example, however, several statements, including those used above, are described.

The Indian Problem

As an illustration of the manner in which BASIC can be used to solve a problem, consider the classical *Indian problem*. The problem is stated as follows: Manhattan Island was sold by the Indians to the settlers in 1626 for $24 worth of beads and trinkets. At a given interest rate, what is the island worth today? A "simple-minded" solution is presented as the following program:

```
10  LET P=24
20  LET R=.06
30  FOR Y=1627 TO 1973
40      LET P=P+P*R
50  NEXT Y
60  PRINT P
70  END
```

Output:*

1.44993E+10

The statements numbered 10 and 20 assign the values 24 and .06 to the principal (P) and the interest rate (R), respectively. The interest for a given year is computed as P*R and the principal at the end of a given year is computed as P+P*R. Statements 30 through 50 constitute a program loop; the principal is recomputed as the year (Y) advances from 1627 to 1973. After the loop is completed (that is, the number of iterations specified in statement 30 has been satisfied), the resulting principal (P) is printed in statement 60.

The PRINT statement can also be used to have several data items printed on the same output line by including those items in the PRINT statement, separated by commas. Thus if statement 60 read,

```
60  PRINT "PRESENT VALUE OF MANHATTAN=";P
```

*1.44993E+10 is the floating-point form of 14,499,300,000.

then the output would be,

PRESENT VALUE OF MANHATTAN= 1.44993E+10

Data items enclosed in quotation marks are printed as descriptive information, whereas the *numerical value* of an expression is printed. (Recall that a variable is an expression.)

In the preceding program, the data of the problem was built into the program (that is, a beginning principal of 24 and a rate of .06). If the user desired to repeat the calculations for different interest rates, then he would have to build a set of data values with a DATA statement, such as

DATA .05,.06,.07,.08

and access the data set with a READ statement, such as

READ R

Thus, a program to compute the present value of Manhattan Island for different interest rates is given as follows:

```
10   DATA .05,.06,.07,.08
20   FOR I=1 TO 4
30      LET P=24
40      READ R
50      FOR Y = 1626 TO 1973
60          LET P = P+P*R
70      NEXT Y
80      PRINT "PRESENT VALUE OF MANHATTAN=";P
90   NEXT I
00   END
```

Output:

```
PRESENT VALUE OF MANHATTAN= 5.40628E+08
PRESENT VALUE OF MANHATTAN= 1.44993E+10
PRESENT VALUE OF MANHATTAN= 3.77035E+11
PRESENT VALUE OF MANHATTAN= 9.51162E+12
```

The program includes a nested FOR loop that has the form:

```
       ⎧FOR...
       ⎪   ...
       ⎪    ⎧FOR...
   A   ⎨  B ⎨    ...
       ⎪    ⎪    ...
       ⎪    ⎩NEXT...
       ⎪   ...
       ⎩NEXT...
```

The interpretation of the nested loops is as follows: For every iteration of loop A, loop B is executed from start to finish. (Thus, if A is executed n times and loop B is executed m times, then a given statement contained in loop B is executed $n \times m$ times.)

Several statements were used in the above examples:

LET—assigns the value of an expression to a variable

FOR—begins a program loop and specifies how many times it is executed

NEXT—ends a program loop and tells the computer to return to the beginning of the loop for the next iteration

PRINT—causes output data to be printed

DATA—creates a set of data

READ—causes data specified in a DATA statement to be accessed (read) and assigned to specified variables

END—ends a BASIC program

Each of these statements is described in more detail in later sections.

Characters and Symbols

A computer program is essentially a coded form of an algorithm for solving a given problem on a computer. The statements of a program are encoded in the alphabet of the language using established conventions. It is necessary to distinguish between characters of the alphabet and symbols of the language. A *character of the alphabet* is an entity that has a representation internally and externally to the computer. The letter "A," for example, is a character of most language alphabets. The majority of characters have no meaning in their own right; for example, the letter "A" only has meaning through the manner in which it is used, which may be as part of a variable, the name of a statement, and so forth. Table 8.1 lists the BASIC alphabet, which consists of approximately 50–55 characters depending upon the equipment involved.

A *symbol of the language* is a series of one or more characters that has been assigned a specific meaning. Typical symbols are the plus sign (+) and

TABLE 8.1 CHARACTERS OF THE BASIC ALPHABET

Alphabetic Characters (26)

A B C D E F G H I J K L M N O P Q R S T U V W X Y Z

Digits (10)

0 1 2 3 4 5 6 7 8 9

Special Characters (19)

Name	Character
Blank	(no visual representation)
Equal sign	=
Plus sign	+
Minus sign	−
Asterisk	*
Solidus (slash)	/
Up arrow	↑
Left parenthesis	(
Right parenthesis	)
Comma	,
Point or period	.
Single quotation mark (apostrophe)	'
Double quotation mark	"
Semicolon	;
Question mark	?
"Less than symbol"	<
"Greater than" symbol	>
"Not equal" symbol	≠
Currency symbol (dollar sign)	$

the comma, used as a separator. A symbol consisting of more than one character is termed a *composite symbol* that is assigned a meaning not inherent in the constituent characters themselves. Typical composite symbols are ** for exponentiation and >= for "greater than or equal to." The symbols of the BASIC language are listed in Table 8.2.

In most implementations of BASIC, lower-case letters can be used interchangeably with upper-case letters. Spaces are ignored in BASIC, except with quotes, so that they can be inserted by the user to promote easy reading.

TABLE 8.2 SYMBOLS OF THE BASIC LANGUAGE

Symbol	Function	Alternate[a]
+	Addition or prefix +	
−	Subtraction or prefix −	
*	Multiplication	
/	Division	
↑	Exponentiation	**
>	Greater than	GT
>=	Greater than or equal to	GE
=	Equal to (also see below)	
<>	Not equal to	≠ or NE
<	Less than	LT
<=	Less than or equal to	LE
,	Separates elements of list or subscripts	
.	Decimal point	
;	Separates elements of list	
=	Assignment symbol	
"	Used to enclose literals	
()	Enclose lists or group expressions	

[a]Some versions of BASIC use alternate composite symbols; frequently, the characters used are a function of the input devices available to the user.

Data Types and Constant Values

Two types of data are permitted in BASIC: arithmetic data and character-string data. An *arithmetic data item* has a numeric value and is stored as either a fixed-point number or a floating-point number, depending on the magnitude and precision of the value and the manner in which the language is implemented on a given computer. A person need not be concerned with how his data is stored and the rules governing integer arithmetic do not apply. An arithmetic data item is referenced through the use of a variable or a constant and may be generated as an intermediate result as part of a computational procedure. BASIC accepts arithmetic constants in three principal forms:

1. As a constituent of a non-DATA statement, such as the number 5 in

LET A = B+5

2. As a constant in a DATA statement, such as

DATA 25,-13.289,.734E-4

3. In response to an input request (from an INPUT statement), such as

?-75,4.56

In general, the arithmetic constant is written in the usual fashion, that is, as a sequence of digits optionally preceded by a plus or minus sign and possibly containing a decimal point. (An arithmetic constant is specified in decimal and the user need not be concerned with how it is stored.) Sample arithmetic constants are –13.5, 12345, 1., +36, .01, –5, and 0. In addition, an arithmetic constant can be scaled by a power of 10 by following the constant with the letter E followed by the power, which must be expressed as either a positive or negative integer. Thus, the constant xEy is equivalent to the expression $x \times 10^y$ in mathematics. To cite some examples, .12E–4 is equivalent to .000012, –3E2 is equivalent to –300, +1.234E3 is equivalent to 1234, and –1E+1 is equivalent to –10. The sign of an arithmetic constant is frequently omitted in expressions by applying elementary rules of arithmetic. Thus, instead of writing A+(-5), most users simply write A-5. Similarly, A-(-5) would ordinarily be written as A+5.

In an arithmetic constant, the E (if used) must be preceded by at least one digit. Thus, 1E2 is a valid constant where E2 is not.

A *character-string data item* is stored as a string of characters and can include any character recognized by the computer equipment. A character-string data item is referenced through the use of a variable or a constant. BASIC accepts character-string constants in three principal forms:

1. As a constituent part of a non-DATA statement, such as

LET F$ = "TEA FOR TWO"

or

IF P$ = "END" THEN 100

2. As a constant in a DATA statement, such as

DATA "BIG", "BAD"

3. In response to an input request (from an INPUT statement), such as

?"EACH HIS OWN"

A character-string constant must be enclosed in quotation marks. Any character within the quotes, including the blank character, is considered to be part of the character string. The length of a character string is the number of characters between the enclosing quotation marks. If it is desired to include a quotation mark in that string, then the included mark must be represented as two consecutive quotation marks. The consecutive quotation marks are a lexical feature of the language and are stored as a single character. Sample character-string constants are:

Character-String Constant	Length	Would Print as
"TEA FOR TWO"	11	TEA FOR TWO
"123.4"	5	123.4
" " "DARN IT" " "	9	"DARN IT"
"DON'T"	5	DON'T

Character-string data are frequently used for printing descriptive information, such as page and column headings, and are occasionally referred to as "label data."

Names

A *name* is a string of alphabetic or numeric characters, the first of which must be alphabetic. In BASIC, names are used to identify scalar variables, array variables, and functions.

A *scalar arithmetic variable* name (also referred to as a simple variable) consists of a single letter or a single letter followed by a single digit. A, I, Z1, and K9 are valid simple variables while A10, DOG, and 3A are not. The initial value of a simple variable is zero and it can only be used to represent arithmetic data.

A *scalar character-string variable* name (also referred to as a simple character variable) consists of a single letter followed by a dollar sign (that is, the currency symbol). The maximum length of a character string that can be assigned to a character-string variable is 18. The initial value of a simple character variable is 18 blanks. Thus, A$, I$, and S$ are valid simple character variables while A1$, 5$, and IT$ are not.

Arrays

An *array* is a collection of data items of the same type (that is, all arithmetic data items or all character-string data items) that is referenced by a single array name. An *arithmetic array* can have either one or two dimensions and uses an identifier that consists of a single letter. An element of an array is referenced by giving the relative position of that element in the array. If the array has one dimension, then an element is referenced by appending a subscript enclosed in parentheses to the array name as follows

$a(e)$

where a is the array name and e is an expression evaluated at the point of reference. Thus, the array reference $a(e)$ selects the eth element of array a. If the array has two dimensions, then an element is selected in a similar manner with an array reference of the form:

$a(e_1,e_2)$

where a is the array name and e_1 and e_2 are expressions evaluated at the point of reference. Thus, the array reference $a(e_1,e_2)$ selects the element located in the e_1th row and the e_2th column of a. The following are valid array references: A(I), B(W4), C(P+1), C(I,J), E(T3/R+13,3*X↑2-1), F(A(2*Q)), and G(B(1),4). The last two examples depict subscripted subscripts. All elements of an arithmetic array are initially set to zero when the program is executed.

A *character-string array* (referred to as a character array) can have one dimension and uses an identifier that consists of a letter followed by a dollar sign. Each element of a character array can contain up to 18 characters and is initially set to 18 blanks when the program is executed. As with an arithmetic array, an element of a character array is referenced by specifying the relative position of that element in the array with a construction of the form

$a\$(e)$

where $a\$$ is the array name and e is an expression evaluated at the point of reference. The following are valid character array references: B$(3), C$(I), D$(2*J-1), and D$(A(K)).

The extent of an array can be declared implicitly or explicitly. An *explicit array declaration* is made through the use of the dimension (DIM) statement, which is used to give the extent of each dimension of the array. Thus, the statement

DIM P(3,4),Q(36),T$(17)

defines a two-dimensional arithmetic array P with three rows and four columns, a one-dimensional arithmetic array Q with 36 elements, and a character array T$ with 17 elements, each element of which can contain a character string of 18 characters. The lower subscript bound for all array dimensions is one; the upper subscript bound is the value declared with the DIM state-ment. The DIM statement is presented in a later section on arrays.

An *implicit array declaration* is made when an array reference with either a single or a double subscript is made to an undeclared array. An array refer-enced in this way with a single subscript is assigned an extent of 10 with lower and upper subscript bounds of 1 and 10, respectively. An array refer-enced in this way with a double subscript is assigned row and column extents of 10; each dimension has lower and upper bounds of 1 and 10, respectively.

Operators and Expressions

Arithmetic and comparison operators are included as part of the BASIC language. Arithmetic operators are defined on arithmetic data and are classed as binary operators and unary operators. A *binary arithmetic operator* is used in the following manner:

$$\text{operand} \left\{ +|-|*|/|\uparrow \right\} \text{operand}$$

where an operand is defined as an arithmetic constant, a function reference, an element of an arithmetic array, or an expression enclosed in parentheses. A *unary arithmetic operator* is used in the following manner:

$$- \text{operand}$$

where "operand" has the same definition as given directly above. The use of a unary operator is restricted to the following cases:

1. As the leftmost character in an expression, provided that two oper-ators do not appear in succession; or
2. As the leftmost character in a subexpression enclosed in parentheses such that the unary operator follows the left parenthesis.

An example of case 1 is $-A+B\uparrow C$ while an example of case 2 is $A*(-B\uparrow(-3))$. The result of a binary or unary arithmetic operation is a numeric value.

An *arithmetic expression* can be an arithmetic scalar variable, an element of an arithmetic array, a numeric constant, a function reference, or a series of these constituents separated by binary operators and parentheses and pos-sibly prefixed by unary operators. Thus, any of the following are valid ex-pressions in BASIC:

```
A1              -(C1↑I-1)      -SQR(X↑3)-J
B+25            SIN(X3)        ((Y+3)*Y+16)*Y-1
```

As stated previously, parentheses are used for grouping and expressions within expressions are executed before the operations of which they are a part. For example, the expression 2*(3+4) evaluates to 14. When parentheses are not used in an arithmetic expression, an operand may appear as though it is an operand to two operators; that is, for example, the operand B in an expression such as,

A+B*C

In this case, operators are executed on a priority basis as governed by the following list:

Operator	Priority
↑ (that is, **)	Highest
unary –	
*, /	↓
binary +, binary –	Lowest

Thus, in the expression, A+B*C, the expression B*C is executed first and the result of that subexpression is added to A. Operators of the same priority are executed in a left-to-right order.

A *character expression* is a character variable, a character array member, or a character constant. Except when they are used in a PRINT statement, character strings are handled in a special way:

1. If the character string contains less than 18 characters, it is padded on the right with blanks so that it can be stored as 18 characters.
2. If the character string contains more than 18 characters, it is truncated on the right so that its length is 18 characters.

(Character strings used in a PRINT statement are given a length determined by the enclosing quotation marks and the above conventions do not apply. No padding or truncation occurs.)

A *comparison expression* has the form:

operand $\{=|<>|>=|>|<=|<\}$ operand

where the "operands" can be either arithmetic expressions or character expressions. (The operands cannot be mixed.) The result of a comparison expression is either a "true" value or a "false" value, which is used in the conditional IF statement. Thus, if A=10, B=15, C$="TEA", and D$="DOG", then the following valid comparison expressions give the indicated results:

A=B yields the value "false"*
A↑2+A*B>=B↑2 yields the value "true"
C$<>D$ yields the value "true"
(A+2.5)↑2>101.5 yields the value "true"
C$<D$ yields the value "false"†

In an arithmetic comparison expression, the arithmetic expressions that serve as operands to the comparison operation are evaluated first; then the comparison operation is performed.

Statement Structure

BASIC is designed to be a terminal-oriented programming language and the structure of the language reflects that mode of operation. Each statement is prefixed with a *statement number* that serves two purposes:

1. BASIC statements are executed in an order determined by the arithmetic value of the statement number; and
2. The statement number is used to reference another statement in statements such as

    GOTO 500

In the first case, the statement number serves as a "line number," so that statements need not be entered in any specific order to facilitate the insertion, deletion, and modification of statements.

The form of a BASIC statement is:

statement-number [statement-identifier] [statement-body]

where "statement-number" is an unsigned integer,‡ "statement-identifier" is a word that identifies a particular type of statement, and "statement-body" is a series of characters that comprise the body of the statement. Sample statements are:

*Arithmetic comparisons use the arithmetic value of the operands.

†When BASIC (and as a matter of fact, any programming language) is implemented, an ordering sequence among characters is defined. Frequently, the ordering sequence is based on the numerical values of the bit representations of the characters.

‡Usually, one to four decimal digits are permitted a statement number.

```
500  LET A=B+C*D
300  LET K3=16
783  GOTO 100
910  IF A>=B THEN 300
440  STOP
999  END
```

Thus, a statement is constructed from a statement identifier, a statement body, or both. Neither a statement identifier nor a statement body is required so that a blank line (except for the statement number) is permitted to improve readability and to serve as a point of reference in a program. Blank lines are ignored by the computer.

A good programming practice is to insert comments to help a person remember what a particular set of statements does. A comment (that is, a remark) can be inserted anywhere in a program with a statement of the form:

statement-number REM[any-character] . . .

For example, the following statements are comment lines:

```
350  REM THIS PROGRAM IS INCORRECT
890  REMARK FNG IS THE GAMMA FUNCTION
```

Comment lines are ignored by the computer.

Program Structure

A program in the BASIC language is characterized by the fact that a complete program must be entered before any part of the program is executed and by the fact that it is usually transparent to the user how the program is executed. In general, the conventions given below apply regardless of whether the operational mode is time sharing or batch processing. The time-sharing mode is used as an example.

After the user identifies himself to the computer, the word "READY" is typed by the computer so that the user knows that the computer is ready to accept a command telling it what to do. (Obviously, commands differ between different implementations of the language.) Assume the user types the word NEW, telling the computer that he wishes to develop a new program, followed by the name of the new program. Another "READY" message is typed by the computer and the user can proceed to enter his program. (If the user had typed the word OLD followed by a program name, then the old program would be retrieved from direct-access storage for use by the terminal user.) The user enters information line by line. Each statement must be preceded with a statement number that is saved as part of the statement. The only restriction on a program is that it must end with an END statement; in other words, the highest numbered statement in a program must be the END statement.

When the user has entered his complete program, he normally enters a command to either RUN the program or to LIST the program. After the computer has performed a requested action, it types "READY" to inform the user that he can again enter either statements or commands.

The user can add or change a statement at any time by simply typing the statement number (of the line to be inserted or modified) followed by the new statement. When the program is run or listed, the statements are sorted by statement number and new statements replace old ones. A statement is deleted by typing its statement number with a blank line.

Once the execution of a program is started, the program executes until a STOP statement is executed, an END statement is reached, or a condition arises that prevents further execution. The following example depicts the preceding concepts:

```
Computer:   READY
User:       NEW TRNGL
Computer:   READY
User:       100 DATA 3,4,5,12,7,24
User:       200 READ  B,H
User:       300 LET D=SQR(B↑2+H↑2)
User:       400 PRINT B,H,D
User:       500 GOTO 200
User:       999  END
User:       RUN
Computer:   3    4    5
            5   12   13
            7   24   25

Computer:   OUT OF DATA IN LINE 200

Computer:   READY

User:       150 PRINT "BASE", "HEIGHT", "DIAG"
User:       RUN

Computer:   BASE    HEIGHT    DIAG
Computer:   3         4        5
Computer:   5        12       13
Computer:   7        24       25
```

```
Computer:  OUT OF DATA IN LINE 200

User:      LIST
Computer:  100 DATA 3,4,5,12,7,24
Computer:  150 PRINT "BASE", "HEIGHT", "DIAG"
Computer:  200 READ B,H
Computer:  300 LET D=SQR(B↑2+H↑2)
Computer:  400  PRINT B,H,D
Computer:  500 GOTO 200
Computer:  999 END

Computer:  READY
```

Thus, the structure of a program in the BASIC language is inherent in the fact that it is a collection of statements ordered by statement number (that is, line number).

The following sections describe the various statements that comprise the core of the BASIC language. The statements are grouped by the functions they perform and examples of the use of each type of statement are given. The first topic is "input and output" and statements relevant to that topic are covered. Other topics covered are: assignment statements, program control, looping, arrays, and functions.

INPUT AND OUTPUT

Input and output statements are used to enter data into the computer and to display results to the user. Four statement types are presented: PRINT, DATA, READ, and INPUT.

The PRINT Statement

The PRINT statement is used to display results on a person's output unit, usually taken to be a terminal device. The form of the PRINT statement is:

```
PRINT  expression [{,|;} expression] . . .
```

where "expression" is an arithmetic or a character-string expression. The format of the PRINT statement denotes that the following cases are valid:

```
PRINT A              PRINT C,D1+3      PRINT H;I
PRINT 25                               PRINT J,K; L
PRINT 2*B                              PRINT 'ABC';M

PRINT A,B,C,D,E          PRINT 2*A↑3+4*A+5
PRINT
```

The key point is that expressions must be separated by a punctuation character that can be either a comma or a semicolon. Normally, the PRINT statement is used in a program as follows:

```
10  PRINT "3↑2=",3↑2
20  END
```

and a result such as:

```
3↑2=           9
```

is produced. A comma is used as punctuation and the output is printed in columns. When it is desired to run the fields together, a semicolon is used as a separator, as in the following example:

```
10  PRINT '3↑2=';3↑2
20  END
RUN

3↑2= 9

DONE
```

When a PRINT statement is completed, the carriage is normally moved up to the next line. The user can prevent the carriage from advancing by ending the PRINT statement with either a comma or a semicolon. The following example illustrates the latter point:

```
10  FOR I = 1 TO 5        10  FOR I = 1 TO 5
20      PRINT I           20      PRINT I;
30  NEXT I               30  NEXT I
40  END                  40  END
RUN                      RUN

    1                        1  2  3  4  5
    2
    3                    DONE
```

```
4
5

DONE
```

A PRINT statement with no statement body simply advances the carriage line. Thus, in the following example:

```
10  PRINT 'FIRST LINE'
20  PRINT
30  PRINT 'NEXT LINE'
40  END
RUN

FIRST LINE

NEXT LINE

DONE
```

a line on the printed page is skipped as a result of the "null" print statement (line 20).

The DATA Statement

The DATA statement is used to create a data list, internal to the computer and has the form:

```
DATA constant [,constant] . . .
```

where "constant" is an arithmetic or character constant. All data specified in DATA statements are collected into a single list; the order of the data constants is determined by the logical order of the DATA statements in the program. The internal data list can be accessed by the READ statement during the execution of a program. Actually, the DATA statement is a nonexecutable statement and the internal data list is created before the program is executed. Thus, DATA statements can be placed anywhere in a program. The logical order of DATA statements is determined by the relative magnitude of associated statement numbers.

The READ Statement

The READ statement is used to assign values to scalar and array variables and has the form:

```
READ variable [,variable] . . .
```

where "variable" is an arithmetic or character scalar variable or a subscripted array variable. A pointer is associated with the internal data list constructed from the DATA statements in a program. Initially, this pointer is set to the first value in the data list. As READ statements are processed, successive values from the data list are assigned to the variables in the READ statements. Logically, the values in the data list are used up as READ statements are executed. Each value from the data list must be the same type as the variable to which it is assigned. Thus, it is the user's responsibility to insure that data values are sequenced in the required order. If an attempt is made to "read" data when the data list is exhausted or the type of a data value and the variable to which it is assigned do not agree, then a READ error results and execution of the program is terminated. A READ error also occurs when an attempt is made to "read" data when no DATA statement exists in the program. Examples of the DATA and READ statements have been given previously. The following example depicts the use of character-string constants, as well as arithmetic constants.

```
 5   PRINT 'GRADE REPORT'
 6   PRINT
10   READ N$,T1,T2,T3
20   PRINT N$
30   PRINT 'AVERAGE IS'; (T1+T2+T3)/3
35   PRINT
40   GOTO 10
50   DATA 'R.ADAMS'
51   DATA 80,90,76
52   DATA 'J.COTTON'
53   DATA 50,71,68
54   DATA 'M.DODGER'
55   DATA   100,86,96
99   END
RUN

GRADE REPORT
```

```
    R.ADAMS
    AVERAGE IS 82

    J.COTTON
    AVERAGE IS 63

    M.DODGER
    AVERAGE IS 94

    OUT OF DATA IN LINE 10
```

The INPUT Statement

In some cases, the data values to be used in a program are not known beforehand and must be entered on a dynamic basis. The INPUT statement allows the user to interact with an executing program and permits data values to be entered. The INPUT statement operates like the READ statement except that data is entered from the user's console on a dynamic basis instead of from an internal data set. The INPUT statement is placed in a program at the point that the data is needed. The computer types a question mark (?) and the execution of the program is suspended until the required data is entered. Since a program can include several INPUT statements, most people precede the INPUT statement with a PRINT statement identifying the data that should be entered. The form of the INPUT statement is:

```
INPUT   variable[,variable] . . .
```

where "variable" is an arithmetic or character scalar variable or a subscripted array variable. The following example depicts the use of the INPUT statement:

```
10  PRINT "ENTER A,B"
20  INPUT A,B
30  PRINT "A+B=";A+B
40  PRINT "A*B=";A*B
50  GOTO 10
60  END
RUN

ENTER A,B
? 2,3
```

```
A+B= 5
A*B= 6
ENTER A,B
?3,4
A+B= 7
A*B= 12
?STOP
PROGRAM HALTED
```

The above program includes what is known as an *input loop*; in other words, program control is always directed to the statement numbered 10 and then to statement 20 (with the GOTO statement in line 50) to input new values for A and B. The user can terminate the loop by typing STOP instead of entering a data value.

ASSIGNMENT STATEMENTS

The assignment statement permits a data value to be assigned to a scalar variable or to a subscripted array variable and includes the "simple" LET statement and the conventional assignment statement.

The Simple LET Statement

The LET statement has the form:

> LET variable=expression

where "variable" is a scalar arithmetic variable or a subscripted arithmetic array variable and "expression" is an arithmetic expression; or "variable" is a scalar character-string variable or a subscripted character-string array variable and "expression" is a character-string expression. The statement means: "Replace the value of the variable with the value of the expression evaluated at the point of reference in the program." The following examples depict valid LET statements:

```
LET   A=10
LET   B$= "TEA FOR TWO"
LET   C1=.00125 *A+3
LET   D(14)=191.8
LET   E$(I+1)="JOKER"
LET   P(K,3*J+1)=A*B(L-2)↑I
```

The Conventional Assignment Statement

The use of the word LET in the assignment statement is a notational convenience and is not required in most implementations of BASIC. The form of the conventional assignment statement is:

```
variable-expression
```

where "variable" and "expression" are the same as defined above. Examples of valid assignment statements are:

```
A=10
B$="TEA FOR TWO"
P(K,3*J+1)=A*B(L-2)↑I
```

and so forth.

PROGRAM CONTROL

As was mentioned previously, statements in a program are executed sequentially until a statement is executed that alters the sequential flow of execution. Six statements are included in the BASIC language to control the manner in which a program is executed: GOTO, IF, END, STOP, FOR, and NEXT. The GOTO and IF statements are presented in this section and are used to alter the flow of program execution on an unconditional and on a conditional basis, respectively. The END and STOP statements are also covered briefly. The FOR and NEXT statements are used for looping and are described in the next section.

The GOTO Statement

The GOTO statement has the form:

```
GOTO statement-number
```

where "statement-number" must be the line number associated with a statement in the program. If the statement number used as the operand to the GOTO statement does not exist in the program, then the condition is recognized and continued execution of the program is not permitted. Several examples of the GOTO statement are given in previous sections.

The IF Statement

The IF statement allows program control to be altered on a conditional basis, depending on the value of a "conditional" expression. The format of the IF statement is:

```
IF comparison-expression THEN statement-number
```

If the "comparison-expression" has the value "true" (in other words, the condition holds), then program control passes to the statement whose statement number is specified. If the statement to which control is branched is a nonexecutable statement (such as a DATA statement), then program control is passed to the first executable statement following the specified nonexecutable statement. If the "comparison-expression" is not "true" (in other words, the condition does not hold), then the execution of the program continues with the first executable statement that logically follows the IF statement.

The following example that computes the average of a list of values depicts the use of a simple IF statement, as well as an assignment statement, a GOTO statement, and a remark statement. The list is terminated when the value –999 is reached.

```
10   READ V
20   IF V=-999 THEN 70
30   REM S AND N ARE INITIALLY ZERO
40   S=S+V
50   N=N+1
60   GOTO 10
70   PRINT "AVERAGE IS"; S/N
80   DATA 24,42,68,50,-999
90   END
```

Output:

AVERAGE IS 46

Other examples of the IF statement are given in subsequent sections.

The END and STOP Statements

Every program written in the BASIC language must end with the END statement, which has the following format:

```
END
```

The END statement serves two purposes:

1. It denotes the logical end of the program, such that statements with statement numbers greater than that of the END statement are ignored by the computer.
2. It causes execution of a program to be terminated when program control flows to it.

The STOP statement, which takes the form:

```
STOP
```

causes execution of the program to be terminated. The STOP statement can be located anywhere in a program, making it unnecessary to branch to the END statement to terminate the execution of a program.

LOOPING

Many algorithms require that a sequence of steps be repeated. An algorithm of this type is usually programmed in one of two ways: (1) The program steps are duplicated the required number of times; and (2) the program is written so that the same program steps are executed iteratively. The second method is preferred in complex programs or when the necessary number of iterations is not known beforehand.

Introduction to Iterative Procedures

A series of statements to be executed repetitively is termed a *loop*; the statements that comprise the loop are termed the *body of the loop*; and one pass through the loop is termed an *iteration*. The number of iterations is governed by a *control variable* that usually operates as follows:

1. The control variable is set to an *initial value*.
2. The value of the control variable is compared with a limit value. If the limit value is exceeded, then the loop is not executed and the first executable statement following the body of the loop is executed.
3. The body of the loop is executed.
4. The value of the control variable is incremented by a specified value— frequently referred to as an *increment* or a *step*. (The obvious implication is that the program "steps" through the loop as the "control variable" assumes a set of values.)
5. The value of the control variable is compared with a limit value. If the limit value is exceeded, then the loop is terminated and program execution continues with the first executable statement following the body of the loop. Otherwise, execution of the loop continues with step 3.

The following BASIC program depicts a simple loop:

```
 10   REM SUM OF EVEN INTEGERS <=N
 15   PRINT "ENTER N";
 20   INPUT N
 30   S=0
 40   I=2
 50   IF I>N THEN 90
 60   S=S+I
 70   I=I+2
 80   IF I<=N THEN 60
 90   PRINT "SUM=";S
100   PRINT
100   GOTO 15
110   END
RUN

ENTER N? 5
SUM= 6

ENTER N? 10
SUM= 30

ENTER N? 2
SUM= 2
```

```
ENTER N? 1
SUM= 0

ENTER N? STOP
PROGRAM HALTED
```

The program depicts each of the above steps. The statement numbered 40 initializes the control variable I (step 1). The statement numbered 50 tests the control variable I against the limit N (step 2). Statement number 60 is the body of the loop (step 3). Statement number 70 increments the control variable (step 4) with a "step value" of 2. Statement number 80 tests the control variable against the limit (step 5); if the value of the control variable is less than or equal to the limit value, then program control is returned to the statement numbered 60 to repeat the loop.

Looping is such a frequently used technique in computer programming that special statements are defined to control the manner in which loops are executed.

The FOR and NEXT Statements

Two statements are included in BASIC to facilitate the preparation of program loops. The FOR statement is used to start a loop; it specifies the control variable, its initial value, its limit value, and the step. The NEXT statement is used to close a loop; it specifies the control variable that should be "stepped." The previous loop written with the use of FOR and NEXT statements is given as follows:

```
10   REM SUM OF EVEN NUMBERS <=N
20   PRINT "ENTER N";
30   INPUT N
40   S=0
50   FOR I=2 TO N STEP 2
60       S=S+I
70   NEXT I
80   PRINT "SUM="; S
90   PRINT
100  GOTO 20
110  END
RUN

ENTER N? 5
SUM= 6
```

ENTER N? 10
SUM= 30

ENTER N? STOP
PROGRAM HALTED

The statements between the FOR and the NEXT statements comprise the body of the loop.

The format of the FOR statement is given as:

```
FOR arithmetic-variable = arithmetic-expression
    TO arithmetic-expression [STEP arithmetic-expression]
```

where "arithmetic-variable" must be a scalar variable and "arithmetic-expression" must be a scalar expression. If the STEP clause is omitted, it is assumed to be +1. The format of the NEXT statement is:

```
NEXT arithmetic-variable
```

where "arithmetic-variable" is the same scalar variable that is used in the corresponding FOR statement.

The FOR and NEXT statements are used in pairs to delineate a FOR loop. The FOR statement establishes the control variable and specifies the initial value, limit value, and step value. (The three values are referred to as *control parameters*.) The NEXT statement tells the computer to perform the next iteration. The control parameters are evaluated when the FOR statement is executed and cannot be changed in the body of the loop. *However, the value of the control variable can be modified from within the body of the loop.* FOR loops can be nested but must not overlap each other.

Effective Use of the FOR and NEXT Statements

It is important to recognize that the use of a FOR/NEXT loop is a means of achieving control in a computer program. It can be used in some cases to eliminate the need for the GOTO statement, as shown in the following program that computes *n* factorial:

```
 10  FOR I = 1 TO 2 STEP 0
 20     PRINT "ENTER N";
 30     INPUT N
 40     F=1
 50     FOR J= 2 TO N
 60     F=F*J
 70     NEXT J
 80     PRINT N; "FACTORIAL IS"; F
 90     PRINT
100  NEXT I
110  END
RUN

ENTER N? 5
5  FACTORIAL IS 120

ENTER N? 7
7  FACTORIAL IS 5040

ENTER N? 1
1  FACTORIAL IS 1

ENTER N? STOP
PROGRAM HALTED
```

The above program depicts a nested loop (that is, a *double loop*, as it is frequently called). The outer loop is executed until a "STOP" is entered in response to the INPUT statement. The same effect could have been achieved with a FOR statement, such as:

```
FOR I = 1 TO 10000
```

where the loop is not expected to execute for the full 10,000 iterations but will be terminated by a special condition, as shown. In a similar fashion, a FOR loop can be used to count the number of times a series of statements is executed; for example:

```
10  DATA  8,10,7,20,15,0
20  REM COMPUTE AVERAGE AND NUMBER OF VALUES
30  FOR N = 1 TO 100
40     READ V
50     IF V=0 THEN 80
60     S=S+V
70  NEXT N
```

```
80   PRINT "AVERAGE="; S/N; "NUMBER OF VALUES =";N
99   END
RUN

AVERAGE = 12   NUMBER OF VALUES = 5
```

In addition, the FOR statement, as defined above, allows several useful options, three of which are mentioned briefly:

1. There can be a nonintegral STEP;
2. There can be a negative STEP; and
3. The value of the control variable can be changed in the FOR loop.

All three cases are described in the following example:

```
10   FOR D=2 TO –2 STEP –.5
20       IF D <> 0 THEN 40
30       D=–1
40           PRINT 1/D
50   NEXT D
60   END
RUN

0.5
0.666667
1
2
0
–2
–1
–0.6666667
–0.5
```

Other examples of the FOR loop are included in the next section on arrays.

ARRAYS

Arrays are an important feature of most programming languages since a great many computer applications utilize the concept of a family of related data, referred to by a single name—the array variable. The subject of arrays is briefly considered in Chapter 7; this section goes into more detail on how arrays are defined and used. First, a very brief review. An *arithmetic array* can have either one or two dimensions; an arithmetic variable name must consist of a single letter. A *character array* must have one dimension only; its variable name must consist of a single letter followed by a dollar sign ($).

Implicitly Defined Arrays

An implicitly defined array is one that is used without being declared. A one-dimensional implicitly defined array has an extent of 10 with lower and upper subscript bounds of 1 and 10, respectively. A two-dimensional implicitly defined array has both row and column extents of 10; lower and subscript bounds, for each dimension, are also 1 and 10, respectively.

Implicitly defined arrays are allowed in BASIC for practical reasons:

1. "Small" arrays are frequently used, especially in an academic environment, and it is a convenience to be able to use an array of this type without having to define it. Also, by not having to specify the size of a "small" array, fewer characters have to be entered into the computer and the chances of making a simple mistake are lessened.
2. Computer storage is sufficiently large to easily handle the storage requirements of implicitly defined arrays.
3. For large arrays, which *do* have to be declared, storage must be managed judiciously.

As an example of a case where the use of an implicitly defined array would be useful, consider the generation of the first 10 Fibonacci numbers, where the ith Fibonacci number is defined as:

$$x_i = x_{i-1} + x_{i-2}, \text{ for } i > 2$$

The first two numbers in the sequence are: 1, 1.

```
10   X(1)=X(2)=1
20   PRINT X(1); X(2);
30   FOR I=3 TO 10
40       X(I)=X(I-1)+X(I-2)
50       PRINT X(I);
60   NEXT I
99   END
RUN

  1  1  2  3  5  8  13  21  34  55
```

Another case might be to store and retrieve a parts list that takes the following form:

Part Index	Part Name	Quantity	Unit Price
1	Plate ZR41T	10	.49
2	Hinge J33	5	1.26
3	.5×3 Bolt	103	.12
4	Washer .5 Alum	97	.01
5	Nut .5 Hex	103	.03
6	PT 4001 T	21	.25

The program, which follows, first stores the "part name" as a string array and the "quantity" and "unit price" as a two-dimensional array; then, the user is allowed to input a part index and the computer prints out the name, quantity, and the value of the inventory.

```
10   REM ENTER INVENTORY DATA
20   READ N
30   FOR J=1 TO N
40       READ P$(J), D(J,1),D(J,2)
50   NEXT J
60   REM RETRIEVE DATA
70   PRINT "ENTER PART INDEX";
80   INPUT I
85   IF I>N THEN 150
90   PRINT P$(I), "QUANTITY ="; D(I,1); "UNIT PRICE ="; D(J,2);
            "TOTAL. VALUE ="; D(I,1)*D(I,2)
95   PRINT
100  GOTO 70
150  PRINT "INDEX ERROR"
151  GOTO 70
200  DATA 6
201  DATA PLATE ZR41T", 10, .49
202  DATA "HINGE J33",5,1.26
203  DATA ".5X3 BOLT",103,.12
204  DATA "WASHER .5 ALUM",97,.01
205  DATA "NUT .5 HEX",103,.03
206  DATA "PT 4001 T",21,.25
999  END
RUN

ENTER PART INDEX?   4
WASHER .5 ALUM   QUANTITY = 97   UNIT PRICE = 0.01
            TOTAL VALUE = 0.97
```

```
ENTER PART INDEX?  7
INDEX ERROR
ENTER PART INDEX?  3
.5X3 BOLT  QUANTITY = 103  UNIT PRICE = 0.12
          TOTAL VALUE = 15.36

ENTER PART INDEX?  STOP
PROGRAM HALTED
```

The value of the elements of an implicitly defined arithmetic array are set initially to zero and the value of the elements of an implicitly defined character-string array are set initially to 18 blanks.

Explicitly Defined Arrays

An array is explicitly dimensioned with the DIM statement that has the following form:

> DIM   array-specification [,array specification] . . .

where "array specification" is defined as:

    arithmetic-variable(integer-constant[,integer-constant])

or

    character-variable(integer-constant)

where "integer constant" must not be zero. The following example depicts valid array specifications:

    DIM A(17), B$(54), C(15,25), D(3,20), E(1000)

A one-dimensional array is specified as:

    DIM $a(n)$

or

    DIM $a\$(n)$

and has an extent of n with lower and upper subscript bounds of 1 and n, respectively. An element of a (or $a\$$) is selected by an array reference of the form $a(e)$ (or $a\$(e)$) where e is an arithmetic expression that is evaluated at the point of reference and truncated to an integer. Similarly, a two-dimensional array is specified as

DIM $a(m,n)$

and has row and column extents of m and n, respectively; the lower and upper subscript bounds for the row extent are 1 and m, respectively, and the lower and upper subscript bounds for the column extent are 1 and n, respectively. An element of a is selected by an array reference of the form $a(e_1, e_2)$, where e_1 and e_2 are arithmetic expressions evaluated at the point of reference and truncated to integers.

The following example computes prime numbers using the Sieve of Eratosthenes. The program requests a number N and then computes and prints the prime numbers less than or equal to N.

```
 10   DIM P(1000)
 20   PRINT "ENTER N";
 30   INPUT N
 40   IF N>1000 THEN 990
 50   FOR I= 2 TO N
 60       P(I)=I
 70   NEXT I
 80   L=SQR(N)
 90   FOR I= 2 TO L
100      IF P(I)=0 THEN 140
110      FOR J= I+I TO N STEP I
120          P(J)=0
130      NEXT J
140   NEXT I
150   PRINT
160   PRINT "PRIMES LESS THAN"; N
170   FOR I= 2 TO N
180      IF P(I)=0 THEN 200
190      PRINT P(I) ;
200   NEXT I
210   PRINT
220   GOTO 20
990   PRINT "TOO LARGE"
991   GOTO 20
999   END
RUN


ENTER N? 100

PRIMES LESS THAN 100
 2  3  5  7  11  13  17  19  23  31  37  41  43  47  53  59  61
67  71  73  79  83  89  97
```

```
ENTER N? 2000
TOO LARGE
ENTER N? 15

2  3  5  7  11  13

ENTER N? STOP
PROGRAM HALTED
```

The program also depicts nested FOR loops and the variable control parameters that were mentioned in the preceding section.

As a final example of the use of one-dimensional arrays, the following program reads a list of numbers and sorts them in ascending order. The program utilizes an exchange technique, depicted as follows:

The program initially sets a flag (F) to zero. When an exchange is made, F is set to 1. If both passes are made through the data without making an exchange, then the values are sorted and the program terminates. Otherwise, the process is repeated. The advantage of the exchange technique is that the process is efficient if the data is sorted or partially sorted beforehand.

```
10   DIM W(100)
20   READ N
30   IF N>100 THEN 990
40   FOR I= 1 TO N
50       READ W(I)
60   NEXT I
70   F=0
80   FOR I= 1 TO N-1 STEP 2
90       IF W(I) <=W(I+1) THEN 140
100        T=W(I)
110        W(I)=W(I+1)
120        W(I+1)=T
```

```
130      F=1
140 NEXT I
150 FOR I = 2 TO N-1 STEP 2
160     IF W(I) <=W(I+1) THEN 210
170     T=W(I)
180     W(I)=W(I+1)
190     W(I+1)=T
200     F=1
210 NEXT I
220 IF F<>0 THEN 70
230 PRINT "SORTED VALUES"
240 FOR I= 1 TO N
250     PRINT W(I) ;
260 NEXT I
270 STOP
500 DATA 12
501 DATA -7,3,9,6,5,1,4,3,8,0,2,7
990 PRINT "TOO MANY VALUES"
999 END
RUN
```

```
SORTED VALUES
-7  0  1  2  3  3  4  5  6  7  8  9
```

Two-dimensional arrays are defined and used in a similar fashion, as depicted in the following example. The program reads in a two-dimensional array and performs some elementary arithmetic operations.

```
 10  DIM A(20,20)
 20  REM READ IN ARRAY DIMENSIONS
 30  READ M,N
 40  REM READ IN ARRAY BY ROWS AND DISPLAY IT
 45  PRINT "ORIGINAL ARRAY"
 50  FOR I= 1 TO M
 60     FOR J= 1 TO N
 70        READ A(I,J)
 75        PRINT A(I,J) ;
 80     NEXT J
 85     PRINT
 90  NEXT I
100  PRINT
110  REM REPLACE SECOND COLUMN WITH ONES
120  FOR I= 1 TO M
130     A(I,2)=1
140  NEXT I
```

```
150   REM DISPLAY ARRAY
160   PRINT "MODIFIED ARRAY"
170   FOR I= 1 TO M
180      FOR J= 1 TO N
190         PRINT A(I,J) ;
200      NEXT J
210      PRINT
220   NEXT I
230   PRINT
240   REM MULT EACH ELEMENT BY A(2,3) AND DISPLAY IT
245   PRINT "ARRAY MULTIPLIED BY A(2,3)"
250   FOR I=1 TO M
260      FOR J=1 TO N
270         A(I,J)= A(I,J)*A(2,3)
280            PRINT (AI,J) ;
290         NEXT J
300         PRINT
310   NEXT I
320   PRINT
500   DATA 3,4
501   DATA -7,3,9,6
502   DATA 5,1,4,3
503   DATA 8,0,2,7
999   END
RUN

ORIGINAL ARRAY
-7  3  9  6
 5  1  4  3
 8  0  2  7

MODIFIED ARRAY
-7  1  9  6
 5  1  4  3
 8  1  2  7

ARRAY MULTIPLIED BY A(2,3)
-28    4  36    24
 20    4  16    48
128   16  32   432
```

The results from multiplying the array by A(2,3) appear to be incorrect but are not because A(2,3) is modified partway through the computation. This example is also simplified in a later section.

Matrix Input and Output

An advanced feature of the BASIC language is a set of matrix statements that allows matrix operations, as defined in mathematics, to be performed. The matrix operations are beyond the scope of this chapter; however, two of the statements allow arrays to be read and printed without the use of a program loop. The MAT READ statement has the form:

> MAT READ arithmetic-array-variable

and causes arithmetic data values to be transferred from the data list (constructed from DATA statements), to the matrix in row order. This means that values are assigned to the first row of the matrix, then to the second row, and so on. The MAT PRINT statement has the form:

> MAT PRINT arithmetic-array-variable

and causes the matrix to be printed in row order at the person's terminal. The following example demonstrates these concepts:

```
10   DIM B(2,3)
20   MAT READ B
30   MAT PRINT B;
40   B(2,1)=0
50   MAT PRINT B;
60   DATA -7,3,9,6,5,1
70   END
RUN

-7  3  9
 6  5  1

-7  3  9
 0  5  1
```

FUNCTIONS

The computer is frequently used in applications that require the use of a mathematical function, such as the sine, cosine, or square root. In the computer, functions such as these are usually approximated to a given degree of accuracy with an algorithm such as the following series expansion for the trigonometric sine:

$$\sin x = x - \frac{x^3}{3!} + \frac{x^5}{5!} - \frac{x^7}{7!} + \ldots$$

Two options exist:

1. Each user can program his own mathematical functions; and
2. A set of frequently used functions can be provided as part of the programming language.

Usually, the second option is selected since not all users are versed in computer approximations and it is convenient not to have to bother with them. Moreover, they can be coded efficiently in assembler language and placed in a program library to be shared by all users.

Built-in Functions

Functions that are supplied as part of the programming language are referred to as *built-in functions*. The form of a function reference is the function name followed by an arithmetic expression in parentheses. The expression is evaluated at the point of reference and the specified function is applied to the value of the expression. The function returns a value that can be used as an operand in the expression. Thus, the expression 2+SQR(25) has the value 7, where SQR is the square root function.

Function name for a built-in function is comprised of three letters that have mnemonic relationship to the function they name. The form of a function reference is:

function-name (arithmetic-expression)

where "function-name" is one of the mathematical functions defined in the implementation of the language. Table 8.3 lists the built-in functions included in the original Dartmouth version of BASIC. All of the functions listed in Table 8.3 take a single argument.

TABLE 8.3 BUILT-IN FUNCTIONS

Function Reference	Definition
SIN (x)	Computes the sine of x radians.
COS (x)	Computes the cosine of x radians.
TAN (x)	Computes the tangent of x radians.
ATN (x)	Computes the arctangent in radians of the argument x; the result is in the range $-90°$ to $+90°$.
EXP (x)	Computes the value of e raised to the x power; that is e^x.
LOG (x)	Computes the natural logarithm (that is, ln $|x|$) of the absolute value of x.
ABS (x)	Computes the absolute value of x (that is, $|x|$).
SQR (x)	Computes the square root of x, where $x \geqslant 0$.
INT (x)	Computes the largest integer $\leqslant x$.
SGN (x)	Returns the sign of x; if $x<0$, then SGN$(x)=-1$; if $x=0$, then SGN $(x)=0$; and if $x>0$, then SGN $(x)=+1$.

The following list gives some mathematical expressions that include functions and their equivalent representation in BASIC:

Mathematical Expression	BASIC Expression
$\sqrt{1-\sin^2 x}$	SQR(1-SIN(X)↑2)
$\cos 30°$	COS(30*(3.14159/180)) or COS(3.14159/6)
$\sqrt{a^2+b^2-2ab \cos c_1}$	SQR(A↑2+B↑2-2*A*B*COS(C1))
$\tan^{-1}(x/y)$	ATN(X/Y)
$\dfrac{e^x-e^{-x}}{2}$	(EXP(X)-EXP (-X))/2
$(|x|)↑3$	ABS(X)↑3

When a function reference is used as an operand, as in SIN(X)↑2 or ABS(X)↑3, the function is applied first and the result of the function is used in the arithmetic operation. In other words, a function reference has a higher priority than any of the arithmetic operators.

Internal Constants

An *internal constant* is a frequently used arithmetic value that is defined in the BASIC language. Three internal constants are frequently used: pi, e, and the square root of 2, and listed as follows:

Identifier	Approximate Value (short form)
&PI	3.14159
&E	2.71828
&SQR3	1.41421

Internal constants eliminate the need to remember and enter frequently used arithmetic values. An internal constant is treated as an ordinary operand.

The use of functions and internal constants is demonstrated in the next section, which gives a variety of simple applications of the BASIC language.

APPLICATIONS

This section further demonstrates how the BASIC language is used by giving some routine applications.

Roots of an Equation

The roots of a quadratic equation of the form:

$$AX^2+BX+C=0$$

are given by the quadratic formula:

$$\text{root} = \frac{-B\pm\sqrt{B^2-4AC}}{2A}$$

For example, the equation $x^2+5x+6=0$ can be factored as $(x+2)(x+3)=0$ and the roots are known as $x=-2$ and $x=-3$. The BASIC program given in Figure 8.1 uses the quadratic formula to solve a quadratic equation.

Trigonometric Functions

Trigonometric functions, such as SIN, COS, and so forth, are included in the BASIC language as built-in functions. These functions require that the argument be expressed in radians where one radian is equal to $180/\pi$ degrees. The BASIC program given in Figure 8.2 constructs a table of degrees, radians, the sine function, and the cosine function for angles ranging from $0°$ to $360°$ in $30°$ steps.

```
LIST

100 READ A,B,C
200 IF A=0 THEN 990
300 LET R1 = (-B+SQR(B↑2-4*A*C))/(2*A)
400 LET R2 = (-B-SQR(B↑2-4*A*C))/(2*A)
500 PRINT "A=";A;" B=";B;" C=";C;" ROOT1=";R1;" ROOT2=";R2
600 GOTO 100
700 DATA 1,5,6
800 DATA 1,3,-40
900 DATA 0,0,0
990 END
READY

RUN
A= 1  B= 5  C= 6     ROOT1=-2  ROOT2=-3
A= 1  B= 3  C=-40    ROOT1= 5  ROOT2=-8

STOP AT LINE 990
READY
```

Figure 8.1 A BASIC program demonstrating the use of the quadratic
formula to solve a quadratic equation.

Permutations

The number of ways that four objects can be arranged is given as
$4 \times 3 \times 2 \times 1$ (or four factorial). This means that the first object can be arranged
in four ways, the second object can be arranged in three ways (after the first
object is fixed), the third object can be arranged in two ways (after the first
two objects are fixed), and the last object can only be arranged in one way.
With five objects taken two at a time, the number of permutations is:

5×4

using the same reasoning. The following mathematical formula exists for
calculating the number of permutations of N things taken R at a time:

$$_N P_R = \frac{N!}{(N-R)!}$$

where $N! = N \times (N-1) \times (N-2) \times \ldots \times 3 \times 2 \times 1$. Thus $_N P_R$ is rewritten as:

```
LIST

1Ø PRINT "DEGREES", "RADIANS", "SINE", "COSINE"
2Ø REM - SIN AND COS USE RADIANS INSTEAD OF DEGREES
25 REM - R IS CONVERSION CONSTANT
3Ø LET R = 3.1415928/18Ø
4Ø FOR D = Ø TO 36Ø STEP 3Ø
5Ø     PRINT D, D*R, SIN (D*R), COS(D*R)
6Ø NEXT D
7Ø END
READY
```

```
RUN
```

DEGREES	RADIANS	SINE	COSINE
Ø	Ø	Ø	1
3Ø	.5235988	.5	.8660254
6Ø	1.Ø47198	.8660254	.5
9Ø	1.570796	1	-.731459E-7
12Ø	2.Ø94395	.8660254	-.5ØØØØØ1
15Ø	2.617994	.4999999	-.8660255
18Ø	3.141593	-.1462918E-6	-1
21Ø	3.665192	-.5ØØØØØ1	-.8660253
24Ø	4.18879	-.8660255	-.4999998
27Ø	4.712389	-1	.2223635E-6
3ØØ	5.235988	-.8660253	.5ØØØØØ2
33Ø	5.759587	-.4999998	.8660255
36Ø	6.283186	.2925836E-6	1

```
STOP AT LINE   70
READY
```

Figure 8.2 A BASIC program demonstrating the use of trigonometric functions. (Some values, such as the cosine of 120°, are not exact because decimal numbers are represented in a binary machine using floating point format.)

$$_N P_R = \frac{N \times (N-1) \times (N-2) \times \ldots \times (N-R+1) \times (N-R) \times (N-R-1) \times \ldots \; 3 \times 2 \times 1}{(N-R) \times (N-R-1) \times \ldots \times 3 \times 2 \times 1}$$

dividing we obtain:

$$_N P_R = N \times (N-1) \times (N-2) \times \ldots \times (N-R+1)$$

which is a computational algorithm for $_N P_R$. The BASIC program given in Figure 8.3 computes the number of permutations of N things taken R at a time using the latter formula.

```
LIST

100 READ N,R
200 IF N=0 THEN 990
300 LET P = 1
400 FOR I = N TO N–R+1 STEP –1
500     LET P = P*I
600 NEXT I
700 PRINT N;"THINGS,";R;"AT A TIME – PERMUTATIONS =";P
800 GOTO 100
900 DATA 5,2
910 DATA 10,8
920 DATA 7,5
930 DATA 0,0
990 END
READY

RUN
   5 THINGS, 2 AT A TIME – PERMUTATIONS = 20
  10 THINGS, 8 AT A TIME – PERMUTATIONS = 1814400
   7 THINGS, 5 AT A TIME – PERMUTATIONS = 2520

STOP AT LINE 990
READY
```

Figure 8.3 A BASIC program that computes the number of permutations of N things taken R at a time.

Largest Factor

One method of computing the largest factor of a number N operates by successively dividing N by the largest possible factor INT(N/2), INT(N/2)–1, INT(N/2)–2, and so on, until either a factor is found or the value 1 is reached. A factor is recognized when N/F=INT(N/F), where F is the factor. The BASIC program given in Figure 8.4 requests that the user enter the lower and upper limits of a set of numbers and computes the largest factor of each number in that set.

```
LIST

100 PRINT "ENTER LOWER AND UPPER LIMIT"
200 INPUT L,U
300 PRINT "NUMBER", "LARGEST FACTOR"
400 FOR N = L TO U STEP 2
500     PRINT N,
600     FOR F = INT(N/2) TO 1 STEP -1
700        IF N/F <> INT(N/F) THEN 950
800        PRINT F
900        GOTO 970
950     NEXT F
970 NEXT N
990 END
READY

RUN
ENTER LOWER AND UPPER LIMIT
?31,50
NUMBER          LARGEST FACTOR
 31             1
 33             11
 35             7
 37             1
 39             13
 41             1
 43             1
 45             15
 47             1
 49             7

STOP AT LINE  990
READY
RUN
ENTER LOWER AND UPPER LIMIT
?501,510
NUMBER          LARGEST FACTOR
 501            167
 503            1
 505            101
 507            169
 509            1

STOP AT LINE  990
READY
```

Figure 8.4 A BASIC program that computes the largest factor of a number N.

Mean and Standard Deviation

The arithmetic mean and standard deviations of a set of numbers are computed by the formulas:

$$\bar{x} = \left(\sum_{i=1}^{n} A_i \right) \Big/ n$$

and

$$\sigma = \sqrt{ \frac{\sum_{i=1}^{n} A_i^2}{n} - (\bar{x})^2 }$$

respectively. The BASIC program given in Figure 8.5 computes $\bar{x}$ and σ by accumulating the sum and sum of squares of the values A_i as they are read in from an internal data list created by DATA statements.

QUESTION SET

1. Study the "Indian program" given in the chapter. Why is it necessary to include the following "program loop"?

```
FOR Y=1627 TO 1973
    LET P=P+P*R
NEXT Y
```

2. Distinguish between a "character" and a "symbol."
3. Can you think of any advantage that the use of the up arrow (↑) has for representing exponentiation over the use of the double asterisk (**)?
4. With regard to the use of exponential notation for writing constants, the following statement is made: "In an arithmetic constant, the E (if used) must be preceded by at least one digit." Why?
5. What function does the dollar sign ($) serve for naming character-string data items?
6. Give errors (if any) in the following BASIC statements.

```
LET AB=16
LET A3=K+10,000
LET F$='DON'T''
REED A,B,C
```

```
LIST

10 DIM A(100)
20 READ N
25 IF N=0 THEN 260
30 LET S1 = 0
40 LET S2 = 0
50 FOR I = 1 TO N
60     READ A(I)
70     LET S1 = S1+A(I)
80     LET S2 = S2+A(I)*A(I)
90 NEXT I
100 REM COMPUTE ARITHMETIC MEAN
110 LET X = S1/N
120 REM COMPUTE STANDARD DEVIATION
130 LET Y = SQR(S2/N-X*X)
140 REM OUTPUT FOLLOWS
150 PRINT "DATA"
160 FOR I = 1 TO N
170     PRINT A(I);
180 NEXT I
190 PRINT
200 PRINT "MEAN=";X: "STANDARD DEVIATION=";Y
205 GOTO 20
210 DATA 5
220 DATA 6,7,10,20,2
230 DATA 10
240 DATA 34,56.1,8,123,7,19.453,7.985,5,23,70.001
250 DATA 0
260 END
READY

RUN
DATA
 6  7  10  20  2
MEAN= 9 STANDARD DEVIATION= 6.0663
DATA
 34  56.1  8  123  7  19.453  7.985  5  23  70.001
MEAN= 35.3539 STANDARD DEVIATION= 35.97575

STOP AT LINE 260
READY
```

Figure 8.5 A BASIC program that computes the mean and standard deviation of a set of numbers.

```
DATA 4E-3
LET A=W+3.12.3
LET K13=-3E-1
```

7. Interpretively execute the following program segments using the material given in the chapter:

```
LET A=3              DIM G(20)
LET B=6              PRINT G(7)+23
LET D=B/A+C
PRINT D
```

8. What is the only statement that must be present in a BASIC program?
9. How do you delete a statement in a BASIC program?
10. How do you replace a statement in a BASIC program?
11. In what order are the statements that comprise a BASIC program executed?
12. Which of the following expressions are invalid?

```
A+-B             (((34)))          Q$+1
+/A              A$<63             T$(3)
A(B(2))          -E+F              X(-4)
D(E+1)           W(-I)             X+Y-1>13.4
```

13. What is an "implicit array declaration"?
14. Give an example of a "character constant."
15. Write a BASIC program to compute the product of the numbers 2E3, 173.89, -14.839, 63.1, and .123E-1 and print the result.
16. Write a BASIC program to evaluate the function

$$y = \frac{e^{ax} - e^{-bx}}{2}$$

as x ranges from 1 to 2 in steps of .01, for the following cases:

(a) a=1, b=1
(b) a=1, b=2
(c) a=.5, b=1
(d) a=.5, b=.5
(e) a=.5, b=1.5

17. A depositor banks $10 per month. Interest is 6% per year compounded monthly. Write a BASIC program to compute the amount the depositor has in his acccount after 20 years.

18. Write a BASIC program that computes N! (that is, N factorial) and operates as follows: The computer requests that the user enter a number (N). After verifying that the number is a positive integer, the computer computes N!, prints it, and then requests another number. Error diagnostics should be printed if the number is not a positive integer.

19. Write a BASIC program to evaluate the polynomial $f(x)=6x^2+4x+7$ as x takes on the values from 1 to 10 in steps of 0.1. Print the results as two columns with column headings.

20. Write a BASIC program that computes B and C for values of A that range from $0°$ to $360°$ in increments of $15°$. B and C are defined as follows:

B=1–2 cos A
C=1+cos 2A–3 $\sin^2$ A

Print the results in labeled columns. (1 radian = $\dfrac{180°}{\pi}$)

21. Fill an array with three rows and four columns with the integers 1,2,. . .,12 by rows. Print the array.

22. Write a BASIC program to sum the numbers less than 100 that are divisible by 7.

23. Given a set of numbers of the form:

DATA $n, x_1, x_2, . . ., x_n$

(Allow for at least 100 values.) Write a BASIC program that computes and prints the following:

(a) Sum of numbers in the list
(b) Largest number
(c) Smallest number
(d) Number of numbers equal to 20
(e) Number of numbers greater than 50 and less than 75

24. Given a set of pay records of the form:

DATA employee-number, name, hours, hourly-rate, tax-rate

such as:

DATA 4439,"JOHN JONES",45,2,10,0.18

Write a BASIC program that computes the following values for each employee:

(a) Gross salary
(b) Tax
(c) Take-home pay

Produce the results as a payroll listing that gives for each employee (that is, each line of the listing): employee number, name, hours, gross salary, tax, and take-home pay. Label the columns. Pay time and one-half for hours over 40. Have the program terminate when a zero employee number is read.

25. Write a BASIC program that reads in an $m \times n$ matrix, by rows, and computes the following:

(a) The smallest value in each row
(b) The largest value in each column

A "saddle point" occurs if the maximum of the row minimums is the same element as the minimum of the column maximums. If this is the case, print out the message "SADDLE POINT" followed by the corresponding value. If no saddle point exists, print out the message "NO SADDLE POINT".

26. Write a BASIC program to read in the following table and sort the entries by key:

Key	Value
10	-13.43
7	81.914
16	-50.1
2	13964.2
9	63.173
24	-.4E-2
11	0
6	2

27. Given the following one-dimensional array:

DIM A(50)

and the following data:

DATA $n, x_1, x_2, \ldots, x_n$

write a BASIC program that:

(a) Prints the values on one line.
(b) Prints the values on successive lines.
(c) Sums the elements of the array and prints the result.
(d) Reverses and prints the elements of the array.
(e) Deletes elements of the array with odd numbered indexes and prints the result.
(f) Rotates the array left by two elements and prints the result.

28. Write a BASIC program that inputs X in radians and computes:

$$\sin x = x - \frac{x^3}{3!} + \frac{x^5}{5!} - \frac{x^7}{7!} + \ldots$$

to 3 decimal places. (That is, if the next item in the series is less than .0005, then terminate the calculations.)

29. A magic square such as

$$\begin{array}{ccc}
8 & 1 & 6 \\
3 & 5 & 7 \\
4 & 9 & 2
\end{array}$$

can be constructed as follows:

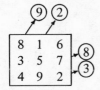

The process always starts in the middle of the top row and numbers are inserted successively by progressing upward and to the right. If the top boundary is reached, continue again at the bottom. If the right boundary is reached, continue again at the left. If another element is reached (that is, 3 to 1), drop down one row (that is, 3 to 4) and continue. The method works for any magic square of order n, where n is odd.

Write a BASIC program to compute a magic square of order n, where n is entered from the terminal.

CHAPTER 9

The Fortran Language

FORTRAN LANGUAGE CHARACTERISTICS

Introduction

The first programming language to be used with any degree of regularity was FORTRAN, which is an acronym for FORmula TRANslation. Under the leadership of John Backus, FORTRAN was developed by the IBM Corporation in the years 1954-1957 for their type 704 computer. The first version of FORTRAN was released for general use in 1957. The language has gone through subsequent evolutionary development and improvement, and a FORTRAN standard was established by the (then called) American Standards Association (ASA) in 1966 and that specification has served as a guideline for subsequent implementations of the language. The level of the FORTRAN language described in this chapter is ASA FORTRAN.

FORTRAN is designed as a mathematically oriented language for the development of scientific computer programs. The objectives of the language are threefold:

1. To provide a programming language that the scientist or engineer can use himself instead of having to communicate his problem to a professional programmer.
2. To provide a programming language that subordinates many of the details ordinarily associated with programming to the compiler so that the lead time to construct programs and the errors involved are minimized.

197

3. To provide a programming language that contributes to the generation of efficient object code by a compiler.

The need for a programming language like FORTRAN was very great and the objectives were well founded because the response to the FORTRAN language has been overwhelming. It is the most widely used of the higher-level programming languages, and has been applied to large and small programs for a wide range of applications.

Fibonacci Numbers

As an example of the general appearance of a FORTRAN program, consider (as we did for the BASIC language) the Fibonacci sequence depicted as follows:

1   1   2   3   5   8   13   21   34   ...

The pattern is that after the first two numbers, each succeeding number is the sum of the previous two numbers. A FORTRAN program that generates Fibonacci numbers less than or equal to 50 is given as follows:*

```
      LATEST=0
      NEXT=1
      WRITE(6,9000)NEXT
10    NEWONE=LATEST+NEXT
      IF (NEWONE.GT.50) STOP
      WRITE(6,9000) NEWONE
      LATEST=NEXT
      NEXT=NEWONE
      GOTO 10
9000  FORMAT(1X,I2)
      END
```

Output:

```
      1
      1
      2
      3
      5
```

*This footnote is intended for the person that is being exposed to FORTRAN for the first time. It is not necessary that the first few programs be completely understood. Only general concepts are required since all topics are covered in later sections.

```
13
21
34
```

Amazing applications of Fibonacci numbers arise in the physical world. For example, Fibonacci numbers can be used to describe the arrangement of stems on a branch and the growth in rabbit population.

The above program is fairly obvious and is not discussed further. After the next example, however, several statements, including those used above, are discussed.

The Indian Problem

As an illustration of the manner in which FORTRAN can be used to solve a problem, consider the classical *Indian problem*. The problem is stated as follows: Manhattan Island was sold by the Indians to the settlers in 1626 for $24 worth of beads and trinkets. At a given interest rate, what is the island worth today? A "simple-minded" solution is presented as the following program:*

```
        PRINC=24.0                                      (1)
        RATE=.06                                        (2)
        DO 10 I=1627,1973                               (3)
     10 PRINC=PRINC+PRINC*RATE                          (4)
        WRITE(6,9000)PRINC                              (5)
        STOP                                            (6)
   9000 FORMAT(29H PRESENT VALUE OF MANHATTAN =,F15.2)  (7)
        END
```

Output:

PRESENT VALUE OF MANHATTAN = 14499279000.00

Statements 1 and 2 assign the values 24 and .06 to the principal (PRINC) and the interest rate (RATE), respectively. The interest for a given year is computed as PRINC*RATE and the principal at the end of a given year is computed as PRINC+PRINC*RATE. Statements 3 and 4 constitute a program loop; the principal is recomputed as the year (I) advances from 1627 to 1973. After the loop is completed (that is, the number of iterations specified in statement 3 has been satisfied) the resulting principal (PRINC) is printed

---

*The student is directed to the BASIC solution to the Indian problem given in the last chapter for an instructive comparison of the two languages.

in statement 5. Statement 6 terminates execution of the program. The WRITE statement is interpreted as follows:

WRITE(6,9000) PRINC

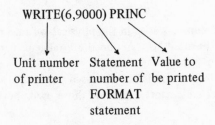

Unit number   Statement   Value to
of printer   number of   be printed
               FORMAT
               statement

The statement numbered 9000 is the FORMAT statement that describes how the result should be printed. It is explained as follows:

9000 FORMAT   (29H PRESENT VALUE
                 OF MANHATTAN = F15.2)

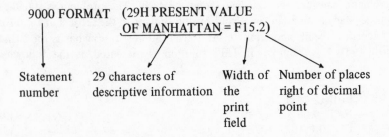

Statement   29 characters of   Width of   Number of places
number   descriptive information the   right of decimal
                                      print   point
                                      field

The END statement denotes the physical end of the program. If program control flows to the END statement, a STOP statement is inserted automatically by the FORTRAN compiler.

In the preceding program, the data of the problem was built into the program (that is, the beginning principal of 24 and a rate of .06). If the user desired to repeat the calculations for different interest rates, then he would have to prepare the different rates as input data and read the values into his program when needed. Assume the desired interest rates were .05, .06, .07, and .08. The user would build a data deck with each value on a different card, placed in a desired position. A corresponding READ statement would access the data values in order.

The following FORTRAN program represents a modification to the above program for entering the interest rate as an input value:

```
10 READ(5,9000)RATE
   PRINC=24.0
   DO 20 I=1627,1973
20 PRINC=PRINC+PRINC*RATE
   WRITE(6,9001)RATE,PRINC
```

```
        GOTO 10
9000 FORMAT(F3.2)
9001 FORMAT(7H RATE=,F4.2,27H PRES. VAL. OF MANHATTAN
     =,F17.2)
        END
```

Input:

```
.05
.06
.07
.08
```

Output:

```
RATE = .05,PRES. VAL. OF MANHATTAN =        540627280.00
RATE = .06,PRES. VAL. OF MANHATTAN =      14499279000.00
RATE = .07,PRES. VAL. OF MANHATTAN =     377035310000.00
RATE = .08,PRES. VAL. OF MANHATTAN = 9511615900000.00
```

The READ statement is interpreted as follows:

READ(5,9000) RATE

Unit number Statement Variable into
of input unit number of which data should
            FORMAT   be read
            statement

Several statements were used in the above examples:

READ—causes data to be entered from an input unit (such as a card
    reader) and assigned to variables.

DO—begins a program loop and specifies how many times it should be
    executed.

WRITE—causes output data to be written to an output unit for printing.

GOTO—causes program control to be directed to a specified statement.

FORMAT—specifies the form of input and output data.

END—ends a FORTRAN program.

Assignment—assigns the value of an expression to a variable.

Each of these statements is described in more detail in later sections.

Characters and Symbols

A computer program is essentially a coded form of an algorithm for solving a given problem on a computer. The statements of a program are encoded in the alphabet of the language using established conventions. It is necessary to distinguish between characters of the alphabet and symbols of the language. A *character of the alphabet* is an entity that has a representation internally and externally to the computer. The letter "A," for example, is a character of most language alphabets. The majority of characters have no meaning in their own right; for example, the letter "A" only has meaning through the manner in which it is used, which may be as part of a variable, the name of a statement, and so forth. Table 9.1 lists the FORTRAN alphabet, which consists of approximately 47-50 characters, depending on the equipment involved.

TABLE 9.1 CHARACTERS OF THE FORTRAN ALPHABET

Alphabetic Characters (26)

A B C D E F G H I J K L M N O P Q R S T U V W X Y Z

Digits (10)

0 1 2 3 4 5 6 7 8 9 10

Special Characters (11)

Name	Character
Blank	(no visual representation)
Equal sign	=
Plus sign	+
Minus sign	—
Asterisk	*
Solidus (slash)	/
Left parenthesis	(
Right parenthesis	)
Comma	,
Decimal point	.
Currency symbol (dollar sign)	$

A *symbol of the language* is a series of one or more characters that has been assigned a specific meaning. Typical symbols are the plus sign (+) and the comma, used as a separator. A symbol consisting of more than one character is termed a *composite symbol* that is assigned a meaning not inherent in the constituent characters themselves. Typical composite symbols are ** for exponentiation and .GT. for "greater than or equal to." The symbols of the FORTRAN language are listed in Table 9.2.

TABLE 9.2 SYMBOLS OF THE FORTRAN LANGUAGE[a]

Symbol	Function
+	Addition or prefix +
−	Subtraction or prefix −
*	Multiplication or repetition
/	Division or separator
**	Exponentiation
.LT.	Less than
.LE.	Less than or equal to
.EQ.	Equal to
.NE.	Not equal to
.GE.	Greater than or equal to
.GT.	Greater than
.AND.	Logical conjunction (AND)
.OR.	Logical disjunction (OR)
.NOT.	Logical negation (NOT)
,	Separator
.	Decimal point
=	Assignment symbol
( )	Enclose lists or group expressions

[a]All composite symbols defined for the FORTRAN language are described in the text. Selected references to the complete FORTRAN language are given at the end of the book.

Blank characters (that is, spaces) are ignored in FORTRAN (except in Hollerith constants) in the statement portion of a line and may be used freely to improve readability. Statements can be labeled with a statement number for reference and some minor conventions on the use of blank characters with a statement number exist. There are covered later.

In general, the question of upper-case and lower-case letters does not apply to FORTRAN and only upper-case letters are defined with the language. However, some implementations of the language, especially in a time-sharing environment, permit upper-case and lower-case letters to be used interchangeably.

Data Types and Constant Values

Six types of data are permitted in FORTRAN: integer, real, double precision, complex, logical, and Hollerith. Integer, real, and Hollerith are presented here. Integer and real are arithmetic data types, associated with numeric values. The Hollerith data type is associated with character data (occasionally referred to as descriptive information).

An *integer data item* is an exact representation of an integer stored in fixed-point form. An integer data item can be positive, negative, or zero but no places to the right of the decimal point are maintained; in other words, the result of an integer expression is always an integer. When an integer data item is stored, the decimal point is normally assumed to be immediately to the right of the low-order digit (rightmost digit) of the integer value.

A name that identifies an integer data item is termed an "integer variable." In FORTRAN, a name can be declared an integer variable or it can assume that attribute by default. This subject is discussed in the next section.

An *integer constant* is a whole number written without a decimal point and optionally preceded by a plus or minus sign. Thus -174, 15, and $+3000$ are valid integer constants while $25.$ is not because it contains a decimal point. Consider the following assignment:

IJOB=NT+15

It specifies that the integer value 15 should be added to integer variable NT and integer variable IJOB should be replaced with the result.

In FORTRAN, a *real data item* is one that is stored in the computer in floating-point notation. It can assume a real value in the mathematical sense; that is, it can be positive or negative and represents a rational or irrational number.

A *basic real constant* is composed of the following constituents in the given order: a sign, an integer part, a decimal point, and a decimal fraction. The sign is optional and the decimal point is required. Either or both of the integer and decimal fraction parts must be present. Thus, $3.$, -25.126, and $+.000123$ are valid basic real constants.

An exponent can be used to scale a numeric value. As in BASIC, an exponent is the letter E followed by a signed or unsigned integer. For example, E2, E-11, and E+4 are valid exponents.

Finally, a *real constant* is one of the following: a basic real constant, a basic real constant followed by an exponent, or an integer constant followed by an exponent. The following are valid real constants: -198.30, $123E-4$, and $1.693E7$. Consider the following assignment statement:

ZT301 = 1.32E-11*Y**(E-34.389)

It specifies that the variable Y is to be raised to the power denoted by the value of the expression E-34.389, and that the result of the exponentiation is to be multiplied by the real constant 1.32E-11, and that the value of the variable ZT301 is to be replaced with the result of the multiplication. E–34.389 is an expression; 1.32E–11 is a real constant. A real constant is stored as a floating-point number.

Hollerith data is character data that is included to serve descriptive purposes, and is permitted in a FORMAT statement used for input and output. There is no Hollerith variable in FORTRAN.

A Hollerith constant takes the form:

$$\underbrace{nHxxx \ldots x}_{}$$

n characters

where *n* is a nonzero positive integer and *x* is any character in the FORTRAN alphabet, including blank characters. The *n* characters comprise the Hollerith data item. The following are valid Hollerith constants:

Hollerith constant	*Characters comprising the Hollerith data item*
3HEQU	EQU
5HDON'T	DON'T
11HTEA FOR TWO	TEA FOR TWO
5HA=B+C	A=B+C
7H%* /–	%* /–

Names

A *name* in FORTRAN is a string of alphabetic or numeric characters, the first of which must be alphabetic. Names are used to identify scalar variables, array variables, and functions.

Names that identify variables may be up to six characters in length, and the same naming conventions apply to scalar and array variables. Each variable has a *type* which may be integer or real. The type of a variable may be specified explicitly or implicitly.

An *integer variable* is declared with the INTEGER statement, and a *real variable* is declared with the REAL statement as shown in the following examples.

```
INTEGER BOW,ITJAM,Z
REAL FOXIT,JELLO,MONKEY,T
```

Each variable is assigned the type specified by its statement identifier. For example, BOW is an integer variable and FOXIT is a real variable. A given variable may not have two types and may not appear in more than one type statement.

A variable that is not specified in a type statement is assigned a type implicitly. Variable names beginning with the letters I, J, K, L, M, or N are implicitly assigned type integer. All other implicitly defined variables are assigned type real. Thus in the statements:

```
I=JERK+13
PETE=TOM+1.23E7
```

I and JERK are implicitly defined as type integer and PETE and TOM are implicitly defined as type real, provided that neither of these variables had been specified in a type statement. If any one of the variables had been specified in a type statement, then it would have been assigned a type governed by the statement identifier of the type statement in which it was included. Thus, a type statement overrides the implicit naming conventions.

Arrays

An *array* is a collection of arithmetic data items of the same type that is referenced by a single array name. An array can have one, two, or three dimensions. An element of an array is referenced by giving the relative position of that element in the array. If the array has one dimension, then an element is referenced by appending a subscript enclosed in parentheses to the array name as follows:

$$a(e)$$

where a is the array name and e is a subscript expression evaluated at the point of reference. Thus, the array reference $a(e)$ selects the eth element of array a. If the array has two dimensions, then an element is selected in a similar manner with an array reference of the form:

$$a(e_1, e_2)$$

where a is the array name and e_1 and e_2 are subscript expressions evaluated at the point of reference. Thus, the array reference $a(e_1, e_2)$ selects the element located in the e_1th row and the e_2th column of a. A three-dimensional array uses an array reference of the following form:

$$a(e_1, e_2, e_3)$$

in a similar manner. The following are valid array references: X(7), A(I), BIG(LEFT), DOG(J+1), I(1,k-3), and FOX(3*J+1,3*L,6). Subscripted subscripts are not allowed in standardized FORTRAN, and elements of an array are *not* initially set to zero when the program is executed.

The extent of an array must be declared explicitly with either a DIMENSION statement, a REAL statement, or an INTEGER statement, which is used to give the extent of each dimension of the array. For example, the statement

```
DIMENSION FOX(10),W(3,4),JLL(10,5)
REAL A(5,5)
INTEGER PILL(100)
```

defines: real array FOX with 10 elements, real array W with 3 rows and 4 columns, integer array JLL with 10 rows and 5 columns, real array A with 5 rows and 5 columns, and integer array PILL with 100 elements. The DIMENSION, REAL, and INTEGER statements are presented in a later section.

Operators and Expressions

Arithmetic and comparison operators are included in this description of the FORTRAN language. Arithmetic operators are defined on real and integer arithmetic data and are classed as binary and unary operators. A *binary arithmetic operator* is used in the following manner:

operand $\{+|-|*|/|**\}$ operand

where an operand is defined as an arithmetic constant, a function reference, an element of an array, or an expression enclosed in parentheses. A *unary arithmetic operator* is used in the following manner:

– operand

where "operand" has the same definition as given directly above. The use of a unary operator is restricted to the following cases:

1. As the leftmost character in an expression, provided that two operators do not appear in succession; or
2. As the leftmost character in a subexpression enclosed in parentheses such that the unary operator follows the left parenthesis.

An example of case 1 is –A+B**C while an example of case 2 is A*(–B**(–3)). The result of an arithmetic operation is always a numeric value.

An *arithmetic expression* can be a scalar variable, an element of an array, a numeric constant, a function reference, or a series of these constituents separated by binary operators and parentheses and possibly prefixed by unary operators. Thus, any of the following are valid expressions in FORTRAN:

```
ALL     -(COWL**I-1)    -SQRT(X**3)-CHI
I+25    SIN(X3)         ((Y+3.0)*Y+16)*Y-1.0
```

As stated previously, parentheses are used for grouping and expressions within parentheses are executed before the operations of which they are a part. For example, the expression 2*(3+4) evaluates to 14. When parentheses are not used in an arithmetic expression, an operand may appear as though it is an operand to two operators; that is, for example, the operand B in an expression such as:

A+B*C

In this case, operators are executed on a priority basis as governed by the following list:

Operator	Priority
**	highest
*,/	↓
binary +, binary −, unary −	lowest

Thus, in the expression A+B*C, the expression B*C is executed first and the result of that subexpression is added to A. At the point in a program that an arithmetic expression is evaluated, the expression has a value that assumes one of the data types mentioned previously, that is, integer or real. Moreover, the operands (including constants) in that expression are restricted to data items of the same type, except that a real value can be raised to an integer power. Thus, if I is an integer variable and A and B are real variables, then the expressions A+B, A+1.0, and I+4 are legal in FORTRAN, while A+I, A+5, and I-3.2 are not.

A *comparison expression* is used to compare two arithmetic values; the result is one of the logical truth values, "true" or "false." A comparison expression consists of a pair of arithmetic expressions separated by a comparison operator, as follows:

operand {.LT.|.LE.|.EQ.|.NE.|.GT.|.GE.} operand

where "operand" is an arithmetic expression, as defined above, and the operands must have the same data type. The following are valid comparison expressions and yield the given truth value if A and B are real variables, I and J are integer variables, and A=10.0, B=15.0, I=3, and J=5.

Valid Comparison Expression	Truth Value
A .GT. B	False
A+B.GE. 19.4	True
A**2+65.3 .LE. B**2	True
I+5 .NE. J	True
J .EQ. 3	False

In a comparison expression, the operands (that is, the arithmetic expressions) are evaluated first; then the comparison operation is performed. Comparison expressions are used for decision making in the logical IF statement.

Statement Structure

The structure of a statement in FORTRAN involves two considerations: statement format and actual statement structure. Statement format involves the conventions for entering a statement into the computer and for labeling a statement. Statement structure involves the manner in which statements are constructed.

A *line* in FORTRAN is a string of 72 characters usually taken as columns 1-72 of a punched card. The characters in a line are numbered consecutively as 1,2,...,72 and are referred to as such, reading from left to right. A line can represent a FORTRAN statement, a continuation to a FORTRAN statement, or a comment.

The first line of a FORTRAN statement is referred to as an "initial line." An *initial line* is characterized by the fact that it is not a comment line (see below) and that column 6 is either zero or blank. Columns 1 through 5 of an initial line can contain the statement number of the statement (also covered below) or must be blank. The actual FORTRAN statement is contained in columns 7 through 72 and most statements are entered as a single line. A statement can be continued on up to 19 continuation lines. A *continuation line* is characterized by the fact that it is not a comment line and that column 6 contains a nonblank nonzero character.

A *comment line* has the character C in column 1 and is ignored by the compiler; it may be used by the programmer to place remarks in a program. A program cannot end with a comment line.

Blank characters are ignored in the statement portion of a line—except in Hollerith constants in FORMAT statements.

A statement is given a *statement number* so that it can be referred to in other statements. A statement number consists of from one to five digits placed in columns 1 through 5 of the initial line of a statement.* A statement number is only a label; thus, the value of the statement number is not significant and statement numbers need not be ordered. Some necessary conventions on the use of statement numbers exist: (1) A statement number must not be zero; (2) the same statement number may not be assigned to more than one statement; and (3) leading zeros in a statement number are not used in distinguishing between statement numbers. Usually, statements in FORTRAN

---

*Statement numbers enclosed in parentheses to the right of examples here are inserted for convenient reference and are not to be confused with actual coded statement numbers.

are assigned a statement number only when they are to be referred to in another statement. However, this is not a necessary condition.

A statement is a string of characters formed by concatenating the characters in columns 7 through 72 of the initial and continuation lines. A statement has the following structure:

```
{ statement-identifier | statement-body |
  statement-identifier statement-body }
```

where "statement-identifier" is a word that identifies a particular type of statement and "statement-body" is a series of characters that comprise the body of the statement. From the statement format, it is obvious that a statement can be composed of a statement identifier, a statement body, or both. A statement without a "statement-identifier" is the assignment statement. A statement may not be blank. The following are valid FORTRAN statements:

READ(5,9010),A,BETA,IFIX	(1)
GOTO 150	(2)
END	(3)
A=B+C	(4)

In statement 1, READ is the statement identifier and the remainder of the statement is the statement body. In statement 2, GOTO is the statement identifier and 150, which is the statement body, refers to the statement number of another statement in that program. Statement 3 depicts an END statement that does not require a statement body. Statement 4 is the assignment statement; it does not use a statement identifier.

Program Structure

A FORTRAN program is composed of a series of statements that are executed sequentially until a statement is executed that terminates execution of the program or a statement, such as GOTO or IF, is executed that alters the sequential flow of execution. Conceptually, the complete program is compiled into machine language and loaded into the computer before any of it is executed. The last statement in a program must be an END statement. FORTRAN is conveniently described with respect to a batch-processing environment, as presented in Chapter 6. A program is compiled and executed using a deck setup similar to the one depicted in Figure 6.1.

A *program* consists of a set of specification statements (such as REAL, INTEGER, or DIMENSION), followed by executable and FORMAT statements, followed by an END statement. Specification and FORMAT statements provide information to the compiler. Executable statements, such as READ or GOTO, result in actual computer processing. FORMAT statements may be interspersed among the executable statements of a program. A program must contain at least one executable statement.

The following FORTRAN program computes the average of a list of numbers:

```
C     FORTRAN PROGRAM TO READ A LIST OF VALUES AND
C     COMPUTE THE AVERAGE
      REAL VALUES(100)
      READ(5,571)N
      READ(5,572) (VALUES (I),I=1,N)
  571 FORMAT(13)
  572 FORMAT(10F8.3)
C
C     PRINT LIST OF VALUES
C
      WRITE(6,573) (VALUES (I),I-1,N)
  573 FORMAT(12H DATA VALUES/(10F10.3)
C
C     COMPUTE AVERAGE
C
      SUM=0.0
      DO 10 I-1,N
   10 SUM=SUM+VALUES(I)
      AVER=SUM/FLOAT(N)
C
C     PRINT AVERAGE AND STOP
C
      WRITE(6,574) AVER
  574 FORMAT(10H AVERAGE =,F10.3)
      STOP
      END
```

Input:

```
/ 28.12  6.20   −14.00  10.08  5.10


/5
```

Output:

```
DATA VALUES
      28.120  6.200  –14.000  10.080  5.100
AVERAGE =       7.100
```

It is important to recognize the following key points:

1. Each FORTRAN statement begins on a new line.
2. The physical order of statements determines the order in which they are executed.
3. Statement numbers are used for statement labeling purposes only.

The following sections describe the various statements that comprise the use of the FORTRAN language. The statements are grouped by the functions they perform and examples of the use of each type of statement are given. The first topic is "input and output" and statements relevant to that topic are covered. Other topics are: the assignment statement, program control, type statements, looping, arrays, and functions.

INPUT AND OUTPUT

Input and output is performed for several reasons: (1) To enter data into the computer for processing; (2) to output results in a form suitable for printing; and (3) to store large amounts of information on a temporary or permanent basis. In the latter case, information may be placed on a mass-storage medium because it is too voluminous to occupy main storage; or information may be placed on a mass-storage medium between distinct runs on the computer. A temporary file used during a sort operation is an example of the former case; a payroll master file is an example of the latter case. The use of input and output facilities for storage purposes is not discussed further; the reader is referred to references at the end of the book.

System Input and Output

Every job that is run on the computer has a system input device and a system output device. Usually, the *system input device* corresponds to the input job stream and allows the user to read the input data that accompanies the program deck. The *system output device* usually corresponds to the line printer and data written to the system output device is formatted for printing. In FORTRAN, each input and output device is assigned a number by the computer installation. The system input device number is frequently 5; the system output device number is frequently 6. These numbers are used here although they may vary at any given installation.

The actual devices are not important. For example, the system input device is sometimes a card reader, sometimes a magnetic tape, and sometimes a magnetic disk. Similarly, the system output device can be a line printer, a magnetic tape, or a magnetic disk. All one needs to know is that input cards are placed on the system input device and lines written to the system output device are eventually printed.

Formatted Input and Output

Formatted input and output uses a FORMAT statement that describes the external appearance of the data. Input and output is performed by routines that are supplied by the FORTRAN compiler and/or the operating system. An input operation is used as an example. The READ statement is compiled into a reference to an input routine; the list of data variables to be read and the format specification are supplied to the routine. The input routine reads a card, converts the data items to internal form using the format statement, and places the results in main storage in the locations assigned to the variables. Program control then returns to the statement following the READ statement. The process is reversed for formatted output.

Figure 9.1 depicts the process of doing formatted input and output. The following comments are useful for understanding Figure 9.1:

1. I format is used for integer data.
2. F format is used for real data without an exponent.
3. X format means "skip characters."
4. H format is used to include Hollerith (that is, literal) data.
5. The first character of the printed line is used for carriage control. (In the example, 1H$\emptyset$, where $\emptyset$ means the blank character, places a blank character in column 1 of the output record and single spacing is used for that line.)
6. Except for X and H formats, a one-to-one correspondence exists between format items and variables.

Figure 9.1 and the above discussion are simply a brief overview. The next section presents the information in more detail.

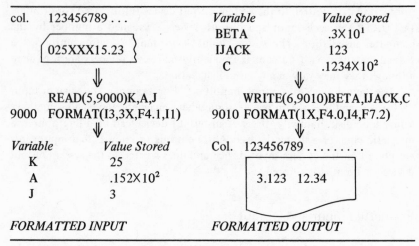

FORMATTED INPUT   FORMATTED OUTPUT

Figure 9.1   Conceptual view of formatted input and output.

The READ and WRITE Statements

The READ statement causes data to be transferred from an external storage medium to main storage under format control. The form of the READ statement is:

    READ(unit, format) [list]

where "unit" is an integer variable or an integer constant specifying an input device number and "format" is the statement number of a FORMAT statement. The "list" is optional and consists of a series of variable names or subscripted array names, separated by commas. An example of a READ statement with a list is:

    READ(5,8193) COW,AL2,JABBER,T(3),BIGY(I,J+1)

The READ statement is rarely used without a list—but it can be. It can be used to read in a Hollerith constant for use in a subsequent WRITE statement (which, for now, takes the same general form as READ); this case is depicted in Figure 9.2.

The WRITE statement causes data to be transferred from main storage to an external storage medium under format control. The form of the WRITE statement is:

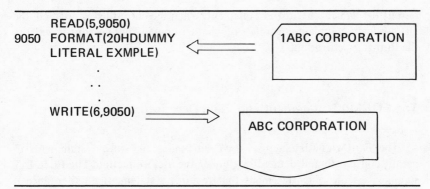

Figure 9.2 A program segment showing how a Hollerith literal can be used to read in descriptive information.

```
WRITE(unit,format) [list]
```

where "unit." "format," and "list" are defined the same as for the READ statement. An example of the WRITE statement is:

```
    WRITE(6,7070)NIL,A(3),WOW
7070 FORMAT(1X,I5,F10.4,F12.6)
```

It should be remembered that the READ and WRITE statements in FORTRAN are used to transfer data between an external storage medium (such as the card reader, magnetic tape, disk, or the line printer) and main storage. Before data can be used, it must be read into main storage. On the other hand, data is still available for use in main storage—even after it has been written out to an output device.

The Line Concept

FORTRAN reads records and writes complete blocks (or lines). This means that each time a read or write statement is executed, a complete line is read or written. Each execution of a READ statement causes the next line to be read from the specified input unit. The amount of data that is taken from the line is determined by the input list. Excess data is ignored. If insufficient data exists to satisfy the input list, then an error condition is generated and execution of the program is terminated in most versions of FORTRAN. Each execution of a WRITE statement causes a line to be written to the specified output unit. The amount of data that is written is governed collectively by the output list and the FORMAT statement. When the output list is satisfied, the output line is complete, regardless of whether unused field descriptors exist in the format specification.

The FORMAT Statement and Field Descriptors

The FORMAT statement is used with input and output statements to permit conversion and data editing under the user's direction. The FORMAT statement is the only statement that requires a statement number since it must be specified in an appropriate input or output statement. The form of the FORMAT statement is:

$$m \text{ FORMAT}(q_1 t_1 z_1 t_2 z_2 \ldots t_n z_n q_2)$$

where:

1. m is the statement number.
2. $(q_1 t_1 z_1 t_2 z_2 \ldots t_n z_n q_2)$ is the format specification.
3. Each q is a series of slashes or is empty.
4. Each t is a field descriptor or a series of field descriptors.
5. Each z is a field separator (comma, slash, series of slashes, or parentheses).
6. n may be zero—in other words, there may be no field descriptor.

A sample FORMAT statement is:

9000   FORMAT(I3,3F12.6/(I2,10I4))

where I3, F12.6, I2, and I4 are field descriptors that correspond on a one-to-one basis with a variable in an input or output list. The 3 before the F12.6 is a repetition factor; thus, 3F12.6 is equivalent to F12.6,F12.6,F12.6. The slash (/) means that the input or output routine should go to the next line. The parentheses around I2,10I4, that is (I2,10I4), is used when the input or output list is not complete but the format specification is exhausted. The input or output routine returns to the first open parenthesis in the FORMAT statement. (When an input or output routine returns to the first open parenthesis in a FORMAT statement, it automatically goes to the next input or output line.) If, for example, a user has a long input or output list and desires to read six values from each input line, he might use statements such as:*

```
        READ(5,9500)(A(I),I=1,1000)
  9500  FORMAT(6F12.5)
```

The repetition factor can also be applied to a parenthesized list of field descriptors. Thus, 3(I4,F10.2) is equivalent to I4,F10.2,I4,F10.2,I4,F10.2. It is *important to recognize* that 3(I4,F10.2) is *not* equivalent to I4,I4,-I4,F10.2,F10.2,F10.2.

A basic set of field descriptors and separators is given in this section.

The *I field descriptor* is used for conversion between an internal integer data item and an external integer in decimal form. The form of an I format specification is:

I*w*

where *w* is the size of the external field, including blanks and a sign. On output, the sign is printed only if the number is negative. A decimal point is not permitted in an input field. For example,† on input, the external values ￠￠12, ￠621￠, and −￠210￠ using format specifications I4, I5, and I6, respectively, cause the values 12, 6210, and −2100 to be stored. For output, the values −987 and 123 using format specifications I5 and I4, respectively, cause the following fields:

￠−987 and ￠123

to be generated.

For all numeric input conversions, leading blanks are ignored and all trailing blanks are treated as zeros. An all-blank field is regarded as zero. For all output conversions, the output field is right justified. Leading blanks are supplied, as required.

The *F field descriptor* is used for conversion between an internal real data item and an external real number in decimal form without an exponent. The form of an F field descriptor is:

F*w.d*

where *w* is the width of the field, including blanks, the sign, and the decimal point and *d* is the number of places to the right of the decimal point. On

---

*The READ statement depicts an "implied DO" list that is covered under arrays.
†The symbol "￠" denotes a blank (or space) character.

input, use of the decimal point is optional. If the decimal point is not used on input, then the rightmost d digits in the field are interpreted as decimal places. If the decimal point is used with input data, then it overrides d. On *output,* the decimal point is always generated with d decimal places to the right of it. Thus, with F field descriptor F6.2, the following input values achieve the same result (where ⱨ denotes the blank character):

  ⱨⱨ–123   ⱨ–1.23   –1.230   –1.23ⱨ

and cause the value $-.123 \times 10^1$ to be placed in main storage. On output, for example, the values $.98134 \times 10^2$ and $-.63472 \times 10^1$ are converted using field descriptors F7.2 and F8.3, respectively, so that the values

  ⱨⱨ98.13 and ⱨⱨ–6.347

are generated.

The *E field descriptor* is designed for use with real data represented in exponential notation on the external medium. The form of an E field descriptor is:

  E*w.d*

where w is the width of the field and d is the number of decimal places. For *input,* the use of an actual decimal point overrides d, as with the F field descriptor. The exponent takes the form: $E \pm ee$, where the sign may be omitted if the exponent is positive and leading zeros in the exponent need not be written. If the exponent is signed, then the letter E may be omitted. The width indicator w must include the exponent. The exponent should be right justified in the field since blank characters are interpreted as zeros. Using an input E field descriptor of E12.5, all of the following fields cause the same real value of $.314159 \times 10^1$ to be stored:

  3.14159E0
  314.159E–2
  314159E0
  .314159+1

For output, the E field descriptor produces a decimal number of the form:

  $$\pm 0.\underbrace{d_1 d_2 \ldots d_n}_{d} \underbrace{ E \pm ee}_{}$$
  $$\underbrace{}_{w}$$

where plus signs are replaced with blank characters during output editing. Thus the statements:

```
        A=987.123
        WRITE(6,9000)A
9000    FORMAT(1X,E15.7)
```

would cause the following value to be printed:

ɸɸ0.9871230E 03

where the ɸ denotes a blank character. As with input, the magnitude of *w* must include space for the exponent.

As implied previously, a field separator is used between field descriptors. A *comma* is simply used to separate distinct field descriptors. For example, the following descriptors:

F20.12I4

could be interpreted as F20.12 and I4 or F20.1 and 2I4. This is a case where a comma is needed. In other cases, it is used mainly for readability. The *slash* (/) causes the input or output routine to go to the next line so that for output, *n* slashes in succession generate *n*−1 blank lines. As an example of the use of the slash for input, suppose it were desired to read a value N with I4 format from a single card and then read N values from subsequent cards in format F12.6 with six values per card. The following statements would be used:

```
        REAL A(100)
        READ (5,9000)N,(A(I),I=1,N)
9000    FORMAT (I4/(6F12.6))
```

The example depicts the use of a slash to go to the next card, a repetition factor, and a return to the first open parenthesis.

The *H field descriptor* is used for Hollerith data, as described previously with regard to READ and WRITE statements without a list. An H field descriptor has the following format

*n*H<u>XXX...X</u>

  n characters

where *n* is an unsigned integer constant that denotes the number of Hollerith characters that comprise the Hollerith literal; the *n* characters from the FORTRAN alphabet follow the H. The H field descriptor is most frequently used for printing comments and headings and does not require a corresponding variable in the input or output list, as demonstrated in the following example:

```
       K=10
       . . .
       WRITE(6,9000)K
9000   FORMAT(13H THE ANSWER = I5)
```

which would generate the following output:

```
THE ANSWER =   10
```

The *X field descriptor* is used to *skip characters* on the external medium during input or output. The format of the X field descriptor is:

$$nX$$

where *n* is an unsigned integer constant that denotes the number of characters to be skipped. For input, *n* character positions of the input line are skipped, regardless of their contents. For example, if columns 1-8 of an input line contained an integer value to be read into KAT and columns 14-25 contained a real value to be read into RAT, then the following FORMAT and READ statements would be used:

```
       READ(5,9030)KAT,RAT
9030   FORMAT(I8,5X,F12.5)
```

For output, the output line for formatted output is initially filled with blanks. Data fields are moved into the output record from left to right as conversions and editing are performed under format control. Use of the X field descriptor simply moves a pointer the indicated number of positions to the right, resulting in blank characters in the output line. Thus, if it were desired to output the values of JOHN and JIM separated by 12 blank characters, the following FORMAT and WRITE statements might be used:

```
       WRITE(6,9040)JOHN,JIM
9040   FORMAT(I5,12X,I5)
```

Carriage Control

Frequently, the eventual disposition of output data written to an output device is the line printer or a computer terminal. In fact, this is always the case with the system output device. Formatted data written to an output device exists as a set of lines; each line is composed of characters. When information in this form is printed, the first character is used for carriage control and is not printed. The following standard for interpretation of the first character of each printed record is established:

Character	*Vertical spacing before printing of that line*
Blank	One line
0	Two lines
1	To first line of next page
+	No advance (overprint of last line)

It is always best for the user to take care of the first character of each record to be printed *explicitly*. For example, to have the values of JOHN and JIM printed, the user should use statements similar to the following:

```
      WRITE(6,9050)JOHN,JIM
9050  FORMAT(1X,2I5)
```

that is, if the user desired single spacing. Users sometimes use an oversized field width for the first field descriptor in a format specification to obtain a blank in column one, as follows:

```
      JOE=10  .
      WRITE(6,9060)JOE
9060  FORMAT(I4)
```

which is essentially the same as

```
      JOE=10
      WRITE(6,9070)JOE
9070  FORMAT(1X,I3)
```

If the nature of the output data is not known, however, surprises frequently result. For example, the statements:

```
      JIL=123
      WRITE(6,9080)JIL
9080  FORMAT(I3)
```

would cause a 1 to be placed in column one. The result: the carriage would be ejected and the 1 would not be printed.

If, on the other hand, the user desired to print on the top of a page (that is, eject the page), he would use statements such as:

```
        WRITE(6,9090)
9090    FORMAT(1H1,20X,15HTITLE OF REPORT)
```

THE ASSIGNMENT STATEMENT

The assignment statement permits a data value to be assigned to a scalar variable or to a subscripted array variable. The form of the assignment statement is:

```
variable = expression
```

where "variable" is a scalar variable or a subscripted array variable and "expression" is an expression, as defined previously, that is evaluated at the point of reference using the current value of the operands of which the expression is composed. The following examples depict valid assignment statements:

```
A=10.5
COW=.00125*A+3.6
D13(14)=191.8
PILL(K,3*J+1) = ALPHA *B(L-2)**I
```

During assignment, only the value of the variable to the left of the equal sign is changed and variable references that are part of the expression retain their original values.

FORTRAN allows a type conversion "across the equals sign" to a limited extent. For example, the following statement is valid (where A is a real variable):

```
A=10
```

and is interpreted to mean: (1) Take the integer constant 10, stored as an integer fixed-point value, and convert it to a floating-point value; and (2) replace the value of A with the result. Similarly, the statement (where I is an integer variable):

I=13.4

is interpreted to mean: (1) Take the real constant 13.4, stored as a floating-point value, and convert it to an integer fixed-point value; and (2) replace the value of I with the result. The reader should recall that mixed-mode expressions, such as (where A is real and I is integer):

10+13.4
I+A
I+13.4
A+10

are illegal in standard FORTRAN. Type conversion during assignment also applies when an intermediate result is computed, as in the following set of statements (where A is real and I and J are integer):

I=5
J=6
A=I+J

which are interpreted to mean: (1) Assign integer constant 5 to integer variable I; (2) assign integer constant 6 to integer variable J; (3) add the value of integer variable I to the value of integer variable J; (4) convert the intermediate result from an integer fixed-point value to a floating-point value; and (5) replace the value of floating-point variable A with the floating-point result.

Table 9.3 lists the conversion rules for type conversion during arithmetic assignment.

TABLE 9.3   TYPE CONVERSION RULES FOR ASSIGNMENT OF THE
            FORM V=E

Type of V	Type of E	Conversion Rule
Integer	Integer	Assign
Integer	Real	Convert to fixed-point and assign
Real	Integer	Convert to floating-point and assign
Real	Real	Assign

PROGRAM CONTROL

Program control statements affect the order in which statements are executed in a program unit. The order is usually sequential, depending on the sequence in which the statements are placed in the source deck. Program control statements allow the normal sequence to be altered.

The GOTO Statement

The GOTO statement unconditionally directs program control to the statement numbered by the specified statement number. The form of the GOTO statement is:

```
GOTO statement-number
```

where "statement-number" is a valid statement number of an executable statement in the program. Examples of the GOTO statement are:

        GOTO 150   575...   GOTO 1436
              .   .   1436...
              .   .
              .   .
              .   .
        150 ...   GOTO 575

The Arithmetic IF Statement

The arithmetic IF statement directs program control to one of three statements, depending on the value of an expression evaluated at the time the IF statement is executed. The form of the arithmetic IF statement is:

```
IF(expression)s₁,s₂,s₃
```

where the "expression" is evaluated at the point of reference and s_1, s_2, and s_3 are valid statement numbers of executable statements in the same program. Program control is directed to the statements numbered by s_1, s_2, and s_3 if the value of the expression is less than zero, equal to zero, or greater than zero, respectively; s_1, s_2, and s_3 need not be unique. Thus, if A=10, B=15, and C=20, then the statement:

    IF(A+B−C)350,50,7324

directs program control to executable statement numbered 7324.

The arithmetic expression in the arithmetic IF statement may be either of the integer or real data types.

The Logical IF Statement

The logical IF statement causes a single executable statement to be executed, depending on the truth value of a comparison operation. The form of the logical IF statement is:

```
IF(comparison-expression) executable-statement
```

where the "comparison-expression" is evaluated at the point of reference and "executable-statement" is any executable statement except a DO statement or another logical IF statement. If the result of the comparison is true, then the executable statement accompanying the logical IF statement is executed. If the result of the comparison is false, then the first executable statement following the IF is executed in sequence.

The executable statement accompanying the logical IF statement can be one that directs program control to another point in the program unit (such as a GOTO statement) and one that does not (such as an assignment statement). If program control is directed to another point in the program, then sequential execution continues from there. Otherwise, the statement is executed and sequential execution continues with the first executable statement following the IF statement.

Examples of the use of the logical IF statement follow:

```
IF(A.GT.B**2) GOTO 560
IF(CLOCK .LT. 0.0) A=0.0
IF(I .EQ. J) IF(I) 160,20,5140
```

In many cases, the logical IF is more convenient than the arithmetic IF. If it were desired to test whether the value of variable A is greater than the value of variable B and branch to statement 7400 if it were true, the arithmetic IF requires a subtraction, a determination of the greater than case, and a statement number on the executable statement following the arithmetic IF. The logical IF requires only a comparison expression and a GOTO statement. Both cases are depicted as follows:

Arithmetic IF	*Logical IF*
IF(A–B)100,100,7400	IF(A .GT. B) GOTO 7400
100 . . .	. . .

The STOP and END Statements

The execution of the STOP statement causes the execution of a program to be halted permanently. The form of the STOP statement is:

```
STOP
```

In an operating system environment, execution of the STOP statement causes an exit to the operating system to terminate program execution. When an operating system is not used, the program simply terminates. The STOP statement can be located anwhere in a program.

Every program written in the FORTRAN language must end with the END statement, which has the following form:

```
END
```

The END statement denotes the logical end of the program and causes the execution of the program to be terminated when program control flows to it.

TYPE STATEMENTS*

The type statements in FORTRAN permit the user to declare INTEGER and REAL variables and to override the implicit typing conventions. The form of a type declaration is:

```
type {name | array-declarator} [, {name | array-declarator}] . . .
```

where "type" is one of the words INTEGER or REAL, "name" is a variable name, an array name, or a function name, and "array-declarator" has the form

*This is a simplified treatment of this topic. The complete FORTRAN language includes other data types that are reflected in type statements.

```
array-variable-name(subscript)
```

where the subscript is composed of 1, 2, or 3 integer constants. The constants are separated from each other with a comma. The constituents declared in a type statement are assigned the type corresponding to the word used in the statement. Thus, the following statement:

    INTEGER ADOG,I3,PIG

specifies that the names ADOG, I3, and PIG are to be assigned the integer data type. Similarly, the statement:

    REAL I,BOY,ZEBRA

declares I, BOY, and ZEBRA as real variables.

The array declarator is used to define an array in addition to specifying its type. The subscript is used to give the size of the named array. This topic is covered in the next section.

A type declaration must be placed at the beginning of a program and can be used to:

1. Confirm implicit typing
2. Override implicit typing

A program may contain any number of type statements with the same word. Thus, the statements:

    REAL K25,X4TP,JONSON
    REAL ABC,LEGGY,I

are equivalent to:

    REAL K25,X4TP,JONSON,ABC,LEGGY,I

The type statement and the FORMAT statement, covered previously with regard to input and output, are examples of what are usually referred to as nonexecutable statements. Use of statements such as the assignment statement and the GOTO cause computation to be performed, hence, the name "executable statement." Nonexecutable statements provide information to

the language processor concerning the manner in which executable statements
are to be processed.

LOOPING

Many algorithms require that a sequence of steps be repeated. An algorithm of this type is usually programmed in one of two ways: (1) The
program steps are duplicated the required number of times; or (2) the program is written so that the same program steps are executed iteratively.
The second method is preferred in complex programs or when the necessary
number of iterations is not known beforehand.

Iterative Procedures

A series of statements to be executed repetitively is termed a *loop*, the
statements that comprise the loop are termed the *body of the loop*, and one
pass through the loop is termed an *iteration*. The number of iterations is
governed by a *control variable* that usually operates as follows:

1. The control variable is set to an *initial value*.
2. The body of the loop is executed.
3. The value of the control variable is incremented by a specified value—
   frequently referred to as an *increment*.
4. The value of the control variable is compared with a *limit* value. If the
   limit value is exceeded, then the loop is terminated and program
   execution continues with the first executable statement following the
   body of the loop. Otherwise, execution of the loop continues with
   step 2.

The following FORTRAN program depicts a simple loop:

```
C       SUM OF EVEN INTEGERS .LE. N                 (1)
        INTEGER SUM                                 (2)
     30 READ(5,8500)N                               (3)
        IF(N .EQ. 0)STOP                            (4)
        SUM=0                                       (5)
        I=2                                         (6)
     50 SUM=SUM+I                                   (7)
        I=I+2                                       (8)
        IF (I .LE. N) GOTO 50                       (9)
        WRITE(6,8600) SUM                          (10)
        GOTO 30                                    (11)
```

```
8500 FORMAT (12)                                              (12)
8600 FORMAT(1X,4HSUM=, I3)                                    (13)
     END                                                     (14)
```

Input:

```
5
10
2
0
```

Output:

```
SUM=  6
SUM= 30
SUM=  2
```

The program depicts each of the above steps. Statement 6 initializes the control variable I (step 1). Statement 7 is the body of the loop (step 2). Statement 8 increments the control variable (step 3) by a value of 2. Statement 9 tests the control variable I against the limit value N (step 4); if the value of the control variable is less than or equal to the limit value, then program control is returned to the statement numbered 50 to repeat the loop.

Looping is such a frequently used technique in computer programming that special statements are defined to control the manner in which loops are executed.

The DO Statement

The DO statement is used to establish a controlled loop, specify the control variable and indexing (or control) parameters, and denote the body of the loop. The form of the DO statement is:

$$DO \ s \ i = n_1, n_2 \ [, n_3]$$

where:

  s is the statement number of the last statement in the range of the DO loop
  i is a scalar integer variable
  n_1 is the initial value given to the control variable
  n_2 is the limit value of the control variable

n_3 is the value by which the control variable is incremented prior to the execution of the loop. If n_3 is omitted, then it is understood to be the value one

n_1, n_2, and n_3 must be integer constants or scalar integer variables

The body of the loop is the statements following the DO statement up to and including the one numbered s. The previous example is written with the use of the DO statement as follows:

```
C        SUM OF EVEN INTEGERS .LE. N
         INTEGER SUM
      30 READ(5,8500)N
         IF(N .EQ. 0) STOP
         SUM=0
         DO 100 I=2,N,2
     100 SUM=SUM+I
         WRITE(6,8600) SUM
         GO TO 30
    8500 FORMAT(I2)
    8600 FORMAT(1X,4HSUM=,I3)
         END
```

Input:

```
    5
   10
    2
    0
```

Output:

```
   SUM=  6
   SUM= 30
   SUM=  2
```

A DO loop is executed in the following manner:

1. The control variable i is assigned the initial value n_1.
2. The body of the loop is executed.
3. The control variable i is incremented by n_3.
4. The control variable i is tested against n_2; if i is greater than n_2, then the loop is terminated and normal execution proceeds with the first executable statement following the range of the DO, that is, the first executable statement following the statement numbered s.

Use of the DO Statement

Several conditions govern the use of the DO statement:

1. At the time the DO statement is executed, the control parameters n_1, n_2, n_3 must be greater than zero.
2. The value of the control variable may not be modified from within the loop. (This restriction results from the fact that the value of the control variable was expected to be placed in an index register.)
3. DO loops may be nested but must not overlap.
4. A DO loop must be entered through its DO statement.
5. The last statement in the range of a DO loop must not be one of the following statements:

   GOTO (of any form)
   Arithmetic IF
   RETURN
   STOP
   PAUSE
   Another DO statement
   Logical IF containing any of these forms

Restriction number 5 presents an operational problem that can be resolved with the CONTINUE statement.

The CONTINUE Statement

Suppose a program were needed to compute the average of a set of numbers, where only numbers greater than or equal to zero are to be included in the average. The number of values (N) is read in, as are the input values. A suitable program is given as follows:

```
C       AVERAGE OF POSITIVE OR ZERO VALUES
        READ(5,9001)N
        SUM=0.0
        COUNT= 0.0
        DO 50 I=1,N
        READ(5,9002) VALUE
        IF (VALUE .LT. 0.0) GOTO 50
        COUNT=COUNT+1.0
        SUM=SUM+VALUE
     50 CONTINUE
        AVER=SUM/COUNT
        WRITE(6,9003)SUM
        STOP
```

```
9001 FORMAT(I3)
9002 FORMAT(F5.2)
9003 FORMAT(1X,8H AVERAGE=,F5.2)
     END
```

Input:

```
3
20.40
-10.36
40.20
```

Output:

AVERAGE= 30.30

The program uses a CONTINUE statement to provide a reference point in the program to complete the loop.

The CONTINUE statement has the form:

```
CONTINUE
```

The execution of the CONTINUE statement causes the normal execution sequence to be continued. It can be used to end a DO loop or as an "entry point" in a series of statements as follows:

```
      SUM=0.0
150   CONTINUE
      READ(5,9000) VAL
      IF (VAL .LT. 0.0) GOTO 5000
      SUM=SUM+VAL
      GOTO 150
```

The CONTINUE statement is sometimes used in the latter fashion to avoid rekeypunching statement numbers when it is expected that statements are to be rearranged in a program.

Nested DO Statements

It is important to recognize that the use of a DO loop is a means of achieving control in a computer program. It can be used in some cases to eliminate the need for the GOTO statement, as shown in the following program that computes *n* factorial (the program terminates when a value of –9 is read):

```
C       FACTORIAL PROGRAM
        INTEGER FACT
        DO 75 I=1,1000
        READ(5,9000)N
        IF(N .EQ. –9) STOP
        FACT= 1
        DO 63 J=1,N
     63 FACT=FACT*J
     75 WRITE(6,9001)N,FACT
   9000 FORMAT(I2)
   9001 FORMAT(1X,I2,1X,10HFACTORIAL=,I5)
        END
```

Input:

```
 5
 7
 1
 0
–9
```

Output:

```
5 FACTORIAL=  120
7 FACTORIAL= 5040
1 FACTORIAL=    1
0 FACTORIAL=    1
```

The above program depicts a nested loop (that is, a *double loop*, as it is frequently called). The outer loop is executed until a value of –9 is read by the READ statement.

Other examples of the DO statement are included in the next section on arrays and subscripts.

ARRAYS AND SUBSCRIPTS

Arrays are an important feature of most programming languages since a great many computer applications utilize the concept of a family of related data, referred to by a single name—the array variable. The subject of arrays is briefly considered in Chapter 7; this section goes into more detail on how arrays are defined and used.

Arrays must be declared in the FORTRAN language and can be of any of the data types mentioned previously, that is, integer or real. The FORTRAN standard allows three dimensions; however, most modern versions of FORTRAN allow at least seven dimensions. Arrays cannot have a variable number of dimensions or even variable-sized dimensions.

Array Specification

Array specifications are made with the DIMENSION statement or with one of the type statements. The DIMENSION statement is used to give the number of dimensions and the size of one or more arrays and has the form:

DIMENSION array-declarator [,array declarator]...

where "array-declarator" has the form:

array-variable-name(subscript)

"Array-variable-name" is the name of the array and "subscript" is one, two, or three integer constants, separated by commas. The subscript in an array declarator gives the number of dimensions and the extent for each dimension. Thus, the statement

DIMENSION A(7,13)

defines a two-dimensional array that has 7 rows and 13 columns. The lower bound for each dimension is one and the upper bound for each dimension is the value specified in the array declarator. The data type of an array may be specified implicitly or explicitly with a type statement. The array A, defined above, is of type REAL because of the implicit type assignments.

Consider the following statements:

DIMENSION IMY(100),A(7,13),RACOB(6,3,2)
REAL IMY
INTEGER RACOB

IMY is a real one-dimensional array that contains 100 elements. A is included in the DIMENSION statement but not in a type statement. It is implicitly given the data type REAL; as an array it is given 7 rows and 13 columns as mentioned above. RACOB is a three-dimensional INTEGER array with extents of six, three, and two, respectively.

The DIMENSION statement is another example of a nonexecutable statement; it supplies information to the language processor on the amount of storage that should be allocated to an array and the manner in which an element of an array should be referenced.

The preceding example has depicted a case in which the same array variable name is used in two different nonexecutable statements (frequently referred to as *specification statements*). For example, the identifier IMY is found in the statement body of the DIMENSION statement and the REAL statement. As mentioned previously, FORTRAN allows a type specification and an array declaration to be made with a type statement. The form of a type statement with this capability was given in the preceding section. Using only type statements, the preceding example can be simplified as:

```
REAL A(7,13),IMY(100)
INTEGER RACOB(6,3,2)
```

Since arrays can be declared in the type statements, the DIMENSION statement is no longer needed in FORTRAN. In fact, it is placed in the "other statements" section of some FORTRAN manuals. However, the DIMENSION statement probably never will be removed from FORTRAN, because of the need to compile programs written for earlier versions of FORTRAN.

Subscripts

A subscript is used to select an element of an array and must contain a subscript expression for each dimension of the array. Subscript expressions are separated by a comma when more than one is needed in an array reference. In standard FORTRAN, a subscript expression is limited to one of the following forms:

$$c * v$$
$$c * v + k$$
$$c * v - k$$
$$v + k$$
$$v - k$$
$$v$$
$$k$$

where c and k are integer constants and v is a scalar integer variable. Thus given:

```
INTEGER ABLE(10,3)
REAL JOE(50)
```

and K=2 and I=4, then ABLE(2*K−1,2) selects the integer value located in the third row and second column of ABLE and JOE(10*I) selects the real value located as the 40th element of JOE.

The elements of an array occupy contiguous storage locations and no array subscript expression may assume a value when evaluated during the execution of a program that is higher than the declared dimensionality for that array. Obviously, this is not a condition that can be detected during compilation and in most versions of FORTRAN, explicit tests of a subscript value are not made during the execution of a program. In general, the results of using an oversized subscript are unpredictable.

Except as specified otherwise, an element of an array can be used anywhere that a constant or a scalar variable of the same type can be used.

Input and Output of Arrays

The FORTRAN language includes a special language facility for reading or writing arrays. Consider the following statements:

```
REAL ALIST(5)
READ(5,9000) ALIST
9000 FORMAT(7F10.2)
```

The READ statement specifies that the entire array ALIST is to be read in; the array specifications for ALIST are determined from the array declaration. Data items must be placed on the input medium by increasing order of array index in accordance with the FORMAT specification. (In the example, the field descriptor reads 7F10.2; however, input is terminated when the list is exhausted. In this case, only the first five fields of the input record are used.)

Input of entire arrays is referred to as *short list input*; output of entire arrays is referred to as *short list output*.

Short list input or output can be used in a conventional input/output list, such as:

```
INTEGER I(5)
REAL FOX(2),JOKER(100)
WRITE(6,9000)DOG,I,JOKER(34),FOX
9000 FORMAT(1X,F5.2,5I3,F16.8,2F10.3)
```

When short list input or output involves two- or three-dimensional arrays, a preestablished convention determines the order in which array elements are transmitted. Arrays are stored in column order in FORTRAN and the short list input and output conventions use that order. Array elements are transmitted in column order such that the first subscript varies most rapidly and the last subscript the least rapidly. Thus, if the following statements were executed:

```
      INTEGER BOY(2,3)
      WRITE(6,9000)BOY
 9000 FORMAT...
```

the array elements are transmitted from main storage to output device 6 in the following order: BOY(1,1), BOY(2,1), BOY(1,2), BOY(2,2), BOY(1,3), and BOY(2,3).

This convention makes the printing of arrays a problem since the line printer effectively prints by row and not by column. For this purpose, a "DO-implied" input and output list is included in the FORTRAN language; a DO-implied list is an extension to the list introduced previously and is defined as follows:

1. A *simple list* is a scalar variable, an element of an array, an array name, or two simple lists separated by a comma.
2. A *DO-implied list* is a list, followed by a comma, followed by an implied DO specification of the form:

$$i = m_1, m_2 \, [,m_3]$$

where i is an integer variable and m_1, m_2, and m_3 are integer values (that is, an integer constant or an integer variable). A DO-implied list means that the list is "effectively copied" where i takes on the values m_1 to m_2 in increments of m_3. If m_3 is omitted, then it is assumed to be one. A DO-implied list is enclosed in parentheses to denote the scope of the specification. Examples follow.
3. A *list* is a simple list, a simple list enclosed in parentheses, a DO-implied list, or two lists separated by a comma.

An example of a DO-implied list is:

```
READ(5,9000)(A(I),I=1,5)
```

where A is a one-dimensional array. This DO-implied list is equivalent to:

```
    READ(5,9000) A(1),A(2),A(3),A(4),A(5)
```

To print the two-dimensional array:

```
    REAL CONV(9,17)
```

therefore, a DO-implied list of the form:

```
    WRITE(6,9000)((CONV(I,J),J=1,17),I=1,9)
```

would be required. This WRITE statement is equivalent to the following DO loop:

```
        DO 321 I=1,9
    321 WRITE(6,9000)(CONV(I,J),J=1,17)
```

provided that the FORMAT statement is written to print one line at a time.

Examples of Array Utilization

The following example computes prime numbers using the Sieve of Eratosthenes. The program reads a number N and then computes and prints the prime numbers less than or equal to N.

```
    C       PRIME NUMBERS
            INTEGER P(999)
            READ(5,83)N
        83 FORMAT(I3)
            IF(N .GT. 999) GO TO 990
            DO 10 I=2,N
        10 P(I)=I
            L=SQRT(FLOAT(N))
            DO 20 I=2,L
            IF(P(I) .EQ. 0) GO TO 20
            II = I+I
            DO 15 J = II,N,I
        15 P(J)=0
        20 CONTINUE
            WRITE(6,84)N
        84 FORMAT(1X, 16HPRIMES LESS THAN, I3)
            DO 30 I=2,N
            IF(P(I) .EQ. 0) GO TO 30
            WRITE(6,85) P(I)
        85 FORMAT(1X,I3)
```

```
   30 CONTINUE
      STOP
  990 WRITE(6,86)
   86 FORMAT(1X,9HTOO LARGE)
      STOP
      END
```

Input:

15

Output:

PRIMES LESS THAN 15

```
    2
    3
    5
    7
   11
   13
```

The program also depicts nested DO loops and variable control parameters.

Another example of the use of one-dimensional arrays involves the sorting of numbers is ascending order. The program utilizes an exchange technique, depicted as follows:

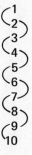

The program initially sets a flag (FLAG). When an exchange is made, FLAG is set to 1. If both passes are made through the data without making an exchange, then the values are sorted and the program terminates. Otherwise, the process is repeated. The advantage of the exchange technique is that the process is efficient if the data is sorted or partially sorted beforehand.

```
      REAL NUMS(100)
      INTEGER FLAG
      READ(5,9000)N
9000 FORMAT(I3)
      IF (N .GT. 100) GO TO 990
      READ(5,9001)(NUMS(I),I=1,N)
9001 FORMAT(2014)
      NN=N-1
   5 FLAG=0
      DO 25 I=1,NN,2
      IF(NUMS(I) .LE. NUMS(I+1)) GO TO 25
      TEMP=NUMS(I)
      NUMS(I)=NUMS(I+1)
      NUMS(I+1)=TEMP
      FLAG=1
  25 CONTINUE
      DO 35 I=2,NN,2
      IF(NUMS(I) .LE. NUMS(I+1)) GO TO 35
      TEMP=NUMS(I)
      NUMS(I)=NUMS(I+1)
      NUMS(I+1)=TEMP
      FLAG=1
  35 CONTINUE
      IF (FLAG .NE. 0) GO TO 5
      WRITE(6,9002)(NUMS(I),I=1,N)
9002 FORMAT(1X,13HSORTED VALUES/(1X,2OI4))
      STOP
      END
```

Input:

```
12
-7 3 9 6 5 1 4 3 8 0 2 7
```

Output:

```
SORTED VALUES
-7 0 1 2 3 3 4 5 6 7 8 9
```

Two- and three-dimensional arrays are defined and used in a similar fashion, as depicted in the following example. The program reads in a two-dimensional array and performs some elementary arithmetic operations.

```
      INTEGER A(20,20)
C     READ IN ARRAY DIMENSIONS
```

```
        READ(5,9000)M,N
   9000 FORMAT(2I2)
C       READ IN ARRAY BY ROWS AND PRINT IT
        WRITE(6,9001)
   9001 FORMAT(1X,14HORIGINAL ARRAY)
        DO 230 I=1,M
        READ(5,9002)(A(I,J),J=1,N)
   9002 FORMAT(20I2)
    230 WRITE(6,9003)(A(I,J),J=1,N)
   9003 FORMAT(1X,20I2)
C       REPLACE SECOND COLUMN WITH ONES
        DO 250 I=1,M
    250 A(I,2)=1
C       DISPLAY ARRAY
        WRITE(6,9004)
   9004 FORMAT(1X,14HMODIFIED ARRAY)
        DO 260 I=1,M
    260 WRITE(6,9005)(A(I,J) J=1,N)
   9005 FORMAT(1X,20I2)
C       MULTIPLY EACH ELEMENT BY A(2,3) AND DISPLAY IT
        DO 270 I=1,M
        DO 270 J=1,N
    270 A(I,J)=A(I,J)*A(2,3)
        WRITE(6,9006)
   9006 FORMAT(1X, 26HARRAY MULTIPLIED BY A(2,3))
        DO 280 I=1,M
    280 WRITE(6,9007)(A(I,J),J=1,N)
   9007 FORMAT(1X,20I4)
        STOP
        END
```

Input:

```
 3  4
-7  3  9  6
 5  1  4  3
 8  0  2  7
```

Output:

```
ORIGINAL ARRAY
-7  3  9  6
 5  1  4  3
 8  0  2  7
```

```
MODIFIED ARRAY
-7  1  9  6
 5  1  4  3
 8  1  2  7
ARRAY MULTIPLIED BY A(2,3)
-28   4  36   24
 20   4  16   48
128  16  32  432
```

The results from multiplying the array by A(2,3) appear to be incorrect but are not because A(2,3) is modified partway through the computation.

FUNCTIONS

The computer is frequently used in applications that require the use of a mathematical function, such as the sine, cosine, or square root. In the computer, functions such as these are usually approximated to a given degree of accuracy with an algorithm such as the following series expansion for the trigonometric sine:

$$\sin x = x - \frac{x^3}{3!} + \frac{x^5}{5!} - \frac{x^7}{7!} + \cdots$$

Two options exist:

1. Each user can program his own mathematical functions; and
2. A set of frequently used functions can be provided as part of the programming language.

Usually, the second option is selected since not all users are versed in computer approximations and it is convenient not to have to bother with them. Moreover, they can be coded efficiently in assembler language and placed in a program library to be shared by all users.

Built-in Functions

Functions that are supplied as part of the programming language are referred to as *built-in functions*. The form of a function reference is the function name followed by an arithmetic expression in parentheses. The expression is evaluated at the point of reference and the specified function is applied to the value of the expression. The function returns a value that can be used as an operand in the expression. Thus, the expression 2.0+SQRT (25.0) has the value 7.0, where SQRT is the square root function.

A *function name* for a built-in function adheres to the naming convention for variables and arrays. The form of a function reference is:

---

function-name (arithmetic-expression)

---

where "function-name" is one of the mathematical functions defined in the implementation of the language. Table 9.4 lists the built-in functions in the FORTRAN language.* All of the functions listed in Table 9.4 take a single argument.

The following list gives some mathematical expressions that include functions and their equivalent representation in FORTRAN:

Mathematical Expression	*FORTRAN Expression*
$\sqrt{1-\sin^2 x}$	SQRT(1.0–SIN(X)**2)
$\cos 30°$	COS(30.0*(3.14159/180.0))
$\sqrt{a^2+b^2-2ab \cos c_1}$	SQRT(A**2+B**2–2.0*A*B*COS(C1))
$\tan^{-1}(x/y)$	A TAN(X/Y)
$\dfrac{e^x-e^{-x}}{2}$	(EXP(X)–EXP(–X))/2.0
$(\lvert x \rvert)^3$	ABS(X)**3

When a function reference is used as an operand, as in SIN(X)**2 or ABS(X)**3, the function is applied first and the result of the function is used in the arithmetic operation. In other words, a function reference has a higher priority than any of the arithmetic operators.

The use of functions is demonstrated in the next section, which gives a variety of simple applications of the FORTRAN language.

APPLICATIONS

This section further demonstrates how the FORTRAN language is used by giving some routine applications.

---

*Double precision and complex functions are omitted since these data types have not been covered.

TABLE 9.4   BUILT-IN FUNCTIONS IN FORTRAN

Function	Definition	Number of Arguments	Symbolic Name	Data Type of: Argument(s)	Data Type of: Function	Example
Absolute value	$|x|$	1	ABS	R	R	ABS(−1.2)↔1.2
			IABS	I	I	
Truncation to Integer	Sign $(x)*$ largest integer $\leqslant |x|$	1	AINT	R	R	AINT(1.2)↔1.0
			INT	R	I	
Modulus (remainder function)	x_1(mod. x_2)	2	AMOD	R	R	AMOD(5.0,2.0)↔1.0
			MOD	I	I	
Largest Value	Max($x_1, x_2, \ldots$)	≥2	AMAX0	I	R	AMAX1(1.0,2.0)↔2.0
			AMAX1	R	R	
			MAX0	I	I	
			MAX1	R	I	
Smallest Value	Min($x_1, x_2, \ldots$)	≥	AMIN0	I	R	AMIN1(1.0,2.0)↔1.0
			AMIN1	R	R	
			MIN0	I	I	
			MIN1	R	I	
Float	Conversion from integer to real	1	FLOAT	I	R	FLOAT(5)↔5.0
FIX	Conversion from real to integer	1	IFIX	R	I	IFIX(5.0)↔5
Transfer of sign	Sign $(x_2)*(x_1)$	2	SIGN	R	R	SIGN(3.1,−6.4)↔ −3.1
			ISIGN	I	I	
Positive difference	x_1−Min(x_1, x_2)	2	DIM	R	R	DIM(2.1,−1.0)↔3.1
			IDIM	I	I	

244

Exponential	e^x	1	EXP	R	R
Natural logarithm	$\log_e(x)$	1	ALOG	R	R
Common logarithm	$\log_{10}(x)$	1	ALOG10	R	R
Trigonometric sine	$\sin(x)$	1	SIN	R	R
Trigonometric cosine	$\cos(x)$	1	COS	R	R
Hyberbolic tangent	$\tanh(x)$	1	TANH	R	R
Square root	x	1	SQRT	R	R
Arctangent	$\tan^{-1}(x)$	1	ATAN	R	R
Arctangent	$\tan^{-1}(x_1, x_2)$	2	ATAN2	R	R

R=REAL   I=INTEGER

```
   10  READ(5,9000)A,B,C
 9000  FORMAT(3F5.1)
       IF(A .EQ. 0.0) GOTO 20
       ROOT1 = (-B+SQRT(B**2-4.*A*C))/(2.*A)
       ROOT2 = (-B-SQRT(B**2-4.*A*C))/(2.*A)
       WRITE(6,9001)A,B,C,ROOT1,ROOT2
 9001  FORMAT(1X,2HA=,F5.1,3H B=, F5.1,3H C=,F5.1,7H  ROOT1=,
       F5.1,7H  ROOT2=,F5.1)
       GOTO 10
   20  STOP
       END
```

Input:

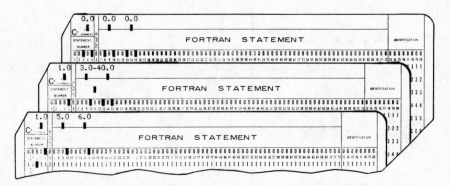

Output:

A= 1.0 B= 5.0 C=   6.0 ROOT1= -2.0 ROOT2= -3.0
A= 1.0 B= 3.0 C=-40.0 ROOT1= 5.0 ROOT2= -8.0

Figure 9.3 A FORTRAN program demonstrating the use of the quadratic formula to solve a quadratic equation.

Roots of an Equation

The roots of a quadratic equation of the form:

$$AX^2+BX+C=0$$

are given by the quadratic formula:

$$\text{root}= \frac{-B\pm\sqrt{B^2-4AC}}{2A}$$

For example, the equation $x^2+5x+6=0$ can be factored as $(x+2)(x+3)=0$ and the roots are known as $x=-2$ and $x=-3$. The FORTRAN program given in Figure 9.3 uses the quadratic formula to solve a quadratic equation.

Trigonometric Functions

Trigonometric functions, such as SIN, COS, and so forth, are included in the FORTRAN language as built-in functions. These functions require that the argument be expressed in radians where one radian is equal to $180/\pi$ degrees. The FORTRAN program given in Figure 9.4 constructs a table of degrees, radians, the sine function, and the cosine function for angles ranging from $0°$ to $360°$ in $30°$ steps.

Permutations

The number of ways that four objects can be arranged is given as $4\times3\times2\times1$ (or four factorial). This means that the first object can be arranged in four ways, the second object can be arranged in three ways (after the first object is fixed), the third object can be arranged in two ways (after the first two objects are fixed), and the last object can only be arranged in one way. With five objects taken two at a time, the number of permutations is:

$$5\times4$$

using the same reasoning. The following mathematical formula exists for calculating the number of permutations of N things taken R at a time:

$$_NP_R = \frac{N!}{(N-R)!}$$

where $N! = N\times(N-1)\times(N-2)\times \ldots \times3\times2\times1$. Thus, $_NP_R$ is rewritten as:

$$_NP_R = \frac{N\times(N-1)\times(N-2)\times \ldots \times(N-R+1)\times(N-R)\times(N-R-1)\times \ldots \times3\times2\times1}{(N-R)\times(N-R-1)\times \ldots \times3\times2\times1}$$

dividing we obtain:

$$_NP_R = N\times(N-1)\times(N-2)\times \ldots \times(N-R+1)$$

which is a computational algorithm for $_NP_R$. The FORTRAN program given in Figure 9.5 computes the number of permutations of N things taken R at a time using the latter formula.

```
         WRITE(6,8000)
   8000 FORMAT(1H1,7HDEGREES,3X,7HRADIANS,5X,4HSINE,6X,
        *6HCOSINE)
   C     SIN AND COS USE RADIANS INSTEAD OF DEGREES
   C     CC IS A CONVERSION CONSTANT
         CC=3.1415928/180.0
         DO 150 I=1,361,30
         DEG=I-1
         RAD=DEG*CC
         SINVAL=SIN(RAD)
         COSVAL=COS(RAD)
    150 WRITE(6,8001)DEG,RAD,SINVAL,COSVAL
   8001 FORMAT(1X,F5.0,2X,3(2X,F9.6))
         STOP
         END
```

Output:

DEGREES	RADIANS	SINE	COSINE
0.	0.	0.	1.000000
30.	0.523599	0.500000	0.866025
60.	1.047198	0.866025	0.500000
90.	1.570796	1.000000	-0.000000
120.	2.094395	0.866025	-0.500000
150.	2.617994	0.500000	-0.866025
180.	3.141593	-0.000000	-1.000000
210.	3.665192	-0.500000	-0.866025
240.	4.188790	-0.866025	-0.500000
270	4.712389	-1.000000	0.000000
300.	5.235988	-0.866025	0.500000
330.	5.759587	-0.500000	0.866026
360.	6.283186	0.000000	1.000000

Figure 9.4 A FORTRAN program demonstrating the use of trigonometric functions.

Largest Factor

One method of computing the largest factor of a number N operates by successively dividing N by the largest possible factor $INT(N/2)$, $INT(N/2)-1$, $INT(N/2)-2$, and so on until either a factor is found or the value 1 is reached. A factor is recognized when $N/F=INT(N/F)$, where F is the factor. The FORTRAN program given in Figure 9.6 requests that the user enter the lower and upper limits of a set of numbers and computes the largest factor of each number in that set.

```
      INTEGER R,P
  100 READ(5,7000)N,R
      IF(N .EQ. 0) GO TO 900
      P=1
      L=N-R+1
      DO 75 I=L,N
   75 P=P*I
      WRITE(6,7001)N,R,P
      GO TO 100
  900 STOP
 7000 FORMAT(2I3)
 7001 FORMAT(1X,I3,8H THINGS,,I3,27H AT A TIME -
     *PERMUTATIONS = ,I8)
      END
```

Input:

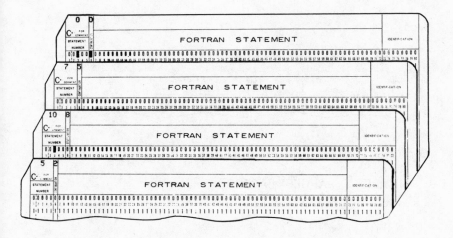

Output:

```
 5 THINGS,  2 AT A TIME - PERMUTATIONS =       20
10 THINGS,  8 AT A TIME - PERMUTATIONS = 1814400
 7 THINGS,  5 AT A TIME - PERMUTATIONS =     2520
```

Figure 9.5 A FORTRAN program that computes the number of permutations of N things taken R at a time.

```
        INTEGER U,F
        READ(5,9000)L,U
        WRITE(6,9001)
        DO 500 N=L,U,2
        K=N/2
        DO 400 M=1,K
        F=K-M+1
        IF(F*(N/F) .NE. N) GOTO 400
        WRITE(6,9002)N,F
        GOTO 500
    400 CONTINUE
    500 CONTINUE
        STOP
   9000 FORMAT(2I3)
   9001 FORMAT(1H1,6HNUMBER,2X,14HLARGEST FACTOR)
   9002 FORMAT(3X,I3,6X,I3)
        END
```

Input:

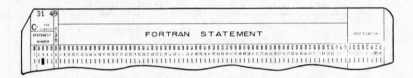

Output:

NUMBER	LARGEST FACTOR
31	1
33	11
35	7
37	1
39	13
41	1
43	1
45	15
47	1
49	7

Figure 9.6 A FORTRAN program that computes the largest factor of a number N.

Mean and Standard Deviation

The arithmetic mean and standard deviation of a set of numbers are computed by the formulas:

$$\bar{x} = \frac{\sum\limits_{i=1}^{n} A_i}{n}$$

and

$$\sigma = \sqrt{\frac{A_i^2}{n} - (\bar{x})^2}$$

respectively. The FORTRAN program given in Figure 9.7 computes $\bar{x}$ and σ by accumulating the sum and sum of squares of the values A_i as they are read in from an internal data set.

```
      REAL A(100)
   20 READ(5,350)N
      IF(N .EQ. 0) GO TO 80
      READ(5,351)(A(I),I=1,N)
C     COMPUTE SUM AND SUM OF SQUARES
      SUM=0.0
      SUMSQ=0.0
      DO 50 I=1,N
      SUM=SUM*A(I)
   50 SUMSQ=SUMSQ+A(I)*A(I)
C     COMPUTE ARITHMETIC MEAN
      XBAR=SUM/FLOAT(N)
C     COMPUTE STANDARD DEVIATION
      SIGMA=SQRT(SUMSQ/FLOAT(N)-XBAR*XBAR)
C     OUTPUT SECTION
      WRITE(6,352)(A(I),I=1,N)
      WRITE(6,353)XBAR,SIGMA
      GO TO 20
   80 STOP
  350 FORMAT(I3)
  351 FORMAT(10F8.3)
  352 FORMAT(1X,4HDATA/(10F8.3))
  353 FORMAT(1X,5HMEAN=,F8.3,20H STANDARD
     *DEVIATION=,F8.3)
      END
```

Input

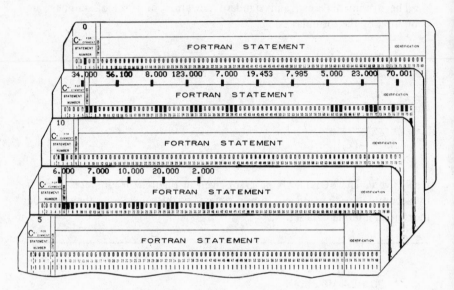

Output

```
DATA
 6.000 7.000 10.000 20.000 2.000
MEAN= 9.000 STANDARD DEVIATION= 6.066
DATA
34.000 56.100 8.000 123.000 7.000 19.453 7.985 5.000 23.000 70.001
MEAN= 35.354 STANDARD DEVIATION= 35.976
```

Figure 9.7 A FORTRAN program that computes the mean and standard deviation of a set of numbers.

QUESTION SET

1. Study the "Indian program" given in the chapter. Why is it necessary to include the following "program loop"?

```
DO 10 I=1627,1973
10 PRINC=PRINC+PRINC*RATE
```

2. Distinguish between a "character" and a "symbol."

3. Write the following FORTRAN real constants in ordinary decimal notation:

    (a) 2E5   (c) .28164E+01
    (b) .104E–6   (d) .4E0

4. Write the following real numbers as FORTRAN real constants using an exponent:

    (a) 5.15×10^{17} (c) .00003629
    (b) 1.369   (d) 651382.

5. Explain what is meant by the statement "The magnitude and precision of a real data item are determined by the size of the exponent and fraction, respectively, of the floating-point format used in storing the numbers."

6. If I=5 and J=2, evaluate the following expressions in the integer mode:

    (a) I/J+2
    (b) 2*I/J
    (c) I/J*2

7. Using the implicit naming convention, identify integer, real, and illegal variable names:

    (a) IDENT   (e) KOUNT   (i) 2IT
    (b) QUOT   (f) PRODUCT (j) WRITE
    (c) XYZ   (g) IO   (k) DIMENSION
    (d) E7   (h) W123   (l) IF

8. Write FORTRAN expressions for the following mathematical expressions:

    (a) $\dfrac{x^3+y^2}{3}$
    (b) $a+bx$
    (c) a^2x-b^3y+abz

9. In what order are the statements that comprise a FORTRAN program executed?

10. Which of the following expressions are invalid?

A+–B	(((34)))	X+Y–1.3 .GT. 13.4
+/A	JILL .LT. 63.4	A**B
A(B(2))	–ELF+F3	TOMICK**1.4
D(I+1)	W(–I)	(((A+B)*3.6–4)

11. Give an example of a Hollerith constant.
12. Write a FORTRAN program to compute the product of the numbers 2E3, 173.89, –14.839, 63.1, and .123E–1 and print the result.
13. Write a FORTRAN program to evaluate the function:

$$y = \frac{e^{ax} - e^{-bx}}{2}$$

as x ranges from 1 to 2 in steps of .01, for the following cases:

    (a) $a=1, b=1$
    (b) $a=1, b=2$
    (c) $a=.5, b=1$
    (d) $a=.5, b=.5$
    (e) $a=.5, b=1.5$

14. A depositor banks $10 per month. Interest is 6% per year compounded monthly. Write a FORTRAN program to compute the amount the depositor has in his account after 20 years.
15. Write a FORTRAN program that computes N! (that is, N factorial) and operates as follows: The computer reads a number N. After verifying that the number is a positive integer, the computer computes N!, prints it, and then reads another number. Error diagnostics should be printed if the number is not a positive integer.
16. Write a FORTRAN program to evaluate the polynomial $f(x)=6x^2+4x+7$ as x takes on the values from 1 to 10 in steps of 0.1. Print the results as two columns with column headings.
17. Write a FORTRAN program that computes B and C for values of A that range from $0°$ to $36°$ in increments of $15°$. B and C are defined as follows:

    B=1–2 cosA
    C=1+ cos 2A–3 sin²A

Print the results in labeled columns. (1 radian = $180°/\pi$)
18. Fill an array of 3 rows and 4 columns with the integers 1,2,...,12 by rows. Print the array.
19. Write a FORTRAN program to sum the numbers less than 100 that are divisible by 7.
20. Given a set of numbers of the form:

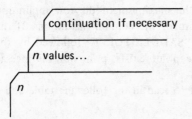

(Allow for at least 100 values.) Write a FORTRAN program that computes and prints the following:

    (a) Sum of numbers in the list
    (b) Largest number
    (c) Smallest number
    (d) Number of numbers equal to 20
    (e) Number of numbers greater than 50 and less than 75

21. Given a set of pay records of the form:

    employee number: columns 1-5
    name: columns 10-35
    hourly rate: columns 40-45, format F6.2
    tax rate: columns 46-49, format F4.2

Write a FORTRAN program that computes the following values for each employee:

    (a) Gross salary
    (b) Tax
    (c) Take-home pay

Produce the results as a payroll listing that gives for each employee (that is, each line of the listing): employee number, name, hours, gross salary, tax, and take-home pay. Label the columns. Pay time and one-half for hours over 40. Have the program "kick out" when a zero employee number is read and tabulate all appropriate columns.

22. Write a FORTRAN program that reads in an $m \times n$ matrix, by columns, and computes the following:

    (a) The smallest value in each row
    (b) The largest value in each column

A "saddle point" occurs if the maximum of the row minimums is the same element as the minimum of the column maximums. If this is the case, print out the message "SADDLE POINT" followed by the corresponding value. If no saddle point exists, print out the message "NO SADDLE POINT".

23. Write a FORTRAN program to read in the following table and sort the entries by key:

Key	Value
10	–13.43
7	81.914
16	–50.1
2	13964.2
9	63.173
24	–.4E–2
11	0
6	2

24. Given the following one-dimensional array:

   REAL A(50)

and the data:

Write a FORTRAN program that:

   (a) Prints the values on one line.
   (b) Prints the values on successive lines.
   (c) Sums the elements of the array and prints the result.
   (d) Reverses and prints the elements of the array.
   (e) Deletes elements of the array with odd numbered indexes and prints the result.
   (f) Rotates the array left by two elements and prints result.

25. Write a FORTRAN program that reads in x in radians and computes:

$$\sin x = x - \frac{x^3}{3!} + \frac{x^5}{5!} - \frac{x^7}{7!} + \cdots$$

to three decimal places. (That is, if the next item in the series is less than .0005, then terminate the calculations.)

26. A magic square such as

$$
\begin{array}{ccc}
8 & 1 & 6 \\
3 & 5 & 7 \\
4 & 9 & 2
\end{array}
$$

can be constructed as follows:

The process always starts in the middle of the top row and numbers are inserted successively by progressing upward and to the right. If the top boundary is reached, continue again at the bottom. If the right boundary is reached, continue again at the left. If another element is reached (that is, 3 to 1), drop down one row (that is, 3 to 4) and continue. The method works for any magic square of order *n*, where *n* is odd.

Write a FORTRAN program to compute a magic square of order *n*, where *n* is read in from cards.

PART III

COMPUTERS
AND SOCIETY

CHAPTER 10

The Scope of
Computer Applications

INTRODUCTION

It is fairly obvious from the preceding chapters that the computer is a tremendous asset to the affairs of the individual, governments, business organizations, and society in general. The general-purpose nature of modern computing machines and the wide range of input and output devices makes the computer appropriate for any application for which we can write a computer program. Programming languages make it easier for us to write programs, and operating systems and time-sharing facilities enable us to utilize our programs effectively—regardless of the precise nature of the application and the mode of operation. Data communications facilities allow the computer to be used from a remote location with an appropriate terminal device. Lastly, mass-storage devices literally permit millions of characters to be stored for ready access in a few milliseconds. Overall, the above concepts and facilities constitute a powerful combination. This chapter is concerned with the scope of computer applications—especially those that span the traditional boundaries of business, government, education, medicine, and law. Some of the more obvious applications, such as payroll processing, have been mentioned briefly in earlier chapters for introductory purposes. This chapter explores these and other areas in more detail.

DATA PROCESSING

Data processing involves the storage, processing, and reporting of information. Although data processing is definitely related to the record-keeping

261

activities of an organization, it is not restricted to those activities and usually encompasses many clerical and time-consuming functions.

One of the more useful applications of data processing is customer billing in a utility-type company. Each customer has a record on a customer file that reflects his name, address, billing rate, credit status, cumulative usage, previous meter reading, and service category. Each month the customer's meter is read by a "meter reader" and the current use is recorded in books. Subsequently, each customer's reading is keypunched, so that each customer's use is reflected in a single card. To the data processing program, each of these cards is referred to as a *transaction*. At the end of the billing period, all transaction cards are sorted by customer's account number and placed on magnetic tape. This is referred to as "batching," since it would be inefficient to run the program separately for each customer. The billing program can now be run using the "old" customer file and the transaction tape as input, as depicted in Figure 10.1. The program processes the customer file and the transaction tape sequentially and a bill for each customer is computed. Output from the billing program is a "new" customer file containing "updated" records, a set of customer bills, and a report that summarizes the processing that was per-

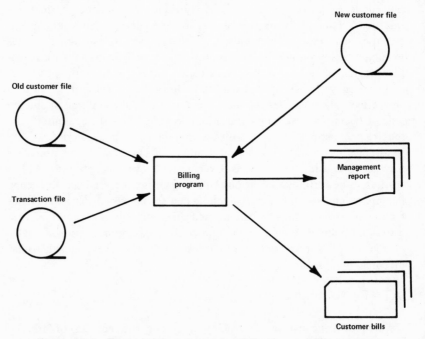

Figure 10.1 Typical data processing application—a billing program.

formed. The "old" customer file and the transaction tape are saved for emergency purposes. The "new" customer file will be used in the next month's run of the billing program.

The process of data processing often combines several operations:

1. Transaction processing
2. Record keeping
3. Bill preparation
4. Management reporting

and almost always involves at least the following input and output files: old master file, transaction file, new master file, and the report file.
Other common data processing applications are:

1. Accounts receivable
2. Accounts payable
3. Inventory control
4. Payroll

In fact, any high-volume operation that must be performed on a periodic basis lends itself to data processing methods. The input operation may vary in data processing; for example, check processing in a bank would involve a magnetic ink character reader and inventory processing in many department stores requires special merchandise ticket readers.

The major advantage of data processing is reduced costs and fewer errors when clerical processing is involved. (In short, the human being has simply priced himself out of the data processing business.) It is also true in many cases that the volume of work has grown to the extent that manual methods are no longer adequate.

The fact that data processing is used to reduce the burden of clerical operations does not simply mean that data processing is a trivial application of computers. The sheer volume of data, in most cases, is a major problem, and to handle that data efficiently is a challenge. For example, a utility for a major city may have more than 500,000 separate accounts.

Another problem involves computer failures. Data processing programs tend to be very long in running, such that a run lasting 12 hours is not unusual. What if the computer fails after 11½ hours? As a means of minimizing the loss in a case such as this, a procedure referred to as "checkpoint" is used. *Checkpoint* refers to the process of saving the status of a job at periodic intervals. Then if the computer fails, the job can be restarted from the latest checkpoint.

PROBLEM SOLVING

The earliest widespread use of computers took place in the areas of scientific and engineering problem solving. This was a normal consequence of the fact that computers were invented and developed by scientifically trained persons who were keenly interested in the computational processes of the central processing unit. The concern for data management and the problems of business and government on a large-scale basis came later in time.

Currently, problem-solving activities with the aid of the computer are not restricted to science and engineering and now encompass business, education, and many other disciplines, such as architecture, medicine, and the humanities. In fact, many problems in this category do not solve a problem but perform a task that lends itself to computers.

A typical engineering problem would be the computation of design parameters for a bridge or a road. Important here is the time factor and the accuracy level. Obviously, engineers have designed and constructed bridges and roads for centuries without the use of computers. With the use of computers, however, the computations can be performed in a very short period of time allowing different design alternatives to be evaluated. Contrary to "semipopular" opinion, computers are extremely accurate,* so that the need for an engineering aid to check calculations is not usually necessary. Accuracy also reduces the amount of redesign that is necessary after construction has begun.

A problem that falls into this category characteristically requires a small amount of input, performs a relatively large number of calculations, and outputs a small number of results. Problems range from simple calculations to complex iterative procedures. A simple problem might be the calculation of compound interest as described by the following formula:

$$V = P(1 + \frac{r}{n})^n$$

where:

P is the principal
r is the interest rate per time period
n is the number of time periods
V is the value of P after n time periods

Similar calculations might be to compute the yield of a bond issue or the predicted size of a herd of cattle after a given number of years.

*Most modern computers include error-checking circuitry to detect errors that occur during computation.

Problem solving encompasses complex problems involving sophisticated concepts in mathematics, statistics, engineering, science, and business. For example, the following equations describe the oxygen deficit of a polluted stream at time t:

$$D_t = \frac{K_d \Lambda_m}{K_i - K_d} \; (10^{-K_d t} - 10^{-K_i t}) + D_o \times 10^{-K_i t}$$

where:

D_t is the oxygen deficit of the stream in mg/liter at time t
K_d is the coefficient of deoxygenation
K_i is the coefficient of reoxygenation
D_o is the initial oxygen deficit in mg/liter
Λ_m is the biochemical oxygen demand for a given mixture of sewage
t is the elapsed time

The key point here is that each of the coefficients must also be calculated and that the calculations are usually performed for varying values of t.

Although textbook problems are usually well defined and the value to be solved for v is readily available, as in:

$$v = f(x,y)$$

many problems in science, engineering, and business take the form:

$$v = f(x,y,v)$$

where the variable to be solved for exists on both sides of the equation and an iterative solution is needed. A common example is Van der Waal's equation for the volume of a gas when the temperature and pressure are known:

$$P + \frac{A}{V^2}(V-B) = RT$$

where:

P is the pressure
T is the absolute temperature
V is the volume—the desired variable
R is the ideal gas constant (0.08205 atm/T)
A and B are constants for the particular gas

This problem requires an iterative solution; that is, successive values of V are calculated until a value that satisfies the equation is found.

Chapters 8 and 9 include a program that uses the quadratic formula for computing the roots of a quadratic equation. Not all equations that we wish to find the root of have well-defined solutions. Figure 10.2 depicts an equation that is assumed not to have a well-defined solution. The root of an equation

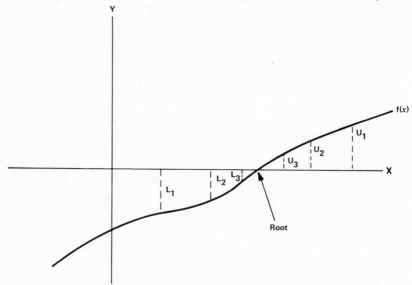

Figure 10.2   The iterative method of interval bisection can be used to calculate the root of the equation.

of this type requires an iterative solution known as "interval bisection." The root of the equation is known to be the point at which the equation $f(x)$ intersects the x-axis. The method of solution successively halves the interval while insuring that $f(L_i)$ and $f(U_i)$ have different signs until a solution with the desired accuracy is reached.

Problems in this category vary in scope and magnitude. Computer programs are used to calculate the trajectory of a space ship from earth orbit to a moon orbit. This is a case of a lot of output for very little input. Data analysis programs, such as those used with the U.S. census, generate a relatively small amount of output in the form of summarized data in response to a tremendous amount of input. In fact, computer programs have been written for practically any problem possessing an algorithmic solution. Programs have been used to calculate the exact ingredients of sausage and to prepare an index for a book. Most of us have even received mail addressed by computer and letters written by the computer.

The dividing line between data processing and problem solving is a fine one. Data processing is characterized by periodic runs involving large amounts of data. Problem solving is characterized by nonperiodic users and a predominance of machine computation. As it turns out, there is no defining characteristic for either category.

MODELS

A *model* is defined as an abstraction of a real-life situation from which we can draw conclusions or make predictions about the future. In a sense, a model is a duplication of a system or subsystem with an emphasis on aspects of interest. Once a model is developed, it is usually more convenient to manipulate the model than work with the actual system. Typical models are the road map and an aerodynamic model used in a wind tunnel.

Models are classified as iconic, analogue, and symbolic. An *iconic model* physically resembles the system it represents; examples are the aerodynamic model, a globe of the world, a photograph, and a blueprint. An *analogue model* establishes a correspondence between a system, subsystem, or variable of a system and an analogous variable in the model. Examples are the bar chart in a sales graph, a schematic, and an electrical analogue. A *symbolic model* uses logic, mathematics, and empirical generalizations (that is, laws of nature) to establish a set of assumptions about a real-life phenomenon from which conclusions can be deduced. Symbolic models are frequently referred to as *mathematical models*, which are the kind used in computer applications.

A familiar mathematical model describes the fall of an object in a vacuum. This law of nature, proposed by Galileo, gives the relationship between distance fallen and time as follows:

$$d = 16t^2$$

If the object is dropped from a height of 10 feet, we can conclude from the model that after one-half second, the object will have fallen 4 feet, or be 6 feet from the ground.

When models are constructed, the determination of the element of the system that needs to be abstracted—or modeled, as they say—is of prime importance. Once a model is developed, its *validity* becomes of immediate concern. In short, it is necessary to know how well the model represents the system being studied.

Symbolic models are used to describe systems and assume the attributes of the system being modeled. When the behavior of a system in response to input conditions can be predicted in advance, then it is classed as a *deterministic system*. When the behavior of a system in response to input conditions can only be predicted within probabilistic limits, then it is classed as a *proba-bilistic system*. Models are classed accordingly and models that represent probabilistic systems use probability theory to establish variables over which the model has no control or are used when the real-life system is sufficiently complicated that it cannot be modeled exactly. Predicting the weather is a good example of the latter. It is well known that the weather system of the world can be described with a set of differential equations. However, the number of variables and equations is so large that today's computers are not fast enough to solve them in the required period of time. As a result, probability is commonly used in weather prediction.

The effective use of models is tricky business. A model used for prediction purposes can be self-fulfilling or self-defeating. A *self-fulfilling prediction* is one that will come true if people believe it and react accordingly. A *self-defeating prediction* is one that will not come true if people believe it and act rationally. An example of a self-fulfilling prediction might occur when economists predict a depression. People who believe the forecast normally respond by reducing spending, payment of debts, and the saving of money so as to better withstand the depression. If enough people believe the prediction and behave in this manner, then the depression will occur. An example of a self-defeating prediction might occur when agriculturists predict a shortage of a certain crop—such as wheat. As a result of the prediction, farmers and food suppliers, expecting high prices for the commodity, would naturally respond by increasing the acreage and production facilities allocated to wheat. Thus, the magnitude of the predicted shortage would be reduced and possibly a surplus would occur.

The utility of a model, therefore, lies not in the mathematics or computer technology involved, but rather in whether or not it led to an effective decision at the time the prediction was made, even if events did not subsequently coincide with the forecast.*

SIMULATION

Simulation is the use of models to obtain the essence of a system without having to develop and test it. One of the most familiar forms of simulation is the "trainers" used to train pilots and astronauts. The objective of such devices is to give the participant experience in a realistic operational environment. A *computer simulation* is a computer model of a real situation; a computer model uses mathematical models, as introduced previously, and computational procedures to achieve a realistic description of a system.

Typical computer simulations involve the description and flow of traffic

*This could be regarded as a form of psychological manipulation.

in a major city, the number of checkout counters needed in a supermarket, and the design specifications of a digital computer. Computer simulation is widely used simply because many processes or systems cannot be described by mathematical equations. However, these same processes or systems can be described with flow diagrams so that a computer program can be written to simulate them. Running the program with various parameters is analogous to the operation of the real system. Thus, a system can be analyzed without having to experiment with real-life situations. Traffic flow in a city is a reasonably good example. In prior years, the traffic commission would establish a one-way street on a trial basis. After a period of time, the change would be evaluated. In the event of a poor design, people had to suffer during the period in which it was being evaluated. With simulation, the traffic flow can be simulated; when a good design is achieved, then the physical implementation can be made.

Simulation is frequently used for convenience, to reduce costs, for training, and for developing competitive strategies. Currently we have simulations of the U.S. economy, sociopolitical simulations of the world, simulations of various companies, and competitive simulations of the marketplace for various consumer products. Many schools employ simulations to train managers and executives.

FEEDBACK AND CONTROL

The terms feedback and control are almost self-explanatory. The most common example of a feedback and control system is the combination of automobile and driver. The output of the system is the path of the automobile; the driver provides the objective of the system and receives "road information" as input. The driver provides control signals to the automobile, as required. Another common example of a feedback and control system is the heating system found in most homes. The thermostat serves as the control mechanism. Output of the system is the heat produced by the furnace. The automobile-driver system is referred to as an *open system* because of the driver in the feedback loop. The heating system is referred to as a *closed system*, because it can operate without human intervention.

In computer control systems, the computer serves as the control mechanism. A typical application might be the control of temperature, among other things, in a chemical process. The chemical-processing equipment contains sensing devices that send signals to an analog-to-digital converter, which serves as an input device to the computer. The computer is programmed to sample the input signals on a periodic basis and compare the values against prescribed limits. If the temperature is too high or too low, the computer generates appropriate output signals to achieve the desired result. The output signal is converted to analog form and serves as input to a control mechanism that is part of the chemical process. The above process is depicted conceptually in Figure 10.3. In actual applications, the monitoring of hundreds

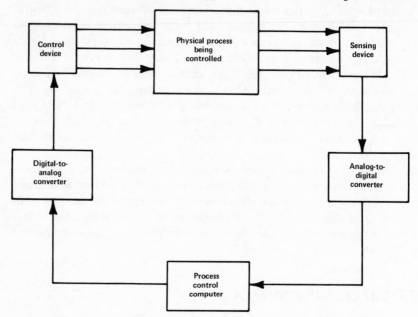

Figure 10.3 Feedback and control system using a digital computer as a control mechanism.

of input signals is not unusual. This application of computers is referred to as *process control*; the technology is widely used in applications that range from control of space vehicles to control of a sewage disposal plant.

Computers are also used in manufacturing engineering through a concept known as *numerical control*. Using conventional machining techniques, the production of a precision part is a time-consuming and costly process. Moreover, successive pieces produced by the same machinist vary in precision, within given tolerance limits, due to human limitations. When using numerical control, a machinist/mathematician, known as a part programmer, describes the piece to be machined in a computer-oriented language. The description of the piece in that language is known as a part program. The machine tool used to machine the part is directed by a control system that accepts signals from the computer and guides the machine tool accordingly. There are two modes of operation. In the on-line mode, the computer is connected directly to the control system. In the off-line mode, a punched tape is produced by the computer and the tape is read by the control system to guide the machine tool.

The advantages of numerical control are that identical parts can be machined by using the same part program and that the techniques are appropriate for high-volume production. Numerical control is widely used in the aerospace industry for producing high-precision structural components on a high-volume production basis.

ON-LINE AND REAL-TIME SYSTEMS

An on-line system is one in which the computer communicates directly with a component external to the computer—regardless of whether that component is a person using a terminal device via telecommunications facilities or is a control system of an independent physical process. The term *real time* refers to two things. In simulation, there is the time of the problem (that is, the time in the system being modeled) and there is the clock time in which the computer executes the simulation program. The clock time is known as real time. The second kind of real time occurs in physical processes or on-line systems in which it is necessary for the computer to respond within time limits in order that the results will be useful in the real world. Thus, an on-line real-time system is analogous in concept to a time-sharing system.

As far as implementation of an on-line real-time system is concerned, the system may be "dedicated" or it may be a time-sharing or multiprogramming system. If the system is *dedicated* to the on-line real-time application, then contention with other jobs for the resources of the computer system is not normally of concern. Problems still arise, however, because many devices that must be serviced in a prescribed period of time usually exist. In a time-sharing or real-time system, an on-line real-time application is serviced by interrupting the executing program on a temporary or permanent basis in order that the real-time requirements of the on-line system can be satisfied.

Two common examples of on-line real-time systems are the airline reservation system and the savings bank system. In an airline reservation system, a central computer records passenger reservation information for scheduled flights. When a customer requests space accommodations, the central computer is queried via a specially built terminal device and telecommunications facilities to determine if the requested facilities are available. If the customer makes a reservation, the amount of remaining available space on the aircraft is reduced and the customer's data is recorded. In a system of this type, the requirements are such that the computer must respond within a specified period (for example, 10 seconds or less) in order to insure customer satisfaction. Flight records, which change dynamically as reservations are made and canceled, must be stored on direct-access storage devices in order to meet the real-time requirements of the application.

In a savings bank system, customer records are stored on direct-access devices at a central computer. Teller stations (that is, input/output terminal devices) are located in each branch of the bank. As deposits, withdrawals, and so on, are made, each transaction is recorded in the customer's records at the time the transaction is made. As a result, banking facilities are available at all times to all customers at all bank branches.

Relatively large on-line systems, such as the airline reservation system and the savings bank system mentioned above, are frequently implemented as dedicated systems because of the volume of transactions and the real-time response requirements. An example of a system that is much smaller in scope might be an inventory control system oriented to the marketing function. Salesmen would use portable terminals. Prior to the completion of each sale, the salesman would query the inventory system to verify that the needed merchandise is available. If the merchandise is available, then the transaction is recorded and the inventory is reduced accordingly. In general, the volume of input in a system of this type would be relatively low, and the program would probably be designed to operate as a high-priority job in a multiprogramming system or on a small computer dedicated to the inventory function.

INFORMATION SYSTEMS

An *information system* is a set of hardware, software, and informational facilities that permits the accumulation, classification, storage, and retrieval of large amounts of information. An information system not only stores data, but also provides facilities for assigning meaning to data—hence, information. The scope and complexity of information systems vary from a deck of punched cards to comprehensive library retrieval systems.

An information system consists of three major components:

1. A large repository for data—called a data base.
2. A means of accessing the data.
3. A means of processing the data for analysis and reports.

A *data base* is defined as a collection of physical data that are related to each other in a prescribed manner. For example, a data base may be the total collection of data known to be in a business, or it may be a central record of all known criminals in a major city. The key point is that all pertinent data is available through a central facility and that access to the facility provides the latest information.

A data base is an adjunct to a conventional large-scale computer system that includes conventional data management, data communications, and job-processing facilities. The scope of an information system is conceptualized in Figure 10.4. The use of a data base is not restricted to on-line systems; a data base serves as a central "data bank" for all users of the computer facility.

The manner in which data are organized in an information system is dependent on the needs of the computer applications that use the system. For example, an information system may contain documents that are retrieved by author, title, or key words; or it may contain customer data (for a data processing application) that is accessed sequentially or by account number.

Information systems are frequently accessed by people that are not computer professionals. Sometimes a query language is used so that an informational request of the form:

IN FILE ALPHA-3
IF AGE>30 AND MALE AND MARRIED
LIST NAME, ADDRESS, EMPLOYEE-NO, YEARS-OF-SERVICE

is entered to retrieve information from the system. Usually, an input request with this general form is interpreted by a program written for that purpose operating in a time-sharing or multiprogramming environment. The program scans the input lines, determines the information required, retrieves the information, and displays it for the user. This is an example of the current trend in information systems. An experienced group of systems analysts and programmers develops a system and a language that can be used by nonprofessional people. The language is frequently "made up" to suit the needs of *that* particular application.

The implications are of course far-reaching. Once a system is developed, practically anyone can use it—and with ease. Thus, safeguards must be implemented to prevent unauthorized people from using the system, and special precautions must be taken to insure the integrity of the data stored in the information system. Several characteristics that are used to describe data in a "desirable" information system are: accuracy, timeliness, completeness, conciseness, and relevancy.

The major difficulty with information systems is obvious from the above discussion. The technical problems can easily be solved. Matters of access, control, and the information that goes into the system are the responsibility of the organization.

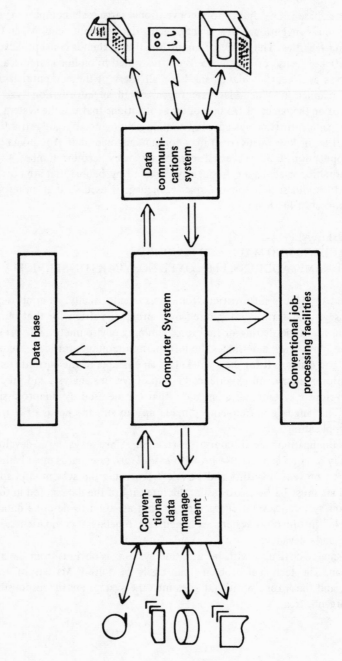

Figure 10.4 The scope of an information system.

ARTIFICIAL INTELLIGENCE

The question "Can a machine think?" is one that has been debated for some time now and is not likely to be answered in this book. However, the subject is fruitful from the point of view of "what the computer can do."

There are various opinions on the subject. Some people say that thinking is an activity that is peculiar to human beings; therefore, machines cannot think. Although thought as something unique to human beings may have been in the minds of philosophers when they first considered the subject of thinking and intelligence, this definition gets us nowhere. Other people maintain that a machine is thinking when it is performing activities that normally require thought when performed by human beings. Thus, adding 2 and 2 must be considered a form of thinking. To continue, some psychologists have defined intelligence as "what an intelligence test measures." In light of the preceding section on information systems, all we need to do is feed enough information into an information system and develop an appropriate query language and we have an intelligent machine. This line of reasoning also gets us nowhere. Perhaps we are wasting our time, but the fact remains that computers are doing some amazing things, such as playing chess, guiding robots, controlling space ships, recognizing patterns, proving theorems, and answering questions, and these applications require much more than the conventional computer program.

Hamming [34] gives a definition of *intelligent behavior* that is useful to our needs:

The ability to act in suitable ways when presented with a class of situations that have not been exhaustively analyzed in advance, but which require rather different combinations of responses if the result in many specific cases is to be acceptable.

The importance of the subject lies in the direction in which society seems to be going. Currently, we use machines for two reasons: (1) The job cannot be done by a human being; and (2) the job can be done more economically by machine. To this list, we must add another entry. Some jobs are simply too dull to be done by humans, and it is desirable from a social point of view to have it done by machine. For this, we require more "intelligent" machines since we seem to be moving outward on a continuum of what we consider to be dull and routine behavior.

Computers are presently used for game playing, theorem proving, symbolic mathematics, question answering, pattern recognition, problem solving, learning and concept formation, and decision making. Although the methods differ widely, one thread seems to run through much of the methodology employed. It is the *problem-reduction* approach that is characterized by the fact that a problem is systematically reduced to subproblems. A solution to a particular subset of the subproblems implies a solution to the original problem. Nilsson [43] gives the example of the problem of driving an automobile from Palo Alto, California, to Cambridge, Massachusetts. The problem could be reduced to the following four subproblems:

1. Drive from Palo Alto to San Francisco
2. Drive from San Francisco to Chicago
3. Drive from Chicago to New York
4. Drive from New York to Cambridge

In this case, solutions to all four subproblems imply a solution to the original problem.

One of the techniques frequently used in artificial intelligence is the strategy tree (or game tree, as it is sometimes called). A complete representation of all possible outcomes of a problem is recorded in a strategy tree; as the problem unfolds, a path is made through the tree. In effect, the branches of the tree at any point in the problem solution denote the options that are available. The technique is best demonstrated by an example. Consider the *game of eight* with the following rules:

1. There are two players.
2. Each player alternates in choosing a number from the set 1, 2, 3 and adding it to a running sum.
3. The first player can choose any of the numbers 1, 2, 3.
4. For each play after the first, a player may not choose his opponent's preceding selection.
5. A player who brings the running sum to 8 wins the game. The player who exceeds 8 loses.

A complete strategy tree for the game of eight is given in Figure 10.5.* One play of the game is represented by one complete path from start to finish. In an artificial intelligence environment, a decision rule would normally be associated with each node, or a general decision rule would be associated with a specific set of nodes, so that the computer can decide which choice to make. This process is frequently referred to as *goal seeking*.

---

*The game of eight is a classic example of the use of strategy trees. A particularly good introductory treatment of game trees and nonnumerical applications is given in Forsythe *et al* [7], pp. 376–378 and pp. 438–444.

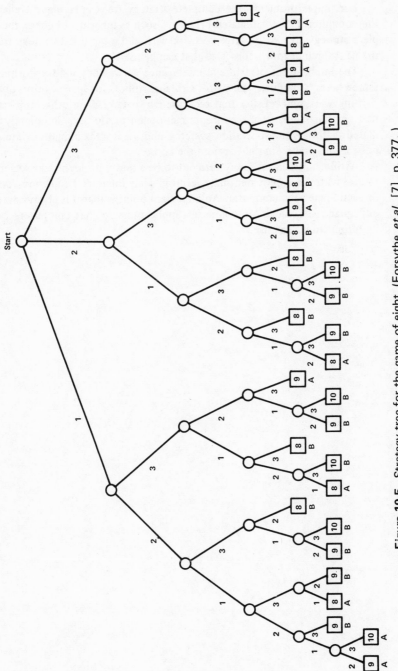

Figure 10.5 Strategy tree for the game of eight. (Forsythe, *et al.* [7], p. 377.)

For simple problems, the complete strategy tree can be made available to the computer. For complicated problems, such as the game of chess, the complete strategy tree is too large to work with and a modified strategy tree for the next three or four nodes is all that can be used.

The implications of artificial intelligence go well beyond the notions presented here. "Computer" pilots for airplanes, robots for space exploration and fighting wars, and missiles that seek their own targets are other applications that combine some of the concepts mentioned previously. Completely automated factories, transportation systems, and medical examinations are other possibilities that seem right around the corner.

Artificial intelligence may turn out to be a messy problem that society has to deal with. Unemployment may result in some quarters. People may distrust or even "hate" the computer. An important point is that it is always better to understand the scope of computer applications so that computers can be better put to human use.

CHAPTER 11

Computers in Organizations

INTRODUCTION

We live in a society dominated by organizations such as businesses, governmental agencies, schools, churches, hospitals, and various social agencies. Most of us belong to more than one organization. An organization is a system; the resources of the system are people, capital, machines, buildings, and so forth. Thus, the resources of an organization are analogous to the components of a system. The various components of the system communicate through information.

Organizations are the primary users of computers. Historically, business has led the way in the use of computers because of the profit motive and because some businesses, such as banks and insurance companies, are essentially information-processing organizations. Currently, most organizations—large or small —use computers. If an organization lacks qualified personnel or finances, it can now share common computing facilities with another organization or have its computing services performed by a computer service company. Many banks, for example, perform payroll services for their customers on a regular basis.

The advantages of computers to the organization have been implied previously:

1. Additional information has become available
2. Information can be made available more quickly
3. Information is more inclusive and accurate
4. Information can be presented in a form that is more useful to the decision maker or the administrator.

Other than problem-solving activities, performed by scientists, engineers, and analysts, and routine data processing, the greatest benefit of computers to organizations occurs in three areas: planning, decision making, and controlling. The precise techniques tend to vary between organizations but generally involve optimization, simulation, prediction, scheduling, and measurement of organizational performance.

When computers are used extensively in organizations, there seems to be a tendency toward *centralization of authority*. Centralization or decentralization is a matter of degree rather than an absolute concept. In organizations that employ decentralization as an operating technique, decisions are made by lower-level administrative or management personnel because of time, distance, and familiarity with the factors affecting the decision. Through the effective use of computer facilities, higher administrative and management personnel can participate in local decision making to a greater extent because they can be supplied with appropriate information in a shorter period of time.

The use of computers does not imply centralization, and the lack of computers does not imply decentralization. Other factors affecting the situation are the size of the organization, management philosophy, physical facilities, the organization growth, and the type of business the company is in. To sum up, the use of computers provides the practical means for centralization—regardless of whether or not an organization decides to go in that direction. However, the use of computers does require organizational changes in both structure and everyday operation. Changes normally occur in the following areas:

1. Departments engaged in data processing
2. Departments engaged in informational services
3. Service departments using computer services
4. Organization and training departments
5. The computer department itself
6. Higher administrative levels that support the computer function

The computer department is and will continue to be a problem to most organizations because operators, programmers, analysts, and capable managers are at present in short supply. On the other side of the coin, the computer department is a good source of quality personnel for the organization. The perseverence necessary to become a good programmer is a valuable trait that can be applied well to other organizational occupations. The typical systems analyst knows a great deal about an organization and is always a prime candidate for promotion into administrative or management positions. Similarly, the data processing manager, because of his managerial and technical background, is frequently picked for an executive position.

Through the years, a sort of mystique has been built up around programmers. Some of the traits attributed to programmers are that they are prima donnas, self-centered, egotistical, hard to work with, and unstable. While this may be true in some research laboratories, overall they seem to have pretty much the same temperament as the average engineer, accountant, or business analyst. Programmers, taking the country as a whole over the last 15 years, have changed jobs more than the average. This is probably because jobs were and are plentiful and a raise in pay usually accompanies a change in jobs. Recently, job changes among programmers have slowed down somewhat and programmers now enjoy an improved status in most organizations. Another factor influencing the turnover of all computer personnel is the lack of a career path that previously existed in *most* organizations. This is another area in which substantial improvement has been made but more is definitely needed.

Another benefit of computers to organizations is standardization. In many cases, the interface between departments is ill defined and the organization essentially operates through informal organizational procedures. Before a computer can be used in a system, that system is usually described in detail and subsequently formalized. Many organizations have benefited considerably from the process of studying how they actually operate. The standardization of reports and time schedules has also helped organizations realize the scope of information that is and can be made available to them.

BUSINESS

The biggest uses of computers in business are in the areas of problem solving and data processing. This has been mentioned previously. Analysts, scientists, and engineers are able to use the computer for numerical calculations and have expanded their functional capabilities to a considerable degree. Data processing is used for operations that involve routine logic and mathematics but require the same processing to be applied to a great many similar transactions. Utility billing, payroll, dividend checks, and inventory records are examples of areas that utilize data processing methods. In addition, many information service companies use computers to provide immediate service to their customers. For example, service companies now exist that will verify the validity of a credit card. To verify a credit card, the businessman makes a toll-free call to the service company, which verifies that the card is neither lost, stolen, or expired. If the card turns out to be "bad," then the service company is held responsible for the charges. Without verification, the acceptance of a "bad" credit card becomes the responsibility of the businessman. Other services, called "information banks," store large amounts of information for use by customers on a demand basis via telecommunications facilities. Computer service companies are regarded as special cases, since their product is essentially the computer.

Businesses that limit their use of the computer to problem solving and data processing, however, tend to gain less from their computer than those that attempt to integrate the computer into the total business system. In other words, information systems should not be justified solely on the basis of cost reduction, but also on the basis of how management can benefit from the increased information.

Essentially, we are talking about a *management information system,* frequently referred to as an MIS. The objective of an MIS is to provide a means for the information of a business to be integrated and dynamically updated so that it can be used for planning, decision making, and control purposes. Conceptually, an MIS is an on-line real-time information system consisting of the following components, facilities, or resources:

1. A centralized *data base* consisting of an integrated set (or subset) of company files.
2. A comprehensive set of data on the company, its operating structure, and the competitive environment.
3. The capability for retrieving data from the data base for analysis and reporting.
4. A set of planning models for use in prediction and planning activities.
5. A set of control models that can be used to monitor performance of the company.
6. A set of decision models to be used for decision making, using the information in the data base.

No one attribute or collection of attributes defines a management information system. Such a system seems to be more of a commitment to the concept of an integrated business system than a set of physical facilities.

Planning is the most widely developed area in which management information systems are used. Planning is known to exist at three organizational levels:

1. *Long-range planning* to develop organizational objectives, establish corporate goals, and set corporate policies.
2. *Tactical planning* to make efficient use of resources, such as money, machines, and men.
3. *Operational planning* to develop alternatives for specific functions or products.

The information necessary for planning is derived from competitive analysis, market research, internal statistics, and from known operational characteristics of the company.

Long-range planning frequently involves the financial status of the organization and its relationship to the business environment. National economic forecasts and political information are frequently used at this level to establish a sound basis for decisions. Information is usually made available to executives in the form of reports.

Tactical planning frequently involves market analysis, competitive strategies, and statistical analysis. Predictions are often used to orient the company and its product line.

Operational planning usually involves optimization and data analysis techniques to organize daily activities. Delivery schedules, trucking routes, and purchase orders are frequently developed by computer because of the number of independent variables involved.

Operational planning is closely related to *decision making* that uses the computer to develop and evaluate alternatives. Statistics and simulation are frequently used for selecting courses of action for the business to follow at each of the above levels of planning.

Computers serve control purposes in businesses in two principal ways: (1) As a means of controlling how the company operates—such as savings bank, credit, and inventory systems; and (2) as a means of measuring performance and alerting appropriate people to "unusual" conditions that need attention. Operation of an organization has been discussed previously. Performance measurement is usually achieved through periodic reports and specific informational requests. This is an area in which a management information system is invaluable. When information is needed for a decision at one of the planning levels, an analysis can be made from the central data base—often within hours when an on-line real-time system is used.

Systems that alert man against the "unusual" conditions are still in their infancy but offer great potential for the future. The basic idea is this. A *business information and control system* is used into which all planning, operational, environmental, and competitive data is entered and maintained on a continual basis—day to day or hour to hour. Routine decisions, such as when to reorder supplies or raw materials, are made by the computer and the departments involved are informed automatically. The computer essentially operates the business by keeping track of *all* information and by making routine decisions. Since the computer serves only a control function, the outward appearance of the business is the same. Many routine clerical jobs, such as ordering pencils, are eliminated and the people are moved into information-gathering positions. Top management has more time to allocate to planning and less time is needed for day-to-day operations. Thus, the human being is doing what he can do best—planning—and the computer is employed in its best capacity—routine operations. The use of this type of control system may be accompanied by a gradual shift in middle management from managing products and resources to managing people.

One of the key features in a business information and control system is that at any point in time, any item of information worth knowing about business is stored in the computer, and it can be accessed by authorized people.

GOVERNMENT AND LAW

One of the major functions of government is to meet the needs of society—whatever they are—and most governmental officials can attest to the fact that it is impossible to please everyone. However, the problems are deeper than that. First, it is difficult to determine what programs are needed and to assess appropriate priorities. Second, it is difficult to determine what has been done. Third, it is impossible to tell if a program is successful until it is past the point of no return in terms of finance and time. And last, it is difficult to manage a governmental agency that is characteristically understaffed and underfinanced.* In the past, governmental officials frequently used the method of "incremental change" for decision making. The *method of incremental change* involves making a small change in a given direction. If the reaction to it is favorable, then another small change in the same direction is made, and so forth. If the reaction to the incremental change is not favorable or if funds for the project dry up, then it is relatively easy to back up and make an effort in a different direction. This description is overly simplified, obviously, but it illustrates an important point. Significant changes often extend over unreasonably long periods of time, which is frustrating to the populace and to the administrator himself. The use of the computer in government has helped alleviate this problem somewhat.

The single biggest user of computers in the United States is the federal government. The objective of most computers installed in the government is increased productivity through information systems. Sanders [49] lists the benefits of information systems to government planners as:

1. The capability with which to make better plans and decisions
2. The capability with which to improve operating efficiency
3 The capability with which to better serve society

*There is almost universal disagreement on this point. However, most governmental administrators will attest to the fact that resources never seem to be sufficient to do the job as it should be done.

There are also some fringe benefits of computers in government. Computers are often regarded as capital expenditures by the government and are not charged to the budget of a particular agency. Thus, the administrator of that agency is given the capability of doing a better job without a significant increase in budgetary expenditures if he decides to utilize computers. The computer has also helped many administrators with their human relations. We live in a socially conscious society, similar in concept to the economically conscious society that existed after the depression of the 1930s. In economics, we have developed a variety of economic indicators, such as the gross national product, that give us an idea of the health of the economy. Although social indicators are not in widespread use among the citizenry, statistical data, available through information systems, has aided many governmental agencies in assessing how well they are serving the needs of society.

Federal Government

It is nearly impossible and certainly impractical to list all of the uses of computers in the federal government. Moreover, many of the applications are either classified for national security or generally not available to the general public. A sampling of computer applications is given in the following paragraphs.

Internal Revenue Service. The agency best known to the average citizen for its computer capability is the IRS. Through the years, the use of computers has reduced the occurrences of "tax cheating" and has substantially increased revenues. The IRS has a network of regional centers and a national center that employ computers. Computers are used to verify the arithmetic on returns and to cross-check reports from employers and banks on income, withholdings, interest, and dividends with actual declarations. Estimated tax as well as name changes, moves from one region to another, and so forth, are also processed. Most IRS regional centers use key-to-tape or key-to-disk systems for data entry from returns, and reports and information are normally available to auditing personnel through CRT-type terminal devices. Regional centers submit tax records to the national center where a record is kept for each taxpayer. (There are 80 million taxpayers and tax-paying entities in the United States.) Tax refunds, delinquent notices, and bills are made through the national center. The computer is also used for auditing purposes. Through the years, IRS personnel have developed criteria with the greatest audit potential. For example, if medical deductions were greater than 70 percent of a taxpayer's income, the computer might signal that the return might be worth looking into. (This, by the way, is an example that is made purposely ridiculous so as not to be interpreted as a fact.) It has been conjectured, but by no means substantiated, that one of the benefits of tax preparation firms is that they supposedly know the limits that can be deducted, and so forth, in each category. It has also been conjectured that these same companies use their customers as guinea pigs to determine what these limits are.

Census Bureau. In the most recent census (1970), the U.S. Bureau of the Census collected and processed information on 205 million people living in the United States. Although the 1970 census resulted in minor criticism because of the personal questions involved, the facts are used to allocate federal funds and to realign the boundaries of congressional districts. The Census Bureau has elaborate procedures to insure the privacy of individual data—even to the extent that they insure that the number of people involved in a sample is large enough to insure individual privacy. Census data is available to researchers, but only after it has been processed to remove any personal information.

Military. The military is another relatively large user of computers in five general areas: the Defense Supply Agency, space observations (that is, satellites), weapon systems, command and control systems, and the area of strategic decision making. The Defense Supply Agency, which is a consolidated source of supplies for all of the services, maintains centralized records on 1.5 million different items. It has been called the world's biggest supermarket. The Air Force SPADATS program, for Space Detection and Tracking System, keeps track of all manmade objects in space. It uses a network of observation stations to detect new objects and verify the existence of old ones. Computers are used in most weapon systems for guidance and trajectory computations. For example, once a ballistic missile is launched, a computer keeps track of its location. Command and control systems use a vast network of radar stations and computers to insure the integrity of United States airspace. Radar data from observed aircraft is entered directly into computers for comparison against flight patterns. If unusual events are detected, strategic forces are alerted. In the area of decision making, computers are used to keep track of ships, planes, and men, and to perform complex statistical analyses regarding military actions. Mobile computers are used in the field, on board ships, and in planes, whenever computational power is needed. Push-button war is largely fiction and local commanders are incorporated into the decision-making loop whenever possible. Simulation techniques are widely used in the military for gaining analytical and decision-making experience through the use of war games, which include both tactical and logistic aspects of a military conflict.

Computers are also used in: (1) The Veterans Administration to process the paperwork associated with hospital, educational, and insurance benefits; (2) the Treasury Department to issue government checks; (3) the Food and Drug Administration to process new drug applications; (4) the Labor Department to assist in the job placement; (5) the Weather Bureau for forecasts of periods up to 30 days; (6) the U.S. Postal Service to speed up postal service with automatic scanners and sorters; and (7) the Social Security Administration for processing earning records and deductions, routine monthly payments, and Medicare and Medicaid systems. The Social Security Administration uses 27 computers and is the largest single computer installation in the world.

Congress. One of the areas of the government that is suffering most from "information overload" is the legislative branch. The computer is needed by legislators to keep track of pending legislation and to assess the needs of their constituents. For example, the 89th Congress considered over 26,000 bills and in the 90th Congress, over 29,000 pieces of legislation were introduced. Legislation has been introduced in the U.S. Congress for an information system for Congress. Other proposals include an electronic voting system and an on-line real-time system that would have access to all federal data bases. At this time, at least five state legislatures (Florida, Hawaii, New York, North Carolina, and Pennsylvania) provide their members with computerized reports on pending bills and other legislative data.

Courts and Law

A major problem that has accompanied the increasing crime rate in the country is the backlog of pending court cases. Persons accused of crimes often have to wait in jail for months—when bail is not available—and in addition to the personal injustices involved, these cases cause overcrowding of jails and a burden to the taxpayers. In both criminal and civil cases, details of the cases are often forgotten by witnesses before the cases come to court. Several states and cities use computers for court administration to keep track of backlogged cases, prepare trial calendars, generate subpoenas and notices to prisoners, and prepare status reports so that lawyers can plan their own schedules accordingly. Another area in which computers have been used successfully is in jury selection.

Although lawyers have been relatively slow to use the computer, many law firms now use computer services for billing, accounting, tax and estate computations, and for legal information retrieval. In the latter case, the computer is used to search for legal precedents. The lawyer, using a terminal device, enters data on his case. The computer searches through voluminous information and generates referrals to specific cases that can be used as legal precedents.

Local Government

The computer has been a boon to state and local governments that are forced by their very nature to deal with messy social problems. Some typical state and local problems are: transportation planning, real estate assessment and tax, water and air pollution, urban and land-use planning, social welfare management, and a variety of other "headaches" such as pest control, pet licenses, and road repair. Transportation, urban, and land-use planning activities frequently use simulation, as discussed in the previous chapter. Computers are also used to prepare land assessments and tax bills and to generate reminders and daily work lists for a variety of other state and local governmental functions.

Computers have helped several welfare programs considerably, especially in large municipalities where a welfare recipient can register at more than one regional center. In New York City, for example, one welfare recipient was eventually caught after receiving welfare checks for several years from different welfare centers in three of New York's five boroughs.

With the current concern over pollution, control computers have been used to improve on the efficiency of various facilities. Recent applications involve the monitoring of a power generating station, controlling a sewage treatment plant, and controlling traffic lights. Traffic control by computer has great potential for the years to come. By controlling traffic lights to meet the needs of the traffic at any point in time, congestion, travel times, and air pollutants are reduced.

Police and Criminal Systems

We live in a mobile society through the use of automobiles, airplanes, trains, and buses. Criminals also benefit from the same advantages, and in the past, all one had to do was "blow town"—as they say—and he was relatively free. The Federal Bureau of Investigation has reduced the problem considerably with its National Crime Information Center (NCIC), which is an on-line real-time computerized information network. The NCIC system stores the arrest records of people and information on wanted persons and stolen property. Local and state law enforcement personnel can query the NCIC system to obtain information on a subject that warrants further investigation.

The Justice Department has also gotten into the act through its Law Enforcement Assistance Administration (LEAA). LEAA has a $7 million research project, called Project SEARCH (System for Electronic Analysis and Retrieval of Criminal Histories), to produce a nationwide on-line information network for exchanging criminal histories. Eventually, local, state, and federal agencies are expected to use the SEARCH system.

Many states have now computerized their motor vehicle registration and driver's license facilities so they can be accessed by state agencies and local police to obtain the name of the owner of an automobile and verify the validity of a registration or a driver's license.

In addition to being connected to the NCIC information system, many state, county, and local law enforcement agencies have information systems of their own. Notable examples of systems that have achieved some degree of success are the Law Enforcement Information Network (LEIN) at Michigan State headquarters in East Lansing, the California Law Enforcement Telecommunications System (CLETS), the Chicago "hot desk" system, the New York State Identification and Intelligence System, and the County Law Enforcement Applied Regionally (CLEAR) system, developed in Cincinnati and Hamilton counties of Ohio and adopted elsewhere. Law enforcement systems of this type are accessed via telecommunications facilities in the station house, the patrol car, or both. From a patrol car, requests are normally radioed to an operator manning a terminal device. The operator, who is experienced at querying the information system, can normally respond in less than a minute to the police officer. Terminals in patrol cars have been implemented for some systems, but it is difficult to tell at this point whether they were installed after a thorough systems analysis or as the result of an aggressive equipment salesman.

Politics

Computers have even been used in political campaigns, vote counting, and election-night broadcasting. The first major political figure to use computers was John F. Kennedy prior to the 1960 presidential election. The Kennedy campaign staff built a model of the voting public from sample data obtained from a public opinion polling company. The model was used to evaluate strategies for dealing with campaign issues—one of which was that Kennedy, if elected, would be the country's first Catholic president. The eventual strategy worked out with the aid of the model was to approach the problem head on rather than sidestepping the issue.

In general, computers are used in political campaigning in two principal ways: (1) As a means of doing routine clerical operations; and (2) as a means of analyzing voter characteristics. In the first category, typical operations are:

1. The compilation and maintenance of voter names, addresses, and voting preferences.
2. The preparation of address labels for mailing campaign literature.
3. The preparation of special appearance letters—generated by computer.
4. Selection of voters from the mailing list (operation 1) that are sensitive to a particular campaign issue so that they can be sent special campaign literature or so that they can be omitted from the mailing of literature sensitive to them.
5. The management of campaign contributors, potential and actual, of campaign funds.

Typical operations in the second category are:

1. Analysis of voters by geographical area taking into consideration income level, ethnic group, past voting habits, race, religion, and a variety of other political factors.
2. Correlations of political issues with geographical areas identified in operation 1.
3. Assessment and prediction of voter behavior through simulation and other modeling techniques.

These and similar techniques were used in Winthrop Rockefeller's campaign for governor of Arkansas in 1966 and Robert Griffin's campaign for senator from Michigan in the same year.

Vote counting is an area in which computers have fared rather poorly. The basic objective, of course, is to have complete election results shortly after the polls close in a voting district. In fact, IBM, the world's largest computer builder, formerly marketed a vote-counting machine that accepted specially punched cards as input. However, late and controversial tabulations in several localities have caused computerized vote counting to be viewed with distrust, and at least 11 states have outlawed the concept completely.

Most of us are familiar with election-night TV reporting where a candidate is declared the winner by the computer after only a small percentage of the vote is in. Almost without exception, the eventual vote count proves the computer to be correct. How is it done? Primarily, predictions are made with statistical techniques and historical voting patterns of that district. The basic thinking behind the methods goes somewhat as follows: If a certain percentage of the voters vote a certain way, there is a given probability that the remaining voters will vote that way also; the prediction is made by putting the two percentages together.

MEDICINE

As a society, we are entering a crisis period as far as medical and health care are concerned; perhaps we are already in one. Services are becoming increasingly expensive, and as an affluent society, we have come to expect better and better care. Lastly, the medical sciences have become exceedingly complex to the extent that available knowledge doubles every five to 10 years. Thus, medical people must know more; we expect more; and services in general are expected to cost more. Increased medical costs are not limited to medical treatment, per se, but are also the result of expanded administrative services—such as hospital drug control, blood bank inventory control, and the control of laboratory tests. It is expected that the effective use of computers in medicine will help reduce or at least help control rising costs and aid medical people in providing better medical and health care.

Dorf [32] lists the primary application of computers in the field of medicine and health services as:

1. Monitoring a patient's condition
2. Storing a patient's medical record
3. Assisting in the diagnosis of diseases
4. Maintaining central information systems

It is important to add to this list the widespread use of computers in medical education and research, and in hospital administration.

Patient Monitoring

The most dramatic use of computers in medicine is in the area of patient monitoring. Control computers are frequently used in intensive-care units to monitor the condition of patients after a severe operation, such as open-heart surgery. The computer monitors and records the patient's heart rate, blood pressure, temperature, and fluid drainage. Obviously, the computer does not perform the monitoring, per se, but controls a variety of sensing and recording equipment that performs the required services. A single computer can monitor hundreds of postoperative patients. The computer is programmed to detect unusual conditions and to administer medication and blood infusions.

Central computers are also used to screen electrocardiograms, so that a patient can receive an electrocardiogram and have it analyzed in less than a minute. Normally, the computer can screen several electrocardiograms at one time.

Medical Records

Physicians are notoriously good at doctoring and notoriously bad at paperwork (and writing). The fact that people move frequently and change doctors only compounds the problem. The information about a patient is recorded, either from written records or with a terminal device, in a centralized medical information system. Medical personnel with the proper authority can retrieve specific facts about a patient, or even his entire medical profile. In today's age of specialization, a patient's records could be scattered among several doctor's offices. With the centralized system, a complete medical history of a patient is available to allow doctors to provide more effective medical treatment.

A recent innovation in medical recording is referred to as "Automated Medical Recording." The method uses computer-administered questioning so that an examination can be tailored to the characteristics of the patient. The physician uses a CRT-type terminal device. Questions are presented on the screen; depending on the question, either the physician, the nurse, or the patient can respond.

Some of the advantages of a centralized medical information system are that records can be analyzed for diseases without outward symptoms that might go unrecognized by doctor or patient and for the early detection of epidemics.

Clinical Decision Making and Treatment

In a book on statistical decision analysis, Raiffa [45] gives a "simple" decision that must be made by a doctor. The doctor does not know whether a patient's sore throat is caused by strep or a virus. If he knew it were strep, he would prescribe penicillin; if he knew it were caused by a virus, he would pre-scribe rest, gargle, and aspirin. Failure to treat a strep throat with medication might result in a serious disease—such as rheumatic heart disease. On the other hand, penicillin should not be prescribed indiscriminately because of a pos-sible reaction or the development of penicillin-resistant bacteria. The doctor could take a throat culture; however, the bacteria could die before the analysis is complete and the presence of streptococci does not guarantee that they are causing the sore throat. The doctor has several possibilities:

1. Take no culture; treat sore throat as viral.
2. Take no culture; treat sore throat as strep.
3. Take no culture; prescribe penicillin for 10 days.
4. Take culture; prescribe penicillin if positive.
5. Take culture and prescribe penicillin; continue penicillin if positive and discontinue if negative.

And a sore throat is regarded as a simple problem!

Dorf lists the four basic steps in diagnosis as:

1. Obtain patient's condition through examination and history.
2. Evaluate the relative importance of the various symptoms.
3. Consider all diseases with similar symptoms and systematically elimi-nate diseases until an appropriate disease category is found.

The computer is used to store all diseases and their symptoms, thereby elimi-nating one of the sources of possible error. In a *clinical decision support system*, the physician uses the computer in an interactive mode for systemati-cally analyzing a decision tree that is constructed from a particular set of symptoms. In the event of multiple diseases, the computer can assist the physician, through modeling and optimization techniques, to determine the best treatment plan.

Clinical support systems are not in widespread use, but it is difficult to determine if the situation is a result of the fact that few systems exist, or because physicians do not want to use them.

Medical Information Systems

Medical information systems encompass two functions: medical record keeping, mentioned previously, and hospital accounting and control systems. It is estimated that approximately 25 percent of all hospital costs are for accounting, billing, medicare and medicaid systems, and for a variety of other clerical and administrative functions. Conventional data processing facilities are usually sufficient for patient accounting; however, many hospitals have gone to on-line real-time systems. Small hospitals frequently share a common hospital accounting system.

Computers have helped enormously in the administration of hospitals and medical centers. Problems of these institutions are unique in the sense that advanced technology is applied whenever possible—meaning obviously, staff and equipment. Within a given operational budget, administrators usually prefer to minimize clerical expenditures and maximize expenditures on staff and equipment to provide the best possible medical care. The use of computers has reduced the "per patient" cost of clerical services and has generally improved medical care.

Other Medical Applications

Other uses of the computer in medicine by hospitals and physicians are:

1. Patient billing by physicians—usually through a computer service bureau.
2. Menu planning in hospitals.
3. Scheduling in clinics and wards.
4. Inventory and drug control.
5. Blood bank management.
6. Control of laboratory tests.

In medical research, computers are used to model the brain, the circulatory system, the side effects of various drug treatments, and for physiological simulation in medical training. In fact, the University of Southern California medical school has a computer-controlled mannequin, complete with heartbeat, blood pressure, breathing action, jaws, eyes, and muscles, for the training of resident doctors. The computer-controlled mannequin can suffer from a variety of diseases and even die. However, this patient prepares a printed report of how well the attending physician performed.

EDUCATION

One of our biggest disappointments has been the use of computers in education, although it may turn out that our original expectations were too great. In our economic society, a good rule of thumb is that increased productivity accompanies increased costs. This has been true in manufacturing, government, marketing, banking, and even medicine. Characteristically, it has not been true in education. The cost of education has skyrocketed, but we continue to be constrained by the traditional teacher-student relationship. It was hoped by many that computers would help in this regard, but substantial results have been slow to arrive. From a performance point of view, most computer-based educational systems and techniques have been successful. The costs of computerized systems are high—perhaps as high as 10 to 1 over conventional methods.

The uses of computers in education can logically be placed into three categories:

1. For clerical operations in educational administration.
2. As a technique and/or tool for use in the educational process.
3. As a field of study—that is, computer science and data processing.

This section is concerned with items 1 and 2.

Administration

One area in which computers *have* reduced educational costs is in the area of administration and control. Many school systems have replaced manual record keeping with a computerized version using conventional data processing methods. Computerized systems are more reliable, more accurate, and can be programmed to produce a variety of reports useful for school administration. Many systems also include medical records so that the data can be used for a variety of analyses. Centralized record keeping is useful when students are frequently moved from school to school, as is the case with the children of migrant farm workers. When a student in this category enters a new school, his complete record can be received in hours and he can be placed immediately. Most school systems currently require medical examinations and inoculations for the various communicable diseases. Students that are transferred are frequently given the same shots—over and over again. With a computerized system, the whole process of changing schools can be made less traumatic to the child involved.

Computers are commonly used for class scheduling, for curriculum planning, and for the grading of examinations. Class scheduling is a cumbersome and time-consuming process. Computer programs are now available for scheduling that optimize the use of classrooms and institutional personnel. Curriculum planning is a recent concept that has great potential in the areas of staffing and physical facilities. It has been shown that future needs of a school can be reliably predicted on the basis of current class enrollments, student aptitudes, and student interests. Because of the newness of this application, sufficient time has not elapsed for results to be achieved and reported. Computer facilities for grading examinations are a welcome resource to teachers at all levels of instruction. The key point is that it frees them for more productive activities. (It should, however, be mentioned that there are negative aspects to computerized paper grading. For example, it eliminates the advantages of using essay and open-ended questions as a testing mechanism.)

Instruction

Computers are used in instruction in three principal ways:

1. As a means of testing skills—for example, in the areas of arithmetic and language
2. As part of a programmed learning program
3. As an analysis and problem-solving tool

As a means of testing skills, a computer system is programmed to present the student with exercises. The student is seated at a terminal device. (The specific type of device is not important.) If the student responds correctly, he is presented with another exercise. If he responds incorrectly, he is given the answer and the session continues with another exercise. The length of the session is usually dependent on achieving a prespecified number of correct answers. (A student pointed out a danger in this method. Playing with the computer terminal is so much fun that it is conjectured that many students make mistakes to prolong the session.)

Programmed instruction (frequently called Computer Aided Instruction or CAI) is more complicated, and requires that a course be synthesized as a set of programmed steps. CAI systems are available for assisting the teacher in "course writing." The student sits at a CAI terminal (usually a CRT-type device) and is presented textual material, which he reads. He is then asked questions. If he responds correctly, the CAI system goes on to the next topic. If he responds incorrectly, he is given the answer and a brief review of the subject matter. The depth to which this process can go is dependent on the course author and the CAI system.

CAI systems are primarily on-line systems that can usually service hundreds of students. The CAI programs take care of sequencing and terminal control. The course author takes care of the course content, which may vary among students using the system at any one time.

The advantage of CAI is that it allows the student to proceed at his own pace and gives him individual attention (note: the word personal was not used) that is not available in many classroom situations. CAI costs are very high—ranging from $200 to $2000 per instructional hour. (Dorf [32])

The use of the computer as a problem-solving and analytic tool in mathematics, science, engineering, and business has been well demonstrated. It has also been used successfully in the social sciences, the humanities, and the arts. Applications range from a simple computer program to generate random poetry to an extensive system for language translation. A few sample uses of the computer in these areas are listed below.

    Study of linguistics
    Language translation
    Concordance generation
    Literary analysis
    Poetry writing
    Attribution study (authorship problem)
    Music analysis
    Programs that solve problems
    Symbolic mathematics
    Simulation of a neurotic person (behavioral science)
    Analysis of census data
    Political simulation
    Simulation of a cell (biology)
    Game plan analysis (football)

In the creative arts, there are:

    Computer-generated art forms
    Music composition
    Creation of motion pictures
    Choreographic description
    Fiction writing

Computers have even been used to generate horoscopes and parapsychological experiments.

This situation with computers in education is well summarized by Sanders:*

A primary purpose of using computers as an instructional tool in the class-room should be to *provide insight* and not merely compute numbers or process documents.

In this regard, we have hardly begun, but in the application of systematic thinking and problem-solving methods, computer training provides a valuable learning experience.

*Sanders [49], p. 304.

CHAPTER 12

Computers and the Individual

INTRODUCTION

The use of computers has changed organizations to the extent that the lives of individuals, both in and out of those organizations, have been markedly influenced. The subject has been treated as an emotional issue by social scientists and journalists and has aroused the fears of society in general. Unfortunately, a large number of these social scientists and journalists have not bothered to investigate the technology they so violently degrade. The following quotations from William Rodgers's book *Think*, a biography of the Watsons and IBM, demonstrate some modern points of view:

E. B. White, a serious humorist and essayist, wrote that he did not believe in computers very much, since the convenience they afforded some people was regarded as more important than the inconvenience they caused to all. "In short," he wrote in *The New York Times*, "I don't think computers should wear the pants or make the decisions. They are deficient in humor . . . The men who feed them seem to believe that everything is made out of ponderables, which isn't the case. I read a poem once that a computer had written, but didn't care much for it. It seemed to me I could write a better one myself, if I put my mind to it." (p. 291)

(Author's comment: It's not obvious from the tone of the above quotation that Mr. White is even talking about a machine.)

Tom Watson at IBM, like Howard Aiken, the designer of the original Mark I, has assured the world that the computer is no more than a tool, a view held by most people who profit by, or in, this field of technology. Others are certain that it is already something of a monster, corrupting values and causing distortion of viewpoints. Some fear it is an instrument that, by compiling a lifetime accumulation of details about each person's life, will doom human beings to a loss of privacy. (p. 294)

The thesis of this book, which is rather obvious at this point, is that fear of computers is diminished through knowledge of the subject matter. A certain amount of apprehension always accompanies new technology. For example: the automobile was disliked because engines were noisy and dirty; and the telephone was initially regarded as an invasion of privacy. However, there are some valid concerns over the computer revolution, which many people feel we are now experiencing. Some of the key issues are:

1. *Automation and Jobs.* Does automation eliminate job opportunities? What kind of jobs exist in a computerized society? Will organizational structure change with an increase in the use of computers? Do we live in a society of specialists?
2. *Personal Issues.* Are information systems destroying our privacy? Is dehumanization a fact or a myth? Are people victims of computers or are computers victims of people? Can we insure the confidentiality of information?
3. *Attitudes.* What are people's attitudes about computers and information systems? Is it possible to do an attitude survey of our own?
4. *The Future.* What does the future hold in a computerized society? Will we still use books in the year 2000? What about leisure time? Specialization? Changing careers?

The computer is here to stay. Let there be no doubt about that. It has changed the way we look at the world to such an extent that we could never retreat back to looking at the "small picture" after experience with the "big picture." Moreover, we have adapted to the pace of change so that we continually expect new and better products, increased productivity, more leisure time—items that the computer has helped to bring about. Like practically everything else in society, we have to take the bad with the good. Are the lack of privacy or the depersonalized education system, for example, the price we have to pay for the benefits of computers? This and other topics are explored in the remainder of this chapter.

AUTOMATION AND JOBS

It *is* true that the computer has displaced some people. Automation always does. It is difficult to generalize about automation because each situation is different and research data is often conflicting. Displaced persons are often absorbed into other units or leave the labor force, through retirement, pregnancy, or for other reasons. In spite of the negative aspects of automation, economists agree that the concept is beneficial to society in the long run and that displacement should not be prevented. It is difficult for the employee being displaced to be philosophical about the matter, and reeducation and retraining are frequently necessary. This should be part of the planning process.

Management and Organization

The effects of automation on management and organization are summarized as follows:*

1. Centralization of planning and control occurs at a higher level of the organization.
2. It has made the middle manager's job more complex. (It was predicted that automation would reduce the number and status of middle management jobs. This prediction never materialized.)
3. It has increased the middle manager's and supervisor's needs for human relations skills.
4. It has reduced the span of supervision, that is, the number of employees a supervisor can effectively manage.

Item 4 is particularly significant in the computer field, where a typical first-line manager may have five to eight programmers or systems analysts reporting to him.

As computers are assigned to routine tasks, more of the energy of the organization is devoted to the solution of nonroutine problems. This requires a certain amount of imagination and creativity that the typical bureaucratic organization, with its rigid structure and personnel pigeon-holing, is not designed to cope with. Therefore, a decline of bureaucratic organizational characteristics tends to accompany a computerized organization. It could be that the Peter Principle†, which states that IN A HIERARCHY EVERY EMPLOYEE TENDS TO RISE TO HIS LEVEL OF INCOMPETENCE, will finally be refuted. In the same book, the authors refer to a type of behavior referred to as *professional automatism*, wherein means are more important

*Davis [31], p. 470

†Peter and Hull, *The Peter Principle* [44].

than ends. More specifically, the paperwork is more important than the purpose for which it was originally designed.

Overall, information systems and decision-making models have enabled executives to reassume many of the decision-making functions that were subordinated to middle management in the previous generation of decentralized organizations. More time can be spent on policy matters and less time "fighting fires." Middle management has more time for planning and control, and lower-level management can devote needed time to the human relations problems associated with a changing society.

Education, Specialization, and the Professions

Automation requires more professional and scientific employees to manage and control the complex systems involved. Clerical workers are moved into more responsible positions; blue-collar workers are upgraded to white-collar jobs. The people who suffer most from automation are the ones lacking in basic education, intelligence, or aptitude for retraining,* because it is difficult to place them in other jobs in the organization. Large organizations tend to be better in this regard for the simple reason that they possess the resources and the job opportunities to do it. In smaller organizations, displaced employees are more likely to be laid off.

The computer revolution has brought about a special breed of "professional specialist," uncommitted to an organization. This modern technocrat is described by Alvin Toffler in *Future Shock*† as follows: "He is willing to employ his skills and creative energies to solve problems with equipment provided by the organization, and within temporary groups established by it. But he does so only so long as the problems interest *him.* He is committed to his own career, his own self-fulfillment." Thus, it can be said that the loyalty of the professional man of the new technology is to his profession and not to the organization that is employing him at any point in time. Specialization increases the number of different occupations and dissolves the traditional boundaries of the bureaucratic organization. On any given team, several levels within the organization may be represented.

Planning and Implementation

The people problems that have arisen through the use of computers are solved through effective planning and careful implementation. People resist change for obvious reasons:

---

*Davis [31], p. 467.
†Toffler [50], p. 134.

1. Possible loss of job
2. Change of working environment (new friends, etc.)
3. Fear of not being able to learn the new skills required
4. Possible loss of status in the community

But people faced with the above fears do not simply say, "I resist." The resistance is manifested in what can be regarded as seemingly irrational behavior, such as forgetting to enter data, withholding output, low morale, and ignoring computer facilities. Many organizations solve the problem by keeping the employees informed of developments, allowing the employees to participate in the new system, and by careful timing of the implementation cycle. Some organizations have even gone so far as to guarantee in writing that the employee will not be displaced when the new equipment (or facilities) is installed.

PERSONAL ISSUES

The "popular" way to feel about computers and information is expressed by McLuhan and Watson in *From Cliché to Archetype* as follows: "As information itself becomes the largest business in the world, data banks know more about individual people than the people do themselves. The more the data banks record about each one of us, the less we exist."* Many other writers in the social arena have expressed similar concerns. Lewis Mumford is concerned with the dehumanizing aspect of computers when he writes:† "The process of automation has produced imprisoned minds that have no capacity for appraising the results of their process, except by the archaic criteria of power and prestige, property, productivity and profit, segregated from any more vital human goals." There are, of course, differing opinions. For example, Alvin Toffler in *Future Shock* believes that the new technology has provided us with too many options at too great a rate. He attributes much of what is bad in our society to this rate of change and not the change itself.

The Number Game

One of the biggest complaints heard from students, customers of a public utility, credit card holders, and so forth is, "I'm just a number to them. They don't know who I am." The problem is actually a matter of necessity, rather than a disregard for human dignity. If it is necessary to record information on thousands of persons, it is simply more efficient to code them by number

---

*McLuhan and Watson [40], p. 13.
†Mumford [42], pp. 192–193.

than by name. Moreover, names are frequently misspelled and abbreviated, and sometimes initials and nicknames are used. Therefore, it is not altogether unreasonable to use numbers inside of the computer. The problem arises when a person is forced to memorize the number. The use of identification numbers is also an outgrowth of traditional batch-processing systems in which the respondent has no means of interacting with the computer. With the widespread use of modern on-line interactive systems, the situation will probably change somewhat since the computer can communicate with the respondent to remove any ambiguities. There are more pressing issues.

Computer Victims

Most Americans have either a credit card, a utility account, a checking account, or a magazine subscription—the average citizen has at least one of each. Many people have experienced the helpless feeling associated with the following sequence of events:

a. The person receives a bill for $0.00 and ignores it.
b. Next month a dunning letter arrives.
c. The person consults with friends and finally sends a check for $0.00.
d. The computer responds by stating it doesn't accept checks for $0.00.

Another recurring case goes somewhat as follows. A person has dinner at a restaurant and uses a credit card. He is never billed. He inquires of the company and is informed, "Be patient, the bill will arrive." Perhaps he does nothing. Subsequently, he tries to use the same credit card. The validity of the card is verified with one of the service companies (see Chapter 10) and he is told that a bill is outstanding and credit will not be accepted.

The person's credit rating may be ruined. (It is also computerized.) However, this is not known until credit is refused and the person investigates the reason why. There are numerous documented cases of persons who have even been turned down for jobs because of poor credit ratings that they did not even know about. The individual is practically helpless. He may have a dispute, for example, with a department store for an erroneous charge. He is given a poor credit rating. The dispute is finally resolved and the erroneous charge is canceled. The store never bothers to inform the credit company, which acts as an information-handling company and takes no responsibility for the accuracy of the data. The individual could consult a lawyer, but that could eventually cost him thousands of dollars. It is no wonder that many people wish the computer would go away.

There has been recent legislation with regard to credit files. The individual can inspect his records and insert a statement of his own. The disadvantages are obvious: (1) The stigma of having a bad report, regardless of whether it can be refuted, cannot be easily eliminated; and (2) the individual usually does not know that he has a bad report until credit is refused—frequently to the victim's embarrassment.

Things are even worse than meet the eye at first glance. Credit card companies, department stores, and the like are profit-making organizations, and they do make a profit regardless of who suffers. Consider the problem of straightening out a customer's account, and suppose the customer is right. There are two options open to the company:

1. Investigate the situation, answer the customer's letters, and seriously attempt to straighten out the matter.
2. Ignore the customer's letters. The customer will either pay the bill, or get angry and cancel his account. (By this time, he has probably said, "To hell with the credit rating.")

From a business point of view, the most profitable course of action might very well be the second one. Many customers will pay their bill—however erroneous—in order to preserve a good credit rating. If the customer does cancel his account, the cost of the advertising necessary to get a new customer is usually far less than the cost of resolving the original problem.

The same reasoning holds true for the correcting of "programming bugs," such as the bill for $0.00 mentioned previously. The programming, checkout, and computer time necessary to correct a simple "bug" may cost thousands of dollars. In light of the situation, it is a wonder that most computerized systems operate as well as they do.

The problem obviously is not the problem of the computer. It is a human problem caused by poor systems design, poor programming, or sloppy input. Not only are people victimized by the computer, but the computer is itself victimized.

Privacy and Confidential Information

Another area of concern to most people is "privacy." Alan F. Westin [52] defines *privacy* as "the claim of individuals, groups, or institutions to determine for themselves when, how, and to what extent information about them is communicated to others." The concern for privacy is nothing new and organizations have always collected information of various kinds. However, the problem has been brought to the public's eye in recent years with the widespread use of computers, information systems, and telecommunications facilities. The use of computers has not created the privacy problem but has enlarged the scope of information gathering. Privacy involves organizations, individuals, and society as a whole. Organizations need privacy to carry out their basic objective—whether it be business, politics, or government. There is a tendency for individuals to invade the privacy of other individuals, for reasons ranging from curiosity to criminal blackmail. Within societies, surveillance techniques are generally accepted when used by authorized agencies against enemies of that society. Thus, privacy is both desirable and undesirable, depending on the factors involved.

From the individual's point of view, privacy is exceedingly important because it provides basic psychological and legal needs. Some of the more obvious of these needs are:

1. *Personal autonomy*—wherein a person's hopes, fears, shame, and aspirations are protected against public scrutiny.
2. *Emotional release*—so that a person can "unwind," "let it all out," or show intimate feelings without fear of events being misinterpreted.
3. *Self-evaluation*—so that a person can employ introspection, observation, and other means to improve himself.
4. *Limited and Protected Communications*—so that a person can seek and utilize counsel (legal, clerical, and so on) without fear of incrimination.

There are other reasons why privacy is important to the individual. First, organizations, such as the federal government, have files on people. Some of these agencies are the IRS, the FBI, the Social Security Administration, the Veterans Administration, and the Department of Justice—to name only a few. Each agency generally has its own procedures for collecting data and insuring its accuracy, value, and appropriateness. Usually, an agency's regulations for the release of information are developed in light of its collection procedures. This is also true of credit companies. But what about when information is shared—as in a data bank? It is also less expensive to obtain information from another agency than to collect it yourself. Once information systems are integrated, the regulations of the collecting agency do not necessarily apply to the agency that is using it.

Another concern about information systems is that the past can very easily get in the way of the future. What does this mean? Suppose a first-grade teacher subjectively remarks in a child's record that he is "hyperactive" or "has a short attention span." It is likely that anyone who might see the child's record could accurately interpret the significance of the remark. But, what about 20 years later when that person is seeking employment. Who knows how a prospective employer might respond to a subjective remark. More importantly, the terms "hyperactive" and "short attention span" might have entirely different meanings in 20 years. Arthur R. Miller* has this to say about the situation: "In the past, there was a limited risk that subjective appraisals by individual teachers would be widely circulated. Now, with mis-

*Miller [41], p. 21.

sionary zeal our well-intentioned information handlers are ready to offer their files 'to anyone who had access to individual school records' as well as to 'prospective employers.' "

In short, we do not have control over information that can be and is released about ourselves. There has been extensive legal consideration of the subject and Miller's book is recommended to the reader for an introduction to what has been accomplished in this regard. Personal factors are just as important. Miller has the following to say about the protection of individual privacy:* "The objective of protecting the individual privacy is to safeguard emotional and psychological tranquility by remedying an injurious dissemination of personal information . . . ."

To complicate the situation, there is even some debate over exactly what constitutes "private" information. This aspect has been studied by Comber [30], who gives the following factors that may apply in determining when an informational item is private:

1. The *context within which the specific information* is embedded
2. The *amount of information* assembled and accessible
3. The *intrinsic nature* of the information
4. The *sophistication of the social values* held by the individuals concerned
5. The *character and scope of the subculture*
6. *Significance of personal attributes* such as age, ancestry, social status, and race

Comber also gives several examples of data items that would be private and not private:

Information that may not be relevant to personal privacy:

Name	Sex
Maiden name	Marital status
Address	Name of spouse
Age or date of birth	Next of kin
Race	

Information that would probably be relevant to personal privacy:

Occupation	Number of children
Education	Ages of children
Income	Taxes paid
Religious preference	History of residence
Political preference	Attitudes toward social issues
Family size	Property ownership

*Miller [41], p. 227.

Value of real property	Record of arrest
Marital history	Ancestry
Drinking practices	Nationality
Hospitalization record	Name of relatives
Medical record	Response to psychological or
Symptoms of illness	medical questions

The end result of our discussion of privacy is that the problem does not lie with computers, but with the discipline and conduct of man who is the designer and user of the information system.

ATTITUDES ABOUT COMPUTERS

Although there appears to be concern by individuals over computers and information systems, one is never really sure until he has collected some data. People appear to be polarized: either they regard them as beneficial to mankind or they regard them as "terrible" machines that dehumanize and threaten the individual.

In one of its periodic surveys (1971) of Minnesota residents, the *Minneapolis Tribune* included some questions relating to attitudes about computers and attitudes about government information files. In one of few reports on the subject, Ronald E. Anderson of the University of Minnesota summarized four of the questions [29]. The four questions and a brief summary of results follow:

Question 1. *Some people say that the relationship between businesses and their customers has become too impersonal because of the computer. Are you inclined to agree or disagree?*

Two-thirds (66 percent) of the interviewees agreed with this statement linking impersonal business with the computer; 28 percent disagreed; and 6 percent gave no opinion. Respondents were next asked the following question:

Question 2. *Have you ever had a mistake made in a transaction that was hard to get cleared up because billing was handled by a computer?*

Only about one-third answered this question affirmatively. In actuality some persons who said they had the computer-based problem may not have known for certain that a computer was involved, but the key point is that these persons *perceived* the computer responsible for the difficulty.

Question 3. *Some people say that American society is threatened by the increase in information that the government collects about individuals from the census, tax returns, social security, and so on. Are you inclined to agree or disagree?*

The key element of this question is the notion of increased collection of information by the government. Centralization of information and links between information files are implicit but not explicit; the question suggests an environment that lacks controls over access to and centralization of information. With the term "threat" the statement expresses a rather strong statement against government information collection, so it is startling that 41 percent of all respondents agreed with this statement; 53 percent disagreed; and 5 percent gave no opinion. The next question asked was:

Question 4. *Which do you think is more important for society to function properly—the government's right to know about its citizens, or the individual's right to privacy?*

An overwhelming two-thirds (66 percent) indicated that privacy was more important for society; 28 percent selected the government's "right to know" over privacy; and 6 percent did not choose one or the other. The raw data is given in Table 12.1. It is interesting to note the following differences: between men and women and between the younger (18–29) age group and the middle (30–59) age group for question 1; between the younger and middle age group, between the urban and rural groups, and between the college-educated and noncollege group for question 2; and between men and women on the issues of privacy in questions 3 and 4. In fact, the response of the sexes to questions 3 and 4 reverses the direction of the response to question 1.

The table is included to encourage further analysis and to give some examples of demographic variables that the student might want to use in a study of his own. For example, do students living in fraternity and sorority housing value privacy (computer privacy, that is) less than students living in other housing? Similar questions could be raised about the use of computers in academic course work, computerized registration and grade reporting, and centralized data banks of test scores and academic records. (The author would be interested in any results you might obtain.)

THE FUTURE

In attempting to assess the immediate future of computer technology, it is always wise to look at other technological innovations to determine how

TABLE 12.1 COMPUTERIZATION RESPONSES WITH DEMO-
GRAPHIC BREAKDOWNS—MINNESOTA POLL STATEWIDE
SAMPLE, JULY 1971

	No. of Persons	Quest 1 Imper- sonal	Quest 2 Billing	Quest 3 Gov't Threat	Quest 4 Privacy
Total	600	66[a]	35	41	66
Sex					
Male	292	60	37	47	70
Female	308	70	33	36	63
Age					
18–29	153	59	34	41	72
30–59	293	71	42	42	65
60+	154	64	27	38	61
Location					
Urban	425	66	40	42	67
Rural	175	63	25	42	66
Education (highest level)					
Grade (some)	119	61	19	43	64
High School (some)	297	68	33	37	62
College (some)	184	65	50	47	75

[a] All numbers in columns under questions 1, 2, 3, 4 are percentages answering the question in the indicated way.

they were absorbed into society. We do not have to look far. The telephone and electric power are example enough. Neither would be in widespread use today if national (and international) networks did not exist, allowing people and organizations to "tie in" to satisfy their particular needs. Fortunately, the same telephone network we use for telephone calls can be used for the computer networks of tomorrow.

John Kemeny, President of Dartmouth College and co-inventor of the BASIC language, has stated we are likely to see the development of huge computer networks in the next decade, similar to airline reservation systems and the time-sharing networks operated by several service companies.

In his "Man and Nature" lectures given at the Museum of Natural History in New York City in the fall of 1971, Kemeny [37] outlined a network of nine regional centers that would service the 80 cities in the United States with populations of 150,000 or over. The nine centers are depicted in Figure 12.1. None of the 80 cities would be more than 500 miles from a regional center

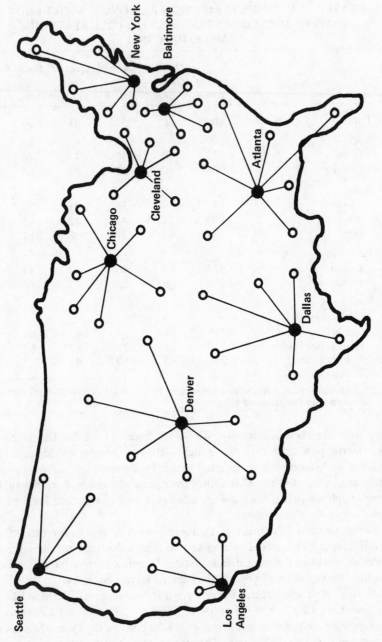

Figure 12.1 Proposed national computer network.

and many suburbs and small cities would also be picked up by the system. In addition to providing service to their respective regions, the centers would be connected together via microwave or high-speed lines to balance the workload and provide emergency service in case of system failure. The regional centers would be used to provide time-sharing service, on-line information systems, and remote job-entry facilities.

It is likely that each regional center will utilize a set of central processing units (a multiprocessing system) sharing the same main storage, direct-access storage, and peripheral input/output units. Systems of this type are in existence today, and network computer service is currently available at many colleges and universities.

In the next decade it is likely that the home terminal will come into widespread use. What will it be used for? The most obvious answer is for computation service and for computer aided instruction (CAI) on a large-scale basis. Kemeny further describes the future "library" system that will allow a person to access a large information system from his own home. With many persons vying for computer service, scheduling will be a problem. Complex operating systems will be used to control computer processing, terminal service, and the running of background jobs.

Kemeny's library of the future will be a complete library stored in the computer. It will be federally funded and maintained on a national basis. Although the costs would be staggering, there are many advantages. The growth rate of libraries in number of volumes doubles approximately every 30 years, and a high percentage of the books are never consulted. By providing access to heavily used information through the computer from the national library system, local library facilities (such as those in colleges and universities) could be reduced considerably. Storage large enough to hold this voluminous amount of information is viewed as a problem, and Kemeny sees books and journals stored as photographic images—similar to the microfilm storage mentioned in this book. Instead of publishing books, publishers will prepare photographable material suitable for entry in the computer. Royalties would be paid on usage and seldom used publications would be removed from the system and stored in conventional libraries to provide faster access to the other information in the system. An added benefit of the concept is that the lead time for publication would be decreased so that available information to researchers and students would be more relevant and up to date.

Kemeny also foresees the day of the *personalized newspaper*, available through the home terminal. Instead of publishing thousands of copies, a newspaper such as *The New York Times* would store information in a computer memory tied to a national computer network. The reporter could type his story directly into the computer, through the network, and the newspaper's staff could perform routine editing and make policy decisions on its contents.

Each reader of the newspaper would have a profile, stored in the computer, of topics of interest to him. For example, the reader might be interested in business, sports, and the society section. (That's some combination.) The computer would display a list of the available news in each topic and the reader would choose the stories of interest to him—in much the same manner that a person scans the headlines while reading the paper in the conventional manner. The computer would then type the story at "normal" reading speed or display it on a CRT-type device. At any point in time, the reader could discontinue reading and go on to the next topic. The advantages are that the reader would be provided up-to-date news on topics of interest to him. What about advertising? Kemeny gives two possibilities: (1) Displaying ads between pages of text; or (2) paying an extra fee for the option of eliminating advertisements.

If all of this sounds farfetched, the following paragraphs will surprise you. Alvin Toffler reports in *Future Shock** that ". . . in the mid sixties, Joseph Naughton, a mathematician and computer specialist at the University of Pittsburgh, suggested a system that would store a consumer's profile—data about his occupation and interests—in a central computer. Machines would then scan newspapers, magazines, video tapes, films and other material, match them against the individual's interest profile, and instantaneously notify him when something appears that concerns him. The system could be hitched to facsimile machines and TV transmitters that would actually display or print out the material in his own living room."

In *Computer Decisions*, Senior Editor Richard Laska† reports that the Information Bank of *The New York Times* is about to go on-line. The information bank will enable users to access and display on their video terminals, information appearing within the last three to five years in *The New York Times* or in some 35 other periodicals. All the user need do is establish a telephone link to the New York Times Information System, enter identifying information, and enter descriptive terms that the system can use to narrow its search. The cost of the service is a flat charge of $1,600 per month, which includes a video terminal, a printer, and unlimited use of the system.

The subject of personal or home computers continues to come up every once in a while. Scientists at M.I.T. are experimenting with a personal computer concept—called OLIVER—for helping to deal with the decision and information overload. OLIVER, which is an acronym for On-Line Interactive Vicarious Expediter and Responder—chosen for Oliver Selfridge—is a computer programmed to store information for an individual, such as his anniversary and his wife's dress size, stock prices, and weather forecasts, and perform routine tasks such as paying bills and ordering food. OLIVER could store a

---

*Toffler [50], p. 249.
†Laska [38], pp. 18–22.

multitude of professional details and serve as a handbook or question-answering device. Moreover, OLIVER could be programmed to identify with its owner to the extent that as its owner's attitudes, likes, and dislikes changed, OLIVER could modify itself accordingly. The M.I.T. people even foresee groups of OLIVERs communicating among themselves to handle routine matters for their masters.

At the more practical level, Kagan and Schear [35] at Western Electric Company are working on a home computer called Home Reckoner—or the H.R. set for short—as an extension to the entertainment center concept. The H.R. set, available in a variety of cabinets and with varying capabilities, could perform diverse functions, such as:

1. Show movies
2. Play party games
3. Run the vacuum cleaner
4. Connect to a computer network

The H.R. set operates as a programmed input/output controller for a variety of devices, such as a TV, stereo set, computer terminal, and vacuum cleaner, with compatible interfaces. Other functions performed by an H.R. set include control of the heating/air-conditioning system, physical security facilities, and home lighting. The authors predict that by 1977 or 1978, an appropriate minicomputer would sell for about $1000.

IN CONCLUSION

In conclusion, it is only fair to admit that it *is* difficult to put the impact of computers on society in perspective. Knowledge of the subject matter is ostensibly the solution to the dilemma, but once one digs in and learns about the field, he can honestly no longer be objective. The best medicine is to call on outside authority. First, a pessimistic quotation on the current state of affairs is from Charles Reich in *The Greening of America:**

The American Corporate State today can be thought of as a single vast corporation, with every person as an involuntary member and employee. It consists primarily of large industrial organizations, plus nonprofit institutions such as foundations and the educational system, all related to the whole as divisions to a business corporation. Government is only a part of the state, but government coordinates it and provides a variety of needed services. The Corporate State is a complete reversal of the original American ideal and

*Reich [46], p. 93.

plan. The State, and not the market or the people or any abstract economic laws determines what shall be produced, what shall be consumed, and how it shall be allocated. It determines, for example, that railroads shall decay while highways flourish; that coal miners shall be poor and advertising executives rich. Jobs and occupations in the society are rigidly defined and controlled, and arranged in a hierarchy of rewards, status, and authority. An individual can move from one position to another, but he gains little freedom thereby, for in each position he is subject to conditions imposed upon it; individuals have no protected area of liberty, privacy, or individual sovereignty beyond the reach of the State.

An appropriate way to end this chapter on computers and individuals is with a contrary opinion with a computer orientation from Donald H. Sanders in *Computers in Society:* *

... the optimists believe that the sophisticated computer systems of the future will permit a more human and personalized society that will further reduce the need for individual conformity. They argue that the complexity of our present society, the millions of people crowded into it, and the inadequacy of our present information systems act to encourage conformity and thus to restrict personalization and human freedom of choice. However, when sophisticated information systems are developed and widely used to handle routine transactions, it will then be possible to focus greater personal attention on exceptional transactions. Therefore, more humanistic attitudes will emerge.

*Sanders [49], p. 252.

PART IV

ON THE PHILOSOPHY OF COMPUTERS AND INFORMATION SYSTEMS

CHAPTER 13

Design Philosophy
for Man-Machine
Information Systems

INTRODUCTION

Many people in responsible positions today, whether in government, hospitals, research labs, or in business, spend a good part of their valuable time attempting to get incorrect and unreliable information on what happened yesterday. Others attempt to negotiate within organizations aided by information systems where the data, statistics, and charted relationships *about* an event far exceed the complexity of the event itself. Obviously, there is a lack of uniformity between needs and means. The situation is not uncommon in science and applies to other specialized activities as well. Any given activity has two aspects. Only the *insider* can understand the training and practice, discipline and method, strategy and imagination, called for in the successful execution of his activity. Yet, at the same time, he may be so close to the activity that its most general features and widest connections begin to escape him. As a result, when it becomes necessary to stand back and appraise the whole discipline, the *outsider* once again has something to contribute. This comment is especially significant in light of the fact that governmental and industrial organizations, unlike biological organisms, do not exist for their own sake but rather to satisfy predefined objectives. Thus, the test of their performance, unfortunately, lies outside the organization itself. It follows that organizations are dependent on effective decisions and well-founded objectives and would naturally turn to computer-based information systems for assistance. Yet these systems have evoked a sort of panic within and outside the organization. Actually, the reasons are more obvious than one might otherwise imagine.

We, as intelligent beings, manage to function remarkably well in a complex environment. Our intellectual functioning is even more noteworthy. In a metaphorical sense, rarely are memories destroyed or programs lost. Yet, when we attempt to organize individuals and add a computer or two, the level of functional efficiency decreases noticeably.

This chapter presents methods and guidelines for formalizing the intelligence activities of an organization. These activities can then be aided by computer-based information systems, but only where feasible, appropriate, and within economic constraints. To some, the material will be a study of organizational structure and its relationship to information systems. To others, it will be a delineazation of which functions an effective information system can be expected to perform.

The ideas are an outgrowth of the study of management information systems and of machine intelligence being pursued at many business institutions and colleges and universities across the country. The techniques employed parallel the concept of "technology" as defined by Kenneth Galbraith [54] in *The New Industrial State*. That is:

Technology means the systematic application of scientific or other organized knowledge to practical tasks. Its most important consequence, at least for purposes of economics, is in forcing the division and subdivision of any such task into its component parts. Thus, and only thus, can organized knowledge be brought to bear on performance.

As it turns out, the mental functions seemingly performed by us humans in everyday information gathering, problem solving, and decision making have apparent analogs in the basic tasks performed within man's more sophisticated counterpart, that is, groups and organizations. A consideration of these basic functions is the subject matter of this chapter. They are identified, discussed, and evaluated in light of the state of the art in information technology. Collectively, the functions provide a "conceptual foundation" for much of the manual and automatic information processing within organizations, thus *formalizing* the intelligence activities within large systems in much the same way that the methodology of operations research formalizes the application of mathematical techniques to appropriate problems within its domain.

KNOWLEDGE, INTELLIGENCE, AND MAN-MACHINE SYSTEMS

Computer and information scientists have unusual ways of assigning unexpected names to common concepts. The world is filled with information. It is inherent in the design of buildings and automobiles, the structure of organizations, and the operations of groups and teams. Yet to a computer or an information scientist, it becomes *data* only when it is recorded on a medium of some kind. It is immaterial whether the medium be a notched stick, as ancient cave men used to count their wives or sheep, or a modern device such as a punched card or magnetic tape. Informally, *information* may be regarded as raw or processed data used for making decisions, although an information scientist would regard it as that which is generated by a change in a unit of storage. Either definition is satisfactory since the notion is rather well defined anyway. *Knowledge* implies organization and is defined as the systematic organization of information and concepts. Knowledge can also be defined as the assignment of meaning to information—and therein lies the difficulty for organizations using computer-based information systems.

What is meaning? Clearly, it is a process of naming or of identification. But it is more than that. It is also the identification of an object or event by name as a result of a common agreed-upon correspondence between an *event* metaphor and a *name* metaphor. It follows that the meaning that we assign to an event metaphor is implicit in our response to it.

One might inquire at this point what all of these definitions have to do with information systems. The answer is, essentially, that intelligence is a behavioral property and that an information system we can use intelligently is one that takes account of the context in which it operates. One might also state that this type of information system must be adaptive and this is certainly true. But the basis of an effective information system is deeper than that. *Intelligent behavior*, on the part of a man, a machine, or both, *is the detection of the change of meaning brought about by a shift of context*. Therein lies the foundation of a useful man-machine information system.

This latter point is discussed further. Many information systems store data and a subset of this data is eventually used for making decisions or preparing reports. For the most part, however, data is single-purpose in that it is collected and used with a small number of objectives in mind. In a large organization, like the city of New York, a significant amount of data is required to support its diverse activities. Applying the ideas given above, a minimal amount of data would be required with its specific meaning being dependent upon the context in which it is used. An accepted name for this would be a *common data base*.

Lastly, proper allocation of tasks between man and machine is essential for an efficient system. Such allocation is an administrative function, and so is the greater part of the complex thinking activity of the organization. It follows that administration will be required to allocate its own tasks between itself and the computer.

BASIC ACTIVITIES IN EFFECTIVE MAN-MACHINE INFOR-MATION SYSTEMS

In complex situations of this sort, it is often useful to explore the activities performed by physiological organisms in response to their environment. Certainly, we fall into this category, but animals do as well. Even they fare much better than many of our man-machine systems. Actually, this physiological exploration is what we perform when studying machine intelligence. In machine intelligence, it is desired to duplicate, by machine alone, the intelligent functions uncovered. Information scientists will attempt only to apply the basic functions to man-machine systems. Let us then explore what we are doing "on-line" and later we can apply our findings to administrative functions and organizations.

Data Gathering

Data comes to us in many forms even if we are not prepared to accept it. It is also true that we as individuals can use the information, in a psychological sense, even if we do not realize that we have received it. The important aspect of the situation, however, is that we must participate in the process in order to collect the data. It is recognized that the discovery of appropriate responses based on the incoming data requires much trial and error, but that is a problem for perceivers and those who infer, as discussed below.

Much of the data used within organizations comes from without and if it is to be used in the continuous information system, then the scope of the information system must be broadened so that it will monitor, on a continuous basis, the critical environmental factors.

Perception

One of the most significant aspects of our existence is the process of perceiving. Our central nervous system senses the stimuli and our brain applies an interpretation to them. It is important to realize, however, that the sensory input is not the event and is only a symbolic representation of it. Therefore, meaning is found in the response that we find appropriate. Further, it should be recognized that the response need not be carried out but may be latent or repressed.

Within the organizational framework, this is analogous to the classification of data. Within most information systems, this function is combined with data gathering—thus limiting the data-gathering operation. That is, we collect only the information we are looking for.

Inferential Analysis

One of the amazing properties of the human organism is the capacity to store cause-and-effect relationships. In fact, much of our behavior is elicited automatically, somewhat like the behavior of a compiled computer program. But we can learn. That is, we can interpret classified information and take appropriate actions without having to experience all situations ourselves. For example, most people do not have to be struck by a moving automobile in order to know that a moving automobile must be avoided.

In machine intelligence, we have an analogy in learning and in theorem proving. In information science, we must be able to predict the consequences of present events, and more importantly, we should be able to infer missing data from data that is available. A similar situation exists in mathematics where a *set* can be defined by listing its elements or by stating a rule that distinguishes between elements that are in the set and those that are not.

Another area of interest is the capacity to derive abstract functional relationships from cause-and-effect data. In a very general sense, this is self-organization, recognizing that only elementary statistical associations are required in the majority of cases.

Recognition of Patterns

In everyday living, we often enter into emergency situations where we have to make a decision with insufficient time or data. Physiologists tell us, on the other hand, that animals do not experience similar situations since by the time an emergency threatens a response is already underway. It follows then that emergencies are in part caused by an overload of the information network such that pertinent information is hidden among the mass of ambiguous data.

In the world of information science, this function is termed *pattern recognition*. After data has been collected and classified, what kind of analysis is performed on it, if any? Or, do we wait and use it once the decision-making process is underway?

The techniques are of importance and involve the notions of *variability* and *deviation*. We must be able to perceive variations, assess their consequences, and initiate appropriate administrative action without the stimulus of a specific organizational need.

Goal Seeking

The concept of the feedback mechanism is fundamental to the science of cybernetics. Although feedback is necessary for the goal-seeking activities of individuals, it is rarely reflected in the computer-based information systems of organizations. Perhaps this is a typically human activity and should remain so.

What are the implications of goal seeking for an information system? The answer is related to the number of times we ask ourselves whether or not we are on the right track. We ask this question about our careers, our children, and even the nation as a whole.

Why then do our information systems not include built-in testing mechanisms to verify that specified conditions are within acceptable limits? Out of tolerance, conditions could then initiate appropriate action in the same way as process-control computers do in the chemical and petroleum industries.

Self-Organization

As participants in the game of life, we are not mere passive observers of incoming data. We constantly adapt to new patterns of information and behavior. It seems that the most meaningful information that can be found is not the raw data but the behavior the system must engage in in order to deal with the raw data. In fact, it is becoming increasingly clear that the degree of participation in the environment is a direct measure of how it is perceived.

How often do we, as computer and information scientists, modify our systems and our own behavior in response to external stimuli? Rarely. The cost is an important factor, but the fact remains that we are not designed for change.

A Brief Summary

It is not intended to imply that the functions of data gathering, perceptions, inferential analysis, pattern recognition, goal seeking, and self-organization must be designed into our computer systems, but rather, that these functions must be present in an effective man-machine information system. In fact, these activities should be recognized when the organization is structured and when the installation of computer systems is in the planning stage.

ADMINISTRATIVE FUNCTIONS AND ORGANIZATION

One can define the administrative needs of organizations in two ways: prescriptively and descriptively. The prescriptive approach starts by defining the types of activities in which administration should be interested and then determines what behavior is necessary for successful pursuit of these activities. The descriptive approach simply defines administrative behavior and determines applicable activities through generalization. The approach taken here is the former.

Planning and Control

The administrative activities of most organizations can conveniently be generalized into two categories: planning and control. Within each of these categories, specific activity can only be justified in light of its value to the organization.

In the area of planning, the following activities can be recognized at most levels of administration:

- Setting objectives
- Developing plans
- Translating objectives and plans into strategies
- Evaluating alternatives
- Budgeting
- Assigning responsibility
- Choosing performance indicators

Similarly, control functions can be defined to support the above activities. They necessarily include:

- Measurement of variations and deviations
- Coordination of activities
- Learning
- Motivation
- Establishment of remedial action
- Causal diagnosis

Information Needs of the Organization

It is relatively easy to relate the planning and control activities of the organization to the functions defined above. We can now define the information needs of the "intelligent" organization without ambiguity. They are listed in order of increasing sophistication:

- Capacity to store modules of raw data
- Capacity to classify data
- Capacity to recognize differences and similarities
- Capacity to store cause and effect relationships
- Capacity to apply heuristics to cause and effect relationships
- Capacity to derive functional relationships from data
- Capacity for modification and extension

Obviously, some activities remain and tend to be those man prefers any-way. What have we gained? We have gained a man-machine information system in which the major components perform the functions for which each is best suited.

CONCLUSIONS

In conclusion, three points should be emphasized. First, it is the essence of economic and technical progress that the time line for the verification of administrative decisions is increasing at a rapid rate. This also pertains to the design and implementation of information systems. Thus, the systems must be appropriate in themselves and must give the administrator, within probabilistic limits, an accurate picture of the future operating environment.

Second, relevant outside events rarely exist in a quantifiable form until after the event has taken place or is certain to take place. The important information to the administrator is the trends and the rate at which they change with time. This information can be provided with an effective information system.

Lastly, the more serious problems faced by administrators arise because of the inadequacy of the older, previously successful systems for dealing with new problems. Often, the problems are the same as the older ones but exist in a different context. The system has not reacted intelligently because it has failed to detect the change in meanings brought about by a change in context.

CHAPTER 14

Toward a Conceptual Basis of Computation

INTRODUCTION

An interesting aspect of computation, these days, is its expansion into new fields of application. The traditional use of computers by mathematically trained people has raised very few conceptual problems. Similarly, data processing problems, although certainly not trivial in scope, have not required that users readjust their thinking to any great degree. Problem-oriented languages have helped in the latter category. It has been said, though, that any ambitious and sustained intellectual work soon overstrains the capacities of common sense. Numerous examples of this exist in the field of modern physics. This discussion of common sense has some serious implications for the computer sciences. The major problems are these: (1) Computer people have solved the easy problems and are now encountering applications in areas where data-handling procedures and analysis techniques are not well defined. (2) Problem originators, although sometimes requiring extensive analysis of data, often do not possess a satisfactory background in the basic concepts of computing. Generally, the problems relate to the following discussion.

In everyday life, few men can comprehend all problems down to a point of decision. In fact, we do well to comprehend only a fraction. This does not disturb most of us since we feel that the major issues can be solved by those who really put their minds to them. Nevertheless, we are functional with respect to these issues as long as we possess a conceptual framework regarding them. It is like the automobile or airplane, for which we often propose very sophisticated uses without necessarily knowing how to operate them and while knowing even less of how they are designed or built. In many new computer applications, however, the possession of a conceptual basis of computation, on the part of the originator, does not exist; that is, their ability to function, in the area of computation, is marginal.

Another aspect concerns computation as a science. Mechanical techniques are certainly well known. An underlying theory, however, is almost nonexistent and only recently has the subject even been considered. Yet, such a theory is a scientific prerequisite.

This chapter does not go very far toward developing such a conceptual basis. What it attempts to present, on the other hand, is a more or less philosophical discussion of techniques for its development along with some preliminary results. At any rate, the problem exists and there is probably some value in simply thinking about it.

ON PHILOSOPHY

One might ask at this point, "What does Philosophy have to do with computers?" A more basic question might be "What is Philosophy?"

William James [62] has the following to say about philosophy:

The word means only the search for clearness where common people do not even suspect that there is any lack of it.

Susanne K. Langer [62] expresses similar feelings in another way:

Philosophy is the pursuit of meanings. It is not a process of finding new facts; the discovery and generalized statement of facts is science. Philosophizing is a process of making sense out of experience, rather than adding to experience itself as factual learning and experimental investigations do.

Historically, significant advances in philosophy have followed periods of fast cultural growth or novel experience. Machine computation certainly falls into one of these categories.

ON THE INADEQUACY OF LANGUAGE

The human use of language is essentially to express ideas about things—to call attention to relations, parts, properties, aspects, and functions. Why then is language not adequate for communicating ideas about computation?

First, in a very real but not a very practical sense, we take language to mean a set of propositions formed from some primitive symbols or statements and repeated use of some prescribed rules. All propositions can be labeled true or false. Unfortunately, not all grammatical propositions are true and not all ungrammatical propositions are false. Any description in this formalism, therefore, would be incomplete, not because of the entity being described, but because of the limitations of the language as we use it. The difficulty is that the language can be used to describe not only parts of the the world but also parts of the language itself. This is what Tarski showed. There are many paradoxes that stem from this concept, such as Russell's class of classes and Richard's paradox. Maron [64], of the Rand Corporation, summarized this concept when he stated:

Human language is richer precisely because we think about ourselves. We cannot eliminate self-reference from human language without thereby turning it from a genuine language of information into a machine language of instructions.

The second limitation is recognized when language is defined as a certain way of organizing experience. Important in the sense of this definition is not the repertory of symbols on which experiences are mapped (vocabularies) but the repertories of the experiences themselves and especially the way experiences are organized. For those with similar experiences, language, of course, is very adequate. The inadequacy of language stems from the "extensional bargain" as recognized by Wendall Johnson and the "continuum of meaning" of Mortimer Taube.

"Extensional bargain" is a term used to describe the agreement among people who speak the same semantic language. You and I make an extensional bargain when we agree not to go beyond a certain point in relating experience to language. The agreement is an implicit kind of thing that is very dependent upon the experience level of the communicants.

Mortimer Taube, in his interesting book entitled *Computers and Common Sense* [70], considers meaning not to be a discrete entity but to fall along a continuum of related meanings. The following quotation from his book perhaps summarizes the limitations of language for the problem at hand:

In the first place, the conjunction or sum of propositions is a proposition in just the same sense that the sum of numbers is a number and the sum of spaces is a space. There is no "longest proposition," any more than there is a "largest number." This establishes the infinity of meaning but not its density and nondenumerability. The set of real numbers which is dense and nondenumerable can represent a similar set of propositions, namely, the totality of the propositions which assert the existence of each real number.

Finally, any meaning, which as a proposition is the characterization of a nexus of actual entities by a selected set of eternal objects, has relevance to a nondenumerable set of possibilities which constitute a nondenumerable penumbra of meanings clustering around any given meaning. The graded relevance of non-realized possibilities to any actual proposition is what gives propositions different meanings to different people. . . .

MODELS

Langer states that the very framework of experience is only thinkable by means of models, which is another alternative in our search for a conceptual basis of computation.

Minsky [66], in his short but stimulating paper entitled "Matter, Mind and Models" defines the term model in this sense:

To an observer B, an object A* is a model of an object A to the extent that B can use A* to answer questions that interest him about A.

More generally, familiar events or processes are models; they can be used to understand more complicated or abstract systems. Moreover, processes can be seen—one in another. The processes of nature can be seen one in another and those that are conceptually unreachable are generally understood only through a model. Death is seen as eternal sleep, youth and age as spring and autumn or winter, life as a flame consuming the candle that sustains it. In fact, the essence of human mentality is the use of models as symbols that may be put together freely, elaborated, and treated as mental pictures of sophisticated events. The use of models to convey concepts is one of the phenomena that distinguish man from animal.

The fact that physical models are indeed useful but inherently limited is also considered by Minsky in the same paper:

In everyday practical thought physical analogy metaphors play a large role, presumably because one gets a large payoff for a model of apparently small complexity. It would be hard to give up such metaphors, even though they probably interfere with our further development, just because of this apparent high value-to-cost ratio. We cannot expect to get much more by extending the mechanical analogies, because they are so informational in character. Mental processes resemble more the kinds of processes found in computer programs—arbitrary symbol-associations, tree-like storage schemes, conditional transfers and the like.

It is felt by some that human mentality projects its own mental processes into everyday life and especially its creative activity. The art of computation is certainly a product of this human mentality. Maron [64] also has *this* to say about models and intelligent behavior:

. . . there is a hierarchical structure to the logical organization of the model which an intelligent artifact embodies, just as there is a hierarchical structure in science itself. This means that whereas there are signal sequences generated on a first level corresponding to predictions about events, other signal sequences, which in turn control the lower-level sequence generators, correspond to predictions about hypotheses.

Actually, the two types of signal sequences constitute distinct dimensions in a continuum of intelligence, or if you will, the ability to process information, as described by Paul Armer of the Rand Corporation in the celebrated book entitled *Computers and Thought* [60]. Clearly, the more elementary mental processes are understood. The question is then, "Why not use Human Mentality, of which we are at least vaguely familiar, as a general model of computation?" This is attempted in the following sections.

ON HUMAN MENTALITY

In the purposeful functioning of any higher information system, purely factual knowledge alone is not sufficient. This is definitely the case with the living brain, which utilizes imagination to develop a continuous world of space and time. In fact, imagination may very well be the most significant force affecting our behavior, and, perhaps, may be another factor that distinguishes man from animal. A quotation of Bronowski [61] from *The American Scholar* will serve as a useful introduction:

The subject of how the mind works as a mechanism, what machinery we can imagine to operate within the brain, has its intrinsic interest in any case. We know that the brain is made of the same stuff as the rest of nature, and its atoms must therefore obey the same natural laws as other atoms do. In that sense, then, it is tempting and even reasonable to say that the brain must be some kind of a machine. But alas, to use the word *machine* in this catch-all sense misses the crux of the question. The real question about the human mind lies deeper; it asks, Is the brain a machine with a formal procedure of any kind that we can now conceive?

On the level of components, codes, and logical organization, the concepts of information theory and cybernetics have been used in an attempt to analyze brain mechanisms in terms of information-processing machines. At this level of comparison, no deep neurophysiological hypotheses have been developed. Another level of comparison relates to their functional similarities, since they both process information in order to derive outputs of a certain kind.

Actual perceptions, often termed stimuli, come and go. But our world is considerably larger than the world of stimuli. What happens is that the human brain uses the sense impressions it receives not only as stimuli to physical action but as material for its specialized function—imagination.

More specifically, one of the processes of imagination, termed *interpretation*, ascribes *meaning* to these stimuli forming facts, and records these facts through *symbols*. Given a stimulus X, attaching meaning to it is the same as asking the question "What is X?" In this context, the question is a request to:

1. Name X, if X refers to an unnamed thing;
2. Describe X or elicit an experience to which X refers, if X refers to a word; or
3. Tell about the nature of X.

In the most general sense, any device whereby we make an abstraction is a *symbol* and conversely, all abstraction involves symbolization. Once defined, symbols representing facts, concepts, experiences, or images can be produced at will and manipulated with great freedom; as a result, we supplement our momentary senses and build an abstract structure of ideas. This must have been what Descartes meant when he stated that the human species has certain specific capacities that distinguish it from automata and other biological species and enable it to manipulate a great variety of symbols in the absence of special trigger stimuli. In many cases, the process of interpreting is performed *automatically*. Instead of having sensations, or receiving stimuli, and judging them to mean the existence of things or the occurrence of events, we seem to perceive things and happenings and become directly aware of facts.

The processes of imagination are not limited simply to the collection and classification of stimuli. Of the other major functions that exist, two are significant here; they involve the development of knowledge structures and the generalization and use of experience.

Knowledge is mentality's mechanism for keeping in step with the outside world. In so doing it uses facts, relations, and constraints. Clearly, relations are perceptible only through symbols. Although imagination implicitly uses them as guides to action, they cannot be explicitly pointed to like physical objects. Compare two unequally sized persons and try to point out the relation "taller than." Relations are abstract and abstract things are embodied in symbolism. One might say then that knowledge is functional through relations similar to the manner in which relations are perceptible only through symbols.

Imagination uses another form of knowledge, in addition to the factual type described in the preceding paragraph. It is often termed *experience* and is evidenced most frequently in problem-solving situations. (The concepts of facts and experience are analogous, in fact, to Minsky's divisions of Coding structures and Knowledge structures [67].) A solution obtained by one's own effort or one obtained elsewhere but followed with interest and insight may provide a *pattern* for solving similar problems. Experience with problem solving results in functional changes of three types:

1. Development of new patterns and the evolution of old ones
2. Extension of methodical multistage processes for problem solving
3. Accumulation of new facts to support problem-solving activity

Patterns for solving problems are related to *models* as discussed previously. Patterns can be seen one in another; it follows that more general patterns may often be comprised of other patterns with less general scopes of applicability. It is precisely this process by which imagination enlarges our world of stimuli. Often, mentality uses new facts as guides to physical action; but the fact that imagination lends support to its own internal functions is not to be ignored.

THE CONCEPTUAL BASIS

It was stated earlier, in discussing models, that processes can be seen one in another; and that familiar events can be used as models for understanding (or even using) unfamiliar or abstract events. The objective is, of course, to use the seemingly comprehensible concept of human mentality as a conceptual model of computation.

Familiarity with certain terms is necessary for discussing computation just as it is in mathematics or any other discipline. Three terms, namely "variables, constants, and quantities," are necessary for this exposition.

Although *variable* is a frequently used noun, few scientists give any more than passing thought to what is behind the word they are using with such effectiveness. The number 7 is not variable; neither are the numbers 8 and e. Even though there are no variable numbers, scientists, in formulating arithmetical assertions, often use letters each of which stand for any element of a specific class of numbers. Such a letter is termed a *number variable*; the said class will be referred to as the *domain* of the variable. In making statements about other objects, scientists use other variables; when considering functions, *function variables* are used. When discussing persons or names, *person variables* or *name variables* are used. Conceptually, assertions using variables are not superior to their verbal counterparts; practically, however, the use of variables affords one the same advantages as models do to human mentality.

Most technical people refer to symbols that stand for single objects as *constants*. In order to avoid inconsistencies, this definition needs some interpretation. Using the above definition, "1/2" and ".5" being different symbols would have to be different constants. In this use of the word constant, we are obviously referring to the number itself and not to the symbols. Such a reference is termed a *number constant*. Other constants, such as " ", "e", or "alpha" may refer to literal values of the symbols and are thus termed *literal constants*.

A *quantity* refers to a pairing of a constant with an object. More precisely, it is an ordered pair whose first member is called the object of the quantity while the second member, which is a constant, is referred to as the value of the quantity. Two quantities are equal if both their objects and values are equal. In some instances, the object of a quantity may be implied by its usage in computation.

The essence of computation is the *program*, which commands the computer to act in a prescribed fashion. A program is composed of quantities called *instructions*; each, in turn, is composed of an operation and one or more operands. In performing interpretative and problem-solving functions, it operates in a manner directly analogous to mental imagination. Formal sequences of instructions are developed that can reference themselves as well as other quantities. This ability for self-reference, or self-modification, imposes a recognized restriction on machine computation. That is, without an exhaustive search, it is impossible to show in advance that the code is free of hidden contradictions.

The ordered sequences of computer instructions resemble patterns for problem solving and contain decision processes for both interpretation and problem solution. As with stimuli, *input data* come and go; the values, per se, are constants as defined above and are inscribed on some sort of input media. The process of interpretation, whether performed explicitly or automatically, ascribes objects to the values, forming *quantities*, and stores this information as occurrences of variable data. The analogy includes the real-time processing of real-time data; this occurs when the quantities are directly associated with the stimuli they represent. In all cases, the *type of the variable* is dependent on the type of quantities involved. Some quantities are used as operands for calculations; others are used as limits (or the range of values) for decision processes. *Decision processes*, which relate, in some fashion, variables to limits, enable a computer program to choose between alternative courses of action.

In a very general sense, computer programs can exhibit knowledge and experience. Knowledge refers to the relation between the input information and the computer program. No knowledge is exhibited when the operating program, functioning in the interpretative mode, assigns meaning (or an object) to the input data (values) before performing the requested calculations.

If, on the other hand, the meaning for input values is implicitly imbedded in the computer programs, the programs, functioning now in the automatic mode, can be said to possess a form of knowledge.

The fact that a program can benefit from its own experience, that is, problem solving, interpretation, and so on, is inherent in an ability for *self-modification.* Computer programs can evolve, therefore, in a manner similar to the way patterns for solving problems are developed in the living brain.

Clearly, the result of computation is the development of new quantities (or facts, if you will) or the verification of old ones. Physical action, resulting from computation, can involve the gamut of electronic or electromechanical devices.

THE MEASUREMENT OF COMPUTATION

In the terminology of quantities, computation is an object to which one can assign a measurement of value. Heretofore, measurements have used execution time, programming time, and even the number of instructions or statements programmed. A complex short program, however, can involve a large amount of actual computer time; similarly, a long simple program can involve a small amount. Finally, either a long program or a complex one can be associated with a significant amount of programming time. In general, it would be desirable to be able to measure computation and have this measurement relate to the complexity of the program and the programming effort involved while not being dependent upon actual computer time, which can vary from computer to computer anyway. We shall look at the problem conceptually from two points of view.

First, suppose we were to throw a coin eight times. More than likely, the heads and tails would be mixed up in the outcome of the throws. Conceivably, however, the first four throws could come up heads and the last four could come up tails. Intuitively it is felt that this arrangement (HHHHTTTT) is more orderly than another arrangement (HTTHTHTH). It is suspected that the amount of order in a situation is measured by the number of words necessary to describe it. Linguistically, usage tends to shorten passages, descriptions, or words. From a programming point of view, therefore, a procedure that can be described briefly indicates one of two things: (1) The procedure is indeed unsophisticated; or (2) the demand for the procedure is great enough to warrant a prewritten program. It is important to emphasize at this point that we are concerned with a distinct programming effort and not the entire realm of programming activity. Then in either of the two cases, discussed just previously, a description of a procedure as written or as seen by a programmer is a reasonable measure of computation. Orderly procedures that are conceptually straightforward or can be delineated briefly possess a proportionately low value for complexity. For example, programs that used "canned" procedures to a great extent might be conceptually straightforward although the "canned" procedures themselves may possess a high degree of complexity. On the other hand, procedures without the attribute of orderliness might tend to fall into the more complex category. Accordingly, the following generalization is developed:

The more common the application, the more redundant the description of it, and the more economical it becomes to develop a general-purpose system to match it and organize appropriate conditional readiness.

Another alternative for measuring computation is to assign an index to it depending upon where the procedures could be placed in a continuum of intelligence; obviously, the words "ability to process information" are more appropriate. In this case, the development of some dimensions for this continuum should be sufficient.

In considering whether or not a computer does what brains do, Mackay [63] has the following to say about elementary machine computations:

When a digital computer solves a problem, is it doing what human brains do when they solve problems? I must confess that I doubt it. I think it would be fair—fair to the computer—to say that a computer does, and of course is designed to do, what people do with tokens and counters: not what their brains do, but what their hands do. This is what makes computers relevant to thinking at all.

Perhaps, this is the level at which computer use began. Let us name this dimension the *Hand Manipulation Level*, characterized as follows:

1. It can manipulate sequences of symbols in the absence of specific trigger stimuli
2. It involves nonpredictive, nonadaptive behavior

Another dimension involves an awareness of external events and a "conditional readiness" to take them into account in the development of relevant action. Accordingly, this is called the *Conditional Readiness Level* and uses adaptive behavior by an organizing structure to maintain and control behavior. The key point is that predictions are generated that match or adapt to the external environment. In general, two types of predictions are recognized:

1. Predictions about events
2. Predictions about hypotheses

They can be likened to low-level subroutines that predict and match and high-level routines that dictate which subroutines should be executed.

The last dimension will be labeled the *Cognitive Level* since it involves:

1. Carrying around a scale model of reality with which to try out various alternatives
2. Free play of the cognitive device to enable inventions outside of the logical processes

It is usually with respect to this latter category that people ask the question "Can machines think?"

Surely computations can be measured; furthermore, the measurements can be compared. The latter is true, however, only when the processes involved are considered within their respective dimensions.

CONCLUSIONS

The chapter is concluded by briefly considering two very popular topics. The first is the social implications of computation and the second relates to discussions of brain/machine functions.

Few people would question the statement that we live in an anxious world. We are constantly being exposed to new ideas and rapid changes. One might say that it is as though we were being swept through a maze of events—many of which we cannot even see or understand. Through social experience, we acquire satisfactory courses of action to follow for most problem-solving or decision situations. (It is to be emphasized that this also applies to ways of *thinking*—that is, we automatically think about certain things according to the class or classes to which they belong.) In a settled society, this is sufficient; the general disorganization of knowledge and the limitations of common sense are of little concern to the average person, who may not even be aware of the obscurities and paradoxes that pop up in our daily lives. In an unsettled society, however, a person begins thinking about things beyond his own realm of life. We immediately become cognizant of the fact that our conceptual powers have broken down. We look to the popular news media—but in many cases find that certain subjects are glamorized well beyond their utility. In short, we are unable to communicate purposefully on modern concepts. What does this mean? It's hard to say. Related to computers, it certainly affects the way we process or even organize our knowledge—whether this knowledge is numerical data, such as bank account records, or factual information, such as that which might be stored in a library. Basically, we are unable to use the best possible tools in dealing with the major issues of everyday life; the issues, in fact, relate to the evaluation of previous results or experience, the development of current goals, and the prediction of future requirements or events. Computation is a means of reducing this complexity—a means of making sense out of experience. So we see the established methods of simply collecting and noting knowledge may no longer be appropriate. The new methods, which can definitely handle the increasing complexities of life, are only useful, however, if they are imbedded in a firm conceptual structure and are accessible to the occasional user.

Currently it is common to hear discussions of the similarities and differences between brain and machine functions. Many computer scientists underscore the similarities. There are some opposite opinions, however, especially by some life scientists who contend that the brain is not electronic and only partly digital. The divergence of opinions indicates that there probably is some value in looking at the similarities and differences.

Operational similarities between the brain and the computer are many; but there is practically no agreement on the implications of these similarities. As an example, let us consider the task of transporting passengers between New York and London by steamship and by jet airplane. The cost is about the same. The number of passengers transported per hour of travel time is also approximately equal. For both modes of transportation, schedules have to be set, tickets have to be sold, reservations made, and passengers have to be transported to and from terminal points. Could the respective designers, in this case, benefit in any gross and obvious way from each other's structures? Clearly no! Could this also be the case with computers and the brain?

On the other hand, structural differences may turn out to be superficial. This is especially significant since much of computer design is based on economical considerations. Magnetic tape drives, cores, drums, and so on, could be easily replaced by electronically operated on-off switches if the cost factor were not so important.

Functional or physiological considerations are other alternatives for similarities or dissimilarities. Immediately we recognize, however, that the many-valued logic and analog nature of neural activity is most unlike modern digital computers—although this is certainly a feasible direction for computer design to go toward.

A quotation of Walter A. Rosenblith [69], professor of communications biophysics at M.I.T. and a member of the famous post-World War II cybernetics supper club, is a fitting conclusion to this discussion:

What conclusions are we to draw from this state of affairs? That the computer is just another, not very appropriate, metaphor? Not quite! Even though detailed structural or functional comparisons may be tantalizing misfits, they have been responsible for many new and penetrating theoretical and experimental questions. Most of these relate to the handling of a commodity that is being called information, even though the formulations of information theory do not directly apply. In the handling of purely abstract or symbolic tasks, where we are as yet unable to point to any specific chain of relevant events in the brain, computer programs are the best systematic descriptions of the way in which men solve such problems; beyond this these programs contribute significantly to an emerging cognitive technology.

Selected Readings
and References

I. COMPUTER CONCEPTS

[1] Cole, R. W. *Introduction to Computing*. New York: McGraw-Hill Book Company, 1969.
[2] Crowley, T. H. *Understanding Computers*. New York: McGraw-Hill Book Company, 1967.
[3] Feldzamen, A. N. *The Intelligent Man's Easy Guide to Computers*. New York: David McKay, Inc., 1971.
[4] Squire, E. *The Computer: An Everyday Machine*. Reading, Mass.: Addison-Wesley, 1972.

II. COMPUTER SCIENCE AND DATA PROCESSING

[5] Awad, E. M. *Business Data Processing*. 3rd ed. Englewood Cliffs, N. J.: Prentice-Hall Inc., 1971.
[6] Davis, G. B. *Computer Data Processing*. 2nd ed. New York: McGraw-Hill Book Company, 1973.
[7] Forsythe, A. I., Kennan, T. A., Organick, E. I., and Stenberg, W. *Computer Science: A First Course*. New York: John Wiley and Sons, Inc., 1969.
[8] Gear, C. W. *Introduction to Computer Science*. Chicago: Science Research Associates, Inc., 1973.
[9] Price, W. T. *Introduction to Data Processing*. San Francisco: Rinehart Press, 1972.
[10] Ralston, A. *Introduction to Programming and Computer Science*. New York: McGraw-Hill Book Company, 1971.

[11] Vazsonyi, A. *Introduction to Electronic Data Processing*. Homewood, Ill.: Richard D. Irwin, Inc., 1973.

[12] Walker, T. M., and Cotterman, W. W. *Introduction to Computer Science and Algorithmic Processes*. Boston: Allyn and Bacon, 1970.

III. COMPUTERS AND SYSTEMS

[13] Abrams, M. D., and Stein, P. G. *Computer Hardware and Software: An Interdisciplinary Introduction*. Reading, Mass.: Addison-Wesley Publishing Co., 1973.

[14] Donovan, J. J. *Systems Programming*. New York: McGraw-Hill Book Company, 1972.

[15] Gear, C. W. *Computer Organization and Programming*. New York: McGraw-Hill Book Company, 1969.

[16] Katzan, H. *Computer Organization and the System/370*. New York: Van Nostrand Reinhold Company, 1971.

[17] Katzan, H. *Operating Systems: A Pragmatic Approach*. New York: Van Nostrand Reinhold Company, 1973.

[18] Kelley, J. F. *Computerized Management Information Systems*. New York: The Macmillan Co., 1970.

[19] Martin, J. *Introduction to Teleprocessing*. Englewood Cliffs, N. J.: Prentice-Hall Inc., 1972.

[20] Stone, H. S. *Introduction to Computer Organization and Data Structures*. New York: McGraw-Hill Book Company, 1972.

IV. PROGRAMMING AND PROGRAMMING LANGUAGES

[21] Coan, J. S. *Basic BASIC*. New York: Hayden Book Company, Inc., 1970.

[22] Elson, M. *Concepts of Programming Languages*. Chicago: Science Research Associates, Inc., 1973.

[23] Katzan, H. *Programming and Computer Techniques*. New York: Van Nostrand Reinhold Company, 1970.

[24] Katzan, H. *Introduction to Programming Languages*. Philadelphia: Auerbach Publishers, Inc., 1973.

[25] Kemeny, J. G., and Kurtz, T. E. *BASIC Programming*. 2nd ed. New York: John Wiley and Sons, Inc., 1971.

[26] Maurer, W. D. *Programming: An Introduction to Computer Techniques*. San Francisco: Holden-Day, Inc., 1972.

[27] McCracken, D. D. *A Guide to FORTRAN IV Programming*. 2nd ed. New York: John Wiley and Sons, Inc., 1972.

[28] Schick, W., and Merz, C. J., Jr. *FORTRAN for Engineering*. New York: McGraw-Hill Book Co., 1972.

V. COMPUTERS AND SOCIETY

[29] Anderson, R. E. "Sociological analysis of public attitudes toward computers and information files." *Proceedings of the 1972 Spring Joint Computer Conference.* AFIPS, Vol. 39, pp. 649-657.

[30] Comber, E. V. "Management of confidential information." *Proceedings of the 1969 Fall Joint Computer Conference.* AFIPS, Vol. 34, pp. 135-143.

[31] Davis, K. *Human Relations at Work.* New York: McGraw-Hill Book Company, 1967.

[32] Dorf, R. C. *Introduction to Computers and Computer Science.* San Francisco: Boyd and Fraser Publishing Company, 1972.

[33] Feigenbaum, E. A., and Feldman, J. (editors). *Computers and Thought.* New York: McGraw-Hill Book Company, 1963.

[34] Hamming, R. W. *Computers and Society.* New York: McGraw-Hill Book Company, 1972.

[35] Kagán, C. A. R., and Shear, L. G. "The home reckoner—a scenario on the home use of computers." *Proceedings of the 1973 National Computer Conference.* AFIPS, Vol. 42, pp. 759-763.

[36] Katzan, H. *Computer Data Security.* New York: Van Nostrand Reinhold Company, 1973.

[37] Kemeny, J. G. *Man and the Computer.* New York: Charles Scribner's Sons, 1972.

[38] Laska, R. M. "All the news that's fit to retrieve." *Computer Decisions.* Volume 4, Number 8 (August 1972), pp. 18-22.

[39] Martin, J., and Norman, A. R. D. *The Computerized Society.* Englewood Cliffs, N. J.: Prentice-Hall, Inc., 1970.

[40] McLuhan, M., and Watson, W. *From Cliché to Archetype.* New York: Viking Press, Inc., 1970.

[41] Miller, A. R. *The Assault on Privacy.* Ann Arbor, Mich.: The University of Michigan Press, 1971.

[42] Mumford, L. *The Myth of the Machine: The Pentagon of Power.* New York: Harcourt, Brace, Jovanovich, Inc., 1970.

[43] Nilsson, N. J. *Problem-solving Methods in Artificial Intelligence.* New York: McGraw-Hill Book Company, 1971.

[44] Peter, L. J., and Hull, R. *The Peter Principle.* New York: William Morrow and Company, Inc., 1969.

[45] Raiffa, H. *Design Analysis: Introductory Lectures on Choices under Uncertainty.* Reading, Mass.: Addison-Wesley, 1968.

[46] Reich, C. A. *The Greening of America.* New York: Bantam Books, Inc., 1970.

[47] Rodgers, W. *Think: A Biography of the Watsons and IBM.* New York: Stein and Day Publishers, 1969.

[48] Rothman, S., and Mosmann, C. *Computers and Society.* Chicago: Science Research Associates, Inc., 1972.

[49] Sanders, D. H. *Computers and Society: An Introduction to Information Processing.* New York: McGraw-Hill Book Company, 1973.

[50] Toffler, A. *Future Shock.* New York: Random House, 1970.

[51] Weiner, N. *Cybernetics: or Control and Communication in the Animal and the Machine.* 2nd ed. Cambridge, Mass.: The M. I. T. Press, 1961.

[52] Westin, A. F. *Privacy and Freedom.* New York: Atheneum, 1967.

VI. DESIGN PHILOSOPHY FOR MAN-MACHINE INFORMATION SYSTEMS

[53] Drucker, P. F. *The Age of Discontinuity: Guidelines to Our Changing Society.* New York: Harper & Row, 1968.

[54] Galbraith, J. K. *The New Industrial State.* Boston: Houghton Mifflin Company, 1967.

[55] Johnson, A. R. "Organization, perception, and control in living systems." *Industrial Management Review.* Winter 1967.

[56] Jolley, J. L. *Data Study.* New York: World University Library, McGraw-Hill, 1968.

[57] Losty, P. A. *The Effective Use of Computers in Business.* London: Cassell and Company, Ltd., 1969.

[58] Toulmin, S. *Foresight and Understanding: An Inquiry into the Aims of Science.* New York: Harper & Row, 1963.

[59] Zannetos, Z. S. "Toward intelligent management information systems." *Industrial Management Review.* Spring 1968.

VII. CONCEPTUAL BASIS OF COMPUTATION

[60] Armer, Paul. "Attitudes toward intelligent machines." In Feigenbaum, C. A., and Feldman, Julian (eds.), *Computers and Thought.* New York: McGraw-Hill Book Company, 1963.

[61] Bronowski, J., Jr. "The Logic of the Mind." *The American Scholar.* Spring 1966.

[62] Langer, S. K. "The Growing Center of Knowledge." *Philosophical Sketches.* Baltimore, Md.: The Johns Hopkins Press, 1962.

[63] Mackay, D. M. "A mind's eye view of the brain." In Wiener, N., and Schade, J. P. (eds.), *Cybernetics of the Nervous System.* Progress in Brain Research, Vol. 17. New York: Elsevier Publishing Co., 1965.

[64] Maron, M. E. "On cybernetics, information processing and thinking." In Wiener, N., and Schade, J. P. (eds.), *Cybernetics of the Nervous System.* Progress in Brain Research, Vol. 17. New York: Elsevier Publishing Co., 1965.

[65] Menger, K. "Variables, constants, fluents." *Current Issues in the Philosophy of Science.* New York: Holt, Rinehart and Winston, 1961.

[66] Minsky, Marvin. "Matter, mind and models." *Proceedings of the IFIP Congress 65*. Washington, D. C.: Spartan Books, 1965.

[67] Minsky, Marvin. "Steps toward Artificial Intelligence." In Feigenbaum, C. A., and Feldman, Julian (eds.), *Computers and Thought*. New York: McGraw-Hill Book Company, 1963.

[68] Rapoport, A. *Operational Philosophy*. New York: Harper and Brothers, 1953.

[69] Rosenblith, W. A. "On Cybernetics and the Human Brain." *The American Scholar*. Spring 1966.

[70] Taube, M. *Computers and Common Sense*. New York: Columbia University Press, 1961.

[71] Wooldridge, D. E. *The Machinery of the Brain*. New York: McGraw-Hill Book Company, Inc., 1963.

Index

345